MAO

A REINTERPRETATION

❧

Lee Feigon

Ivan R. Dee

CHICAGO

The paperback edition of this book carries the ISBN 1-56663-522-5.

Library of Congress Cataloging-in-Publication Data:
Feigon, Lee, 1945–
    Mao : a reinterpretation / Lee Feigon.
      p. cm.
    Includes bibliographical references and index.
    ISBN: 978-1-56663-522-6
     1. Mao, Zedong, 1893–1976. 2. China—History—1949–1976. I. Title.

DS778.M3 F44 2002
951.05—dc21
                                        2002073309

To my mother, Ethel S. Feigon

Contents

MAO
A Reinterpretation

The Image

IN THE MOVIE *Mao: The Real Man*, Chairman Mao's older brother emigrates to Chicago in the early 1900s. There he becomes a mob kingpin nicknamed Wasp. His chief rival is another immigrant, Nikita Khrushchev. In the 1930s Wasp returns to China and secretly takes his brother's place as leader of the Chinese Communist party; Mao retires to a monastery in Tibet. Years later, Khrushchev goes back to Russia. The two old competitors begin the Sino-Soviet dispute.

Despite its crazy plot line, the film so skillfully weaves actual details of Mao's life with bizarre fictional elements that it took me a while to be sure the movie was a fantasy. The Hungarian director Szilveszter Siklosi has said he made the film to show how easy it is to confuse fact with fiction[1] — a central problem for today's writers when the subject is Mao Zedong.

In the 1960s the Chinese government proclaimed Mao the "sun in the sky," and many foreigners more or less agreed that Mao was the nearest thing in the modern world to a Sage King. Some thirty years later, Mao's reputation plummeted among opinion-makers East and West. In a 1993 speech celebrating Mao's hundredth birthday, Jiang Zemin, secretary general of the Chinese Communist party, honored the chairman's great contribution to the early stages of the Chinese revolution but decried Mao's departure "from his own correct principles" in his final decades.[2]

Both in and out of China today it is commonplace to compare Mao to Stalin, Hitler, or other great villains while nonetheless acknowledging that in the early years of his life Mao was an original and heroic figure for his accomplishments in reuniting China.

The truth is that from the 1920s through the 1940s, Mao was not as innovative in his thoughts and actions as popular opinion would have it. He was much more indebted to Stalin's help than he later admitted and than many have been led to believe. It was not until the late 1950s that Mao became a genuinely creative and original thinker and actor. He showed himself to be one of the few rulers willing to take on authoritarian, corrupt bureaucrats, and in doing so he challenged the very people and the very system he had earlier staked his life and reputation to establish. By carrying out first the disastrous Great Leap Forward and then the much more successful Cultural Revolution—movements which have in recent years been almost universally condemned—Mao forced China to break with its Soviet past. Had the Communist bureaucrats who still rule China not aborted the changes that Mao promoted in the 1960s, China would probably have been much further along on the road to political reform than it is now.

Westerners routinely write about these Communist bureaucrats as helpless victims of Mao's campaigns or, even worse, as heroes for resisting his efforts to eliminate China's Soviet-style bureaucracy. Indeed, Mao is condemned almost universally for his attacks on these bureaucrats in the late 1960s. But the irony is that these are the same officials responsible for many of the problems that still plague China today. In effect the Communist bureaucrats that Mao tried to eliminate have been allowed to shape our understanding of Mao. They have created a world in which the perpetrators of evil have often come to be seen as its victims.

These false ideas about Mao—and by connection about China—have been readily accepted because Mao is often viewed not as a real historical actor but as an icon. But these distorted representations are also the projections of our own feelings and political circumstances. In the 1960s Americans disillusioned with U.S. policies in the cold war and in Vietnam were willing to accept Chinese exaltations of Mao. In recent years, wanting to believe that China has been transformed by foreign goods and ideas, we have been too willing to blame China's past backwardness on Maoist leadership and too quick to credit China's present rulers with moving the country onto the right track.

As we have shaped our view of China to match our own projections, we have remolded Mao into a villain. Scholars and journalists who now suggest that Mao was China's Stalin or Hitler are also continuing a practice that has long dominated Western writing about Asia. We picture Asian leaders in black and white: they are good or bad, demonic or messianic, holy or debased. This either-or attitude has confused and confounded Western views of Asia for some years now, the pendulum swinging from one extreme to the other every decade or so. We caricature Mao as saint, then sinner, manipulating the true facts of his life with as much facility as the Szilveszter Siklosi film.

Mao's reputation first rose in the 1930s when the American journalist Edgar Snow published his best-selling book *Red Star over China*, in which Snow described Mao as a simple, uncorrupt populist hero. At a time when the West was recovering from the Great Depression and struggling against supposedly evil authoritarian Asian leaders in Japan, Mao was made into an icon of the good, hard-working, incorruptible Asian with whom we wanted to ally. When Mao—as we should have understood—turned out to be a Marxist, a disappointed Western public, caught up in anti-Communist hysteria, reinterpreted Mao as a godless Antichrist who had ousted the Western-leaning Christian, Jiang Kaishek.

By the early 1950s, as the United States was preparing to fight Chinese forces in Korea, American journalists were writing wild tales about the frailty of Mao's health and about the supposed diabolical scheming and dissipation in the inner sanctums of the Chinese Communist hierarchy. In *Red Star over China*, Edgar

Snow, anxious even then to squash rumors about Mao's health, had reported on Mao's intellectual vigor and provided an eyewitness account of a medical checkup in which physicians certified Mao's lungs as healthy, despite his heavy smoking habit. But by the 1950s Stewart Alsop was reporting in the *New York Herald Tribune* that Mao was very ill and might soon suffer "the kind of convenient 'heart attack' which has ended the careers of numerous European Communists." Three years later, on April 12, 1954, *Time*'s suggestion that Mao had "mysteriously vanished from the public eye" and might have died of cancer seemed credible. A decade later, on May 27, 1962, Tilman Durdin wrote in the *New York Times* that "Mao Tse-tung is known to be in failing health, with his mental powers faltering." Harold Schechter repeated virtually the same story in *Time* seven years after that, on September 26, 1969. His editor was apparently not concerned that *Time* and others had been wrong about it every time before.[3]

At the same time a number of Western writers were insinuating that Mao's revolution was failing, Mao appeared similarly concerned—but for different reasons. Shortly after 1949 he warned his followers not to succumb to the "sugar-coated bullets" of success. In the late 1960s, concerned about the direction in which his presumptive heirs seemed to be taking the country, Mao launched the Cultural Revolution. His goal was to use youthful revolutionaries to eliminate the party hacks he worried would stymie the country's continuing transformation.

Mao's encouragement of student attacks on government bureaucracy and ideological orthodoxy excited a generation of Western student activists disillusioned by the Vietnam War. Their favorable views of Mao often became as distorted as the anti-Maoist views of the 1950s.

In 1969 I attended a talk at the University of Chicago on the origin of Maoist ideas by the eminent Western biographer of Mao, Stuart Schram. Campus radicals filled the hall. Mischievously I turned to the student sitting next to me and suggested that he ask

Schram what all this had to do with the struggle for women's liberation on the campus.

"Good idea," he replied unsmilingly, and to my astonishment interrupted Schram to ask the question.

Schram cast about for a few minutes and then began to talk seriously about Mao's opposition to foot-binding and arranged marriages during the 1920s and 1930s, and how this could serve as an example to the students at the University of Chicago. I was amazed to see everyone nodding in agreement, apparently finding no reason to doubt that the tactics used against foot-binding in rural China should be just as effective in helping women students achieve equal opportunity at the University of Chicago in the 1960s.

Students on American campuses were not the only ones to fall under Mao's spell in that decade. The French novelist and minister of culture André Malraux received great critical and scholarly acclaim for his account of a 1965 meeting with Mao. In *Anti-Memoirs*, Malraux promoted the image of Mao as a modern-day Sage King. He described how he sat for hours with Mao, exchanging philosophical subtleties about the state of the world. It later developed that Malraux's account was pure fiction. After examining transcripts of the meeting, Simon Leys noted in the *New York Review of Books* (May 29, 1997): "The three-hour cosmic dialogue between two philosophico-revolutionary giants of our century had in fact been limited to a routine exchange of diplomatic platitudes that barely lasted thirty minutes."[4]

Not everyone was easily swayed by the new fashion for Mao. The Beatles and Andy Warhol, among other artists, satirized the cult of Mao during the late sixties and early seventies—the Beatles in "Revolution 1," and Warhol in his famous series of silk-screen portraits of the chairman. Despite this skepticism, Mao's image did not begin to change in the West until after his death in September 1976. Within a few years Deng Xiaoping had become the new Chinese leader, and he soon took credit for jump-starting the

Chinese economy and opening up China to the Western world. As Deng's reputation grew, Mao's declined. A Western public inclined to view China in black and white began to push Mao into the shadows as Deng moved into the light.

Western writers have usually credited Deng with ending China's period of isolation, apparently forgetting that it was the United States that refused to establish relations with China during Mao's rule, not the other way around. In 1956 Secretary of State John Foster Dulles refused even to shake hands with Mao's foreign minister Zhou Enlai. In 1971, when the Nixon administration reversed America's China policy, Mao was in charge, not Deng. One of the few people to remember this was Henry Kissinger. Writing in *Newsweek* following Deng's death in 1997, Kissinger recalled that Mao had told Nixon in 1971 that the major obstacle to U.S.-Chinese relations—Taiwan—didn't matter, a position to which the supposedly nonideological Deng never fully acceded, and which according to newly released transcripts Kissinger himself did not really believe either.[5]

Not only did Mao begin the process of opening up China to the outside world, he also created the industrial infrastructure that laid the basis for the resuscitation of the Chinese economy during the Deng years. Chinese industrial output increased thirtyfold from 1949 to 1976. By 1952 Mao had restored China from the devastation of Japanese occupation and the war between Chinese Communists and Nationalists to the highest level it had achieved in the prewar, prerevolution years. Between 1952 and Mao's death in 1976, industrial output increased an average of 11.2 percent per year, an amazing rate of growth by any reckoning. Even during the so-called wasted decade of the Cultural Revolution, the country had almost no inflation and an industrial growth rate of between 8 and 10 percent.

Legitimate questions remain about the human costs of the economic expansion achieved under Mao, as well as disputes over exact numbers. But the assertion that the Chinese economy stagnated under Mao and did not begin to grow until his successors imported Western economic methods is sheer nonsense.

Deng's successful decentralizing of the Chinese economy in the 1980s and 1990s has often been contrasted with Mao's supposedly centralist policies. Yet it was Mao who in the late 1950s insisted on departing from the centralized, Soviet model of development and began to decentralize China's economy. Deng Xiaoping's transfer of the control of investment funds to local governments, regional enterprises, and the banking system in the 1980s was a continuation of, not a radical break with, Mao's policies. The transfer would never have occurred if Mao had not spent much of the 1960s destroying the legitimacy of the country's Stalinist bureaucracy.

Why do these Maoist achievements now receive so little credit in the West, when once they received so much? The most obvious answer is that for every good Chinese leader, Western writers seem to need a bad one. When Snow exalted Mao, it was to despoil the reputation of Jiang Kaishek. When Deng and his cronies became popular, Mao grew unpopular.

But this juxtaposition is not simply the fault of Western writers. It is also the result of Chinese efforts. What better way is there for China's present leaders to magnify their achievements and slight their own failings than to talk about how much the country has developed since Mao held the reins?

China has, of course, changed a great deal in the years since Mao. Cities like Shanghai, Canton, and Beijing now boast impressive new buildings, shiny cars, and fast-food restaurants that were unimaginable only a few years ago. For those like myself who first began going to China in the 1970s, this is a remarkable change. The blinding poverty I saw when I first entered China in 1975, expecting to find a socialist paradise, no longer exists openly in most urban areas. Foreign ideas and techniques are now widely applied.

Workplace cadres no longer control all aspects of a person's life. The country appears a much less sinister place than it did under Mao.

But during the Mao period it was actually Deng Xiaoping who led the menacing and bloody 1957 anti-rightist campaign against ideological dissidents. The Dalai Lama, who spent time in Beijing in the 1950s, has often spoken rather fondly of Mao, but never of Deng. Americans were shocked by the actions of Deng Xiaoping during the 1989 Tiananmen Square massacre. Perhaps we would not have been so disappointed had we not painted Deng in such saintly robes.

On my first trip to China I recall getting into a political argument with staff at my hotel, who confronted me about America's imperialist policies after I accused them of gouging me on a bill. "If you think American policies are bad, what about Deng Xiaoping?" I taunted them. My barb quieted my opponents, who were themselves confused about how Deng, regarded as a leading enemy of the people during the Cultural Revolution, could have been rehabilitated as a leading official by Mao. They muttered something about Deng's situation being complicated, and then let the matter drop. I felt pretty proud of myself for exposing the inconsistencies of Chinese politics. I hadn't realized that twenty-five years later I would be writing about equally fickle American attitudes toward Chinese leaders.

The attempt to turn Mao into an icon prevents us from confronting our confusion about China. Is China like us and is Mao "one of us," as he clearly seems in Edgar Snow's writings, or is he "not one of us," as we now seem to believe? Did he actually threaten us, as he appeared to do in our post-1949 version of him? Or was he our friend, as Snow implied? Much of the Western view of Mao turns out to have been an extraordinarily sophisticated mix of theoretical fictions—inventions disguised as facts.

Writers who avoid the temptation to oversimplify Mao have found themselves being interpreted within this distorted framework. In his compact yet masterful biography, *Mao Zedong*, Yale historian and MacArthur Fellow Jonathan Spence judiciously synopsizes Mao's career, carefully laying out the chairman's successes and failures. Philip Short, a former foreign correspondent for the *London Times*, the BBC, and the *Economist*, provides an equally sober and much more comprehensive assessment in *Mao: A Life*. Yet many of the reviews of both these books focused not on the merits of the authors' analyses but on the question of to what degree Mao should be considered a monster. The normally balanced Ian Buruma spent several pages attempting to show that no matter what the two biographers reported to the contrary, Mao was a psychopathic killer. Buruma suggested that once the facts of Mao's life became as well known in China as they have become in the West, balanced assessments of the former Chinese leader would be tossed aside, and everyone would agree that Mao was a monster.[6]

There are not many more facts about Mao to expose. Scholars have unearthed and published virtually every word Mao ever wrote and have attempted to describe his every action in exhaustive detail. They have even translated and analyzed the notes he scribbled in the margins of his boyhood schoolbooks, and have documented his bowel movements before various battles.

My purpose is not simply to repeat the same old facts about Mao but to write an interpretive study of him that may begin to clear away some of the myths about Mao. I hope to show that the real Mao was neither as smart and independent as earlier versions of him suggest, nor as evil as later interpretations have it. While Mao justly receives credit for uniting China and creating a new unified government in 1949, he also deserves credit for realizing that he had made a mistake in trying to follow a Soviet model for China, and for spending the last two decades of his life trying to tear China away from the Soviet road. Without discounting the horrific damage done by Mao's Great Leap Forward and the Cultural Revolution, one cannot overlook the positive impact of these movements, which gave birth to the present China—indeed, they are more responsible for China's change in recent years than its trade with the West. My goal is to put Mao in perspective as neither a youthful savior nor an old tyrant but a committed, canny revolutionary who shaped China's history.

TWO

Growing Up Normal

AT THE HEIGHT of Mao Zedong's popularity, his image adorned billions of inexpensive commemorative pins. In many of these depictions he strides forth boldly in long, flowing robes—the savior of the Chinese people. But outside China, and in later years within, the comparisons have been less flattering—Mao portrayed as Hitler or Stalin.

In fact the clean-shaven Mao had little in common temperamentally or psychologically with the mustachioed tyrants. Unlike Hitler, he was not a failed art student but successful in his early endeavors. Unlike Stalin, he was not tainted by an illicit past. Furthermore, Mao reached adulthood without undergoing the kind of shock that Lenin had experienced when his beloved elder brother was executed as a revolutionary. Mao never suffered the stigma of social rejection or the wounds of a broken family, as the others did.

Writers who have attempted to find something fundamentally wrong with Mao from an early age have come up empty-handed.[1] What they find instead is a relatively typical childhood—hardly fodder for a revolutionary tyrant. Mao was a good-looking boy who came from a well-off country home. He possessed no famous or even wealthy ancestors, but he was not born in the Chinese equivalent of a log cabin. His father served as a soldier and then scraped together enough money to buy a small parcel of land. Slowly the old man increased his holdings. He hired two laborers to do most of the farm work and spent much of his own time as a grain merchant and moneylender.[2] In 1915 one of Mao's teachers, impressed by his new student, noted in his diary that Mao had told him: "His father . . . was previously a peasant, but has now become a trader."[3]

The family house was large, and Mao, his two younger brothers, and his adopted sister all had their own rooms, an unusual luxury. By Chinese rural standards it was a comfortable life, though not as privileged as that of many other early leaders of the Chinese Communist party, who came from well-to-do landlord families. Life in the Mao household was more challenging than what was to be found in these gentry families. Meat and eggs were rare treats. Mao, his brothers, and his sister all helped with farm work. As a teenager Mao was already tall and muscular. At "the age of fourteen or fifteen" he was as big as his father and "could carry on his broad shoulders two of the heavy manure baskets which had to be taken to the fields several times each day."[4]

Mao's youth was also noteworthy because of the presence of both his parents. This fact may not seem remarkable until it is viewed in contrast with virtually every other early Chinese revolutionary figure, most of whom lost a father (and often a mother too) during their youth, casting them psychologically and often physically adrift from their culture and society. But Mao's mother remained alive until after Mao had become a grown man, and Mao's father continued to support Mao well into adulthood. Toward the end of his mother's life, she spent long periods of time living in a neighboring village with her own family, perhaps because her husband had taken on a mistress.[5] But there was nothing unusual about this by Chinese rural standards.

Of course the mere presence of his parents during Mao's formative years did not guarantee a life without friction. In his interviews with the American journalist Edgar Snow in the 1930s, the chairman described his father as a tyrant and his mother as loving but ignorant. His father, Mao related, had had only two years of schooling, his mother none. Well before he was a teen, Mao became "the family 'scholar.'" At the age of thirteen, Mao left school to work in the family fields and keep the account books for his father. He described his father as "a severe taskmaster."

> ... He hated to see me idle and if there were no books to be kept he put me to work at farm tasks. He was a hot-tempered man and frequently beat both me and my brothers. He gave us no money whatever, and the most meager food. On the fifteenth of every month he made a concession to his laborers and gave them eggs with their rice, but never meat. To me he gave neither eggs nor meat.[6]

As much as he claimed to resent him, however, Mao showed considerable ambivalence toward his father.

> Reflecting on this, I think that in the end, the strictness of my father defeated him. I learned to hate him and we [Mao, his mother, and his brothers] created a real United Front against him. At the same time, it probably benefited me. It made me most diligent in my work; it made me keep my books carefully, so that he should have no basis for criticizing me.[7]

Mao told Snow that he had to run away from home to continue his studying. He may have run off, but he did not stay away for long. His father permitted Mao to enroll in school after Mao raised money from friends and relatives not only for his own tuition but also for his father to hire a laborer to do Mao's work.[8] If it is true that his father was initially reluctant to support Mao's schooling, he clearly warmed to it. By the time Mao was sixteen, his father supported the boy's attendance in a new-style school in the neighboring district. Although the father was stingy, he wished to see his son advance. He continued to support him when Mao left the district school for greater educational opportunities in Changsha, the provincial capital of Hunan.

Mao's descriptions of the hostility between himself and his father, like his tales of his father's refusal to support his efforts at education, were probably overstated. Stories of youthful rebellion against one's family and tales of horrible fathers were wildly popular among young Chinese intellectuals at the time Snow first interviewed Mao. Throughout the 1930s the anti-family novel *Jia*, or *Family*, by the anarchist writer Ba Jin, was a best-seller in China. As someone attuned to the needs of the era, Mao, like other radicals and revolutionaries at the time,[9] seems to have repeated this anti-father theme in describing his own life in order to attract idealistic Chinese youth to the cause. Mao told Snow that his early life was distinguished by rebellion against a vicious father. In reality his family supported him.

Compared with many other revolutionaries, Mao was close to his family. In the spring of 1919, when he learned that his mother was ill, he resigned his job at Beijing University and returned to Hunan to help care for her. Researchers have unearthed the letter that Mao sent to his uncles and aunts reporting on his mother's condition and on his ministrations to her. When she died in the fall, Mao delivered a funeral oration noting his mother's "abundant virtues and her hatred of injustice. . . . She never lied or cheated. She was always neat and meticulous. Everything she took care of she would put in order."[10] In spite of Mao's belief then that its family system was one of the major causes of the evils plaguing Chinese society (an idea current in intellectual circles early in the century), he was deeply rooted in his own family.

Mao did not venture far from his family until he was seventeen, when he moved to Changsha to attend middle school. It was an opportune time. Six months later, on October 10, 1911, a poorly organized insurrection broke out in the central Chinese town of Wuhan. In ensuing days, similar actions occurred in towns and provinces throughout southern and central China. At the close of 1911 the central government collapsed, ending the more than 250-year rule of the Qing dynasty and resulting in the temporary establishment of a republic. To ensure support from gentry and military leaders, the revolutionaries chose the former Qing strongman Yuan Shikai to head their new government. After Yuan dissolved the newly elected parliament, he resisted an effort in 1913 to overthrow him. But Yuan proved unable to reestablish the monarchy, and by 1917 China had disintegrated into a variety of military satrapies. A nominal central government remained, but warlords, some previously allied with the revolutionaries, others former Qing dynasty officers, ruled the various provinces as their personal fiefdoms, often supported by Western powers vying for influence in China.

These events were to have a profound impact on Mao. In the immediate aftermath of the Wuhan insurrection, like many other idealistic young Chinese, he chose to participate in the revolution. But he was a relatively prudent young revolutionary. Having heard that Wuhan was a rainy place, Mao first decided to borrow a pair of waterproof shoes from a friend outside the city. While he was on his way to fetch the shoes, the revolution reached Changsha. Mao watched the violence from the sidelines, galoshes in hand.[11]

And while many of his fellow students joined a special Changsha student army, Mao, who had witnessed the violent, duplicitous actions of other revolutionary participants, decided that this army was "too confused." He sensibly and cautiously enlisted in the regular army. Now on the side of the revolutionaries, this force had previously been under the command of the Qing dynasty. Mao became a common soldier, though he did not live like one. He later poked fun at himself, noting that because he was a student, he refused to "carry in water from outside the city" but instead "bought it from water-peddlers."[12]

A few months later, after the elimination of the Qing had been assured, Mao left the army to return to school. He considered police training, soap-making, and the law. To the delight of his father, he finally entered a business school. The classes were mostly in English, a language Mao did not know. He quit, and with the consent and support of his family entered the Hunan Normal

School. He remained there for five years. He told Snow that his one bad habit as a student was to subscribe to many newspapers and to be a constant buyer of journals and books—extra expenses that his father groused about.[13]

His teachers liked him. One of them, Yang Changji, a well-known scholar who had studied in Europe, wrote about Mao in his journal:

> And yet it is truly difficult to imagine someone so intelligent and handsome [as Mao]. Since many unusual talents come from peasant families, I exhorted him using the examples of Zeng Desheng and Liang Rengon. Student Mao had worked as a peasant for two years and had also been a soldier for half a year at the time when the Republic superseded the empire. He has truly had an interesting life history.[14]

Among his classmates, Mao enjoyed a similar reputation. Although in the summertime he preferred going bare-chested to display his handsome physique, at school he usually wore the blue wool school uniform, keeping it until long after it had worn thin. He sometimes wore over it a grey cotton *changpao*, the long gown favored by the upper-class literati. From the first day, his classmates noticed that he had a charming smile that made him appear "genuinely sincere."[15]

The margins of Mao's books are filled with the ideas he was imbibing in the Hunan Normal School. He notes in a book on German philosophy his adamant disagreement with Schopenhauer, suggesting that while it is true that people act in their own self-interest,

> It is also of our nature to extend this to helping others. This is one and the same human nature, so working for the interests of others is in my own self-interest. . . . Self-interest is primarily benefiting one's own spirit, and the flesh is of no value in benefiting the spirit. Benefiting the spirit means benefiting the feelings and will.[16]

A belief in the group is what distinguished Mao. Although some of the new Chinese writers that his teachers urged him to read attacked all Confucian ideals as bankrupt and advocated the destruction of traditional Chinese values, Mao wished to preserve and integrate these old values into a modern idea system.

While a student, he helped establish an evening school to promote universal education among the common people and teach them practical knowledge, like how electricity works. As Mao wrote in his journal, "Schools and education are extremely critical for creating a new generation of citizenry, and obtaining talented people capable of promoting development."[17]

He was not an athlete, but he liked to exercise. Influenced by his teacher Yang Changji, he believed that lack of physical activity had weakened many Chinese intellectuals, to the detriment of their country. Using the pen name "Twenty-eight-stroke Student" (the number of character strokes in his name), he published his ideas on the subject in the influential national journal *New Youth*, one of the most important publications of its time. He argued in the article that "When the body is strong, one can advance speedily in knowledge and morality and reap far-reaching advantages." Mao criticized those who spent every day inside studying, observing that "when they climb a hill they are short of breath, and when they walk in the water they get cramps in their feet." He commented positively on such seemingly diverse practices as German fencing, the Japanese spirit of bushido, and the self-strengthening regimen of President Theodore Roosevelt.[18]

Years later, Mao recalled:

> We also became ardent physical culturists. In the winter holidays we tramped through the fields, up and down mountains, along city walls, and across the streams and rivers. If it rained we took off our shirts and called it a rain bath. When the sun was hot we also doffed shirts and called it a sunbath. In the spring winds we shouted that this was a new sport called "wind bathing." We slept in the open when frost was already falling and even in November

swam in the cold rivers. All this went under the title of "body-training." Perhaps it helped much to build the physique, which I was to need so badly in many marches back and forth across South China and on the Long March from Kiangsi to the Northwest.[19]

After graduation in June 1918 at the age of twenty-four, Mao moved to Beijing, passing up an opportunity to travel to France with many of his student activist friends. France was the flashier choice. Staying in China allowed him to stay in touch with the people and organizations he had cultivated as a student. He told some friends that he could not make the trip because of money problems, though he seemed to be able to borrow funds for other activities. In 1936 he explained to Snow: "I felt that I did not know enough about my own country, and that my time could be more profitably spent in China." A year later he was still considering the idea of going abroad, suggesting in a letter written in February 1920 that he now wanted to study in Russia instead of France.[20] In the end, though, he remained in China.

In Beijing, Mao's former ethics professor, Yang Changji, helped him get a job at Beijing University's library, working under the head librarian, Li Dazhao. Mao had moved to Beijing at a time when the New Culture movement was at its height. It marked a period of new ideas and experimentation ignited by Chen Duxiu's articles in the pages of *New Youth*. The movement particularly embraced science and democracy. New journals modeled after *New Youth* appeared almost daily, espousing every new fad from the West. New Culture participants believed that China's tradition-laden culture had created an oppressive politics which had divided China into warlord regimes. The movement aimed to root out Confucian thought, attacked Chinese family structure, and promoted the use of the vernacular in Chinese writing. In this atmosphere, Mao was soon inhaling the literary, cultural, political, and scientific ideas sweeping Chinese intellectual circles.

But even as he struck out on his own, Mao remained within a kind of familial orbit. Yang Changji, who had become a member of the faculty of Beijing University and a member of the inner circle of the New Culture movement, acted as a substitute father for Mao. After his benefactor's unexpected death in 1920, Mao married Yang's daughter.

In 1919, after Mao returned to Hunan to help care for his ailing mother, he took a teaching job in Changsha. As one of the few important young Hunanese activists who had not departed for France, he soon became the principal student leader in Hunan. He helped found a liberal journal, *Xiang River Review*, and worked to convey the May Fourth anti-Japanese spirit to his new followers, urging them to listen to the call of "world revolution," unite together, and liberate their thought.[21]

Although this rhetoric sounds heated—and it was certainly annoying to the warlord family then ruling Hunan—Mao himself has acknowledged, "I was then a strong supporter of America's Monroe Doctrine and the Open Door." When Chen Duxiu, then the leader of the New Culture movement, was arrested, Mao protested the arrest, bemoaning that "the masses of the people haven't the faintest glimmer of democracy in their mentality, and have no idea what democracy actually is. Mr. Chen has always stood for two things. He once said that our only crimes against society have been for the sake of 'science' and 'democracy.'"[22]

Mao wrote this article at a time of growing stridency among students and intellectuals. On May 4, 1919, irate student demonstrators in Beijing protested the news that participants at the Versailles Peace Conference planned to transfer the former German concessions on the Shandong Peninsula to the Japanese rather than returning them to China. In the days that followed, protests spread throughout the country. In many cities, workers joined the students. Although the May Fourth Movement is often considered synonymous with the New Culture movement, May Fourth marked the beginning of a more overt and radical politicization of the left-leaning Chinese intelligentsia, discouraged by the betrayal of Western promises at Versailles. Political groups began to coalesce among such New Culture leaders as Chen Duxiu.

Responding to this new atmosphere, Mao also argued that the victorious powers in the world war had mistreated Germany at the Versailles Peace Conference. Mao described Germany as a once-proud nation that had been the home of great philosophical thought—Nietzsche, Fichte, Goethe, and Paulsen. He argued that Germany, like China, was on the verge of great revolutionary change, which would restore its place in the world.[23]

Mao's idea of how revolution would change China politically and culturally was presented in his most important and influential early article, "The Great Union of the Popular Masses." In this piece, Mao for the first time saw "aristocrats" and "capitalists" as the enemy, though his inspiration on this theme derived more from the Russian anarchist Pyotr Kropotkin than from Karl Marx.[24]

He had earlier argued that a small elite would bring change to China. Now he believed that the popular masses could take up the burden. The masses, he declared, should join together through their existing groups. Peasants, workers, students, women, schoolteachers, rickshaw boys, policemen—all needed to form their own groups, which would in turn join together into one great union to transform China.

> Our Chinese people possess great inherent capacities! The more profound the oppression, the more powerful its reactions. . . . I venture to make a singular assertion: one day, the reform of the Chinese people will be more profound than that of any other people, and the society of the Chinese people will be more radiant than that of any other people. The great union of the Chinese people will be achieved earlier than that of any other place or people.[25]

Mao did not advocate violent and sudden deep-seated change. He preferred to focus on the smaller problems confronting each of the various groups. As they solved their own problems, each group would then gradually join with others to effect a more far-reaching transformation. It was the moderate, American-educated Hu Shi, a student of the pragmatist theorist John Dewey, to whom Mao looked for inspiration, not radicals like his former employer at the Beijing University library, Li Dazhao, who by that time had become increasingly partial to Communist ideas.[26]

Mao's philosophy was also shaped by Tao Yi, one of the best women students at the Hunan Normal School and one of the first female members of the New People's Student Society. The two developed a romantic relationship, and though they later split over ideological differences (she opposed communism), Mao and Tao remained on friendly terms.[27]

Over the course of their involvement Mao became a vehement advocate of women's rights. He railed against the impracticality of women's clothing. He called for the formation of a women's army.[28] The Chinese family system, he complained, caused women to be slaves of their families and then their husbands. After a woman named Miss Zhao committed suicide rather than agree to the marriage her parents had arranged for her, Mao wrote a number of articles about her situation, insisting that love, not society or family, should be the major determinant of marriage.

Mao could boast personal experience on the subject. When he was about fourteen, his parents had arranged a marriage for him — common for a rural youth at the time — to an older woman from an influential local family. She apparently died after they had been married for just two years. Mao told Snow that he "never lived with her" and "did not consider her my wife." That does not seem to have been accurate. Jonathan Spence notes that it was immediately after her death that Mao went off to school; perhaps her demise gave Mao an opportunity he might not otherwise have had.[29]

Mao spent a great deal of time thinking about families and relationships. Perhaps reflecting his own lonely situation after he moved away from his home in order to further his education, Mao advocated the formation of a new village structure that would fuse together families, schools, and other social systems. Students would be liberated from much classroom time and would spend part of their day in agricultural and practical work. After graduation they would then no longer think they had "to live in the cities rather than in the rural areas. They are not used to village life and therefore do not like it."[30] In this new village, students would cease to be at odds with the society. They would become joined to it and would work within it to create their own new families.

Mao wrote the letter advocating the new village structure on December 1, 1919. His mother had passed away in October. After returning to his village to speak at her funeral and help attend to family affairs, he again left Hunan for Beijing. In Beijing he discovered that his beloved Professor Yang was critically ill. He died in January 1920, around the same time that Mao's own father unexpectedly passed away. Suddenly Mao found himself on his own.

Less than a year later his professional situation changed again. A new political group came into power in Hunan in July 1920, and Mao returned to Changsha, where he announced the formation of a bookstore and publishing house known as the Cultural Book Society, a venture that Spence suggests Mao may have funded with part of the inheritance he received from his father.[31]

At about this time Mao became a vocal advocate of Hunan separatism, an idea then popular with many liberal businessmen in his home province. Years later in talking to Edgar Snow, Mao still gushed with provincial pride. He noted that his taste for spicy red peppers, which he liked so much that he even baked them into his bread, was a Hunanese provincial attribute. He told Snow that "pepper-adoring peoples" are more likely to be revolutionaries, listing as examples Spain, Mexico, Russia, and France as well as his native Hunan. In 1920 he effused about his native province: "It is like Switzerland in the West or Japan in the East."[32] Hunan's independence, he argued, would allow its industry and agriculture to take root.

Mao was never a simple provincial chauvinist. He believed that larger organizations burdened smaller ones, and that provincial autonomy would lay the foundation for a greater China. Paraphrasing a proposal put forward by Hu Shi, the moderate, American-educated thinker he then admired, Mao suggested, "Now, I propose not talking about the politics of the central government for twenty years. The people of every province should focus all their attention on their respective provinces and adopt a provincial Monroe Doctrine, namely, that every province close its doors and ignore what happens outside its doors."[33]

In 1920 Mao was almost twenty-seven. Life was going well for him. He was writing articles that had won respect from intellectuals throughout the country. His Cultural Book Society was thriving. Business was so good that after initially hiring three salesmen, within a short period of time Mao employed four or five more.[34] Numerous memos survive of Mao's careful organization of events to advertise the book society, and the detailed ledgers he kept attest to the enterprise's profitability. Although he had dropped out of business school because of his poor English, he had clearly benefited from the record-keeping work he had done for his father. As Jonathan Spence has suggested, in both action and thought Mao seemed to have carved out a niche for himself as a successful educator and businessman.[35]

He had rewarded the trust and admiration of his teachers and elders by becoming an increasingly affluent and well-regarded member of the literary community. He was a respectable citizen on his way up, one with a clear devotion to the various groups to which he belonged—his family, his friends from the Cultural Book Society, his province, and his country. In these kinds of small groups, he believed, the future of China would be decided.

THREE

Party Man

❧ IF MAO'S YOUTH lacked the misery of Hitler's and Stalin's, it also lacked the refinement that many future revolutionaries acquired. Deng Xiaoping and Zhou Enlai, like Lenin and Trotsky before them, spent years away from their native countries learning sophisticated new habits. Deng Xiaoping acquired a taste for croissants; Trotsky often dressed like a dandy.

Mao, who never went abroad, kept to his folksy ways. As a student in Changsha, he bathed so infrequently that his strong body odor sometimes led fussier upper-class students to keep their distance from him.[1] But Mao's earthiness connected him to everyday Chinese life. And while many of his compatriots denounced their families, or at least stayed clear of them, Mao frequently visited his old home and retained strong ties to the village and province where he had grown up.

Thus the young Mao stayed grounded, avoiding the extremes that may have shaped the temperaments of the tyrants to whom he has been compared. Hitler preached his odious ideas while still young, long before he rose to power. The young Stalin was known for his willingness to take on the draconian and often unpleasant tasks that others disdained. Lenin early articulated an autocratic program of potentially violent action by a small, deeply committed elite. But Mao was initially reluctant to embrace the idea of violent revolution. After becoming a Communist, he advocated making the party as inclusive as possible toward the various groups in Chinese society.

Mao differed from these other major revolutionary figures not only in his early ideas but also in his situation. Future Soviet leaders such as Lenin, Trotsky, and Stalin attacked a ruling elite to which they never belonged, or of which they were at best marginal members. The same was true of Hitler, a failed art student who was wounded and gassed in World War I. But by the time Mao became a Communist, he was a respected member of the Hunan provincial establishment.

When the political climate in Hunan changed in July 1920, the warlord Zhang Jingyao, whom Mao opposed, was driven out of the province. One of the new Hunan educational commissioners, Mao's old teacher and friend Yi Peiji, invited Mao to be the director of the First Hunan Primary School, a position of prominence. Mao assumed his new job in September 1920. Late that year he married Yang Kaihui. She was the petite, attractive daughter of Mao's recently deceased teacher, Yang Changji. A friend described her as "small in stature and round-faced, with deep-set eyes and pale white skin."[2] Mao's marriage to her meant that he not only had a prestigious job but was now part of the family of one of China's most prominent intellectuals. What he did next was to join the Chinese Communist party.

In 1920 the Communist party was the place to be for a member of China's intellectual elite. Shortly after the success of the October 1917 Bolshevik Revolution, Li Dazhao, the distinguished head librarian at Beijing University, had become interested in Marxist ideas. It was Li who employed Mao when he came from Hunan to visit the city. Chen Duxiu, the former dean of the College of Arts and Sciences at Beijing University, also was attracted to Marxism. Chen was the founder of New Youth magazine as well as a close friend and associate of the well-known politician and intellectual, Zhang Shizhao (an Hunanese reformer). In April 1920, after Chen moved to Shanghai because his increasingly radical ideas and activities had gotten him into trouble in Beijing, Mao visited him. Mao later told Edgar Snow: "Chen's own assertions of belief had deeply impressed me at what was probably a critical period of my life."[3]

In August 1920 Chen Duxiu, with the encouragement of a Comintern agent sent to meet with him, established a Communist cell in Shanghai. Li Dazhao did the same in Beijing a month or two later. Mao's two mentors encouraged him to establish a Hunan branch of the party.

Mao's good friend Cai Hesen and some of the other Hunan students in France wrote to Mao that they too had been inspired by the ideals of the Russian revolution. Cai urged Mao to help organize a Communist revolution in China.

Still, Mao hesitated to embrace this radical new ideology. Then, in September, Tan Yankai, the progressive new leader of Hunan, called off the free elections that Mao and his associates had advocated. Tan appointed his own candidates to the Hunan self-government convention that Mao had championed.[4] In November the warlord Zhao Hengti overthrew Tan. Mao's job as principal of the primary school was not in jeopardy, but with his political ambitions derailed by the change in government, he began to rethink his options.

In December he wrote to Cai Hesen and to his other friends in France that while he still believed in a gradualist approach, he now agreed that only a Russian-style revolution could transform China. Casting off the idea of Hunanese independence, Mao now lauded socialism's "cosmopolitan" nature: "Each of us is a member of the human race, and do not want to complicate the matter by belonging to some meaningless country, family, or religion and becoming slaves to these. . . . This is precisely what is called socialism. All socialisms are international in nature and should not have any patriotic coloration."[5]

At twenty-seven, Mao was ten years older than Trotsky had been when he first declared himself a Marxist and nine years older than Lenin had been when he grew interested in Marxism. Yet Mao's understanding of the ideology was superficial. It would be almost twenty more years before he would undertake the kind of deep study of Marxist writings that the two Russian leaders had made while teenagers. As late as 1927, only ten of Marx's works had been published (and some only in part) in China. As one historian has noted, "Such key sociological categories as 'proletariat,' 'bourgeoisie,' 'class,' and so forth had just begun to get their equivalencies in Chinese, but the translations did not always transfer the meaning of the appropriate term in exact form. Distortions were frequent as terms were adjusted to Chinese reality."[6]

As a consequence, Mao's early Communist writings were influenced as much by anarchist thought as by Marxist doctrine. Indeed, many of the early party members considered themselves anarchists, not Communists. The early party was eclectic and open. The chapter established in Hunan, organized mostly around Mao's associates in the New People's Study Society and the Cultural Book Society, was loose, even by what were then the standards of the party.[7] The man credited with founding the Hunan branch, He Minfan, was a Confucian scholar.

In May 1921 Mao was one of two people invited to represent the Hunan group at the first formal organizational meeting of the Chinese Communist party in Shanghai, called at the urging of the Comintern representative in China. The clandestine gathering elected Chen Duxiu as the party's first secretary general, in spite of the fact that neither he nor Li Dazhao, the other party founder, was present at this first meeting. Chen Duxiu was then the head of the Education Committee of Guangzhou province (in effect the provincial minister of education) under the warlord Chen Chiongming. It was the sort of position that would have been unthinkable for any of the Russian Communist leaders before the Bolshevik Revolution.

After the Shanghai meeting, Mao returned to his job as principal of the First Hunan Primary School. A few months later he received a grant from the local government to establish the Hunan Self-Study University. The institution derived its name from a term suggested by John Dewey's disciple Hu Shi, a man whose moderate views had had considerable influence on Mao during his time in Beijing.[8] The official sponsor of and provider of space for this new school was the Wang Fuzhi Society, a group set up by the provincial elite to promote the ideas of the famous Ming dynasty Confucianist. Mao became the director of the newly established university.

The school never grew to more than twenty-four students. Tension developed between Mao and the headmaster, He Minfan, who saw himself as the leader of the Communists in Hunan and resented Mao's increasingly successful attempts to cast himself as head of the local party. An elder gentleman, He Minfan became irate after Mao taught classes and walked around the institution on a steaming hot day wearing nothing but a towel—and when confronted about his dress showed no contrition.[9]

Few of the students were put off by Mao's behavior. A number became party activists. By 1923 most of the Chinese students in Moscow at the Communist University for the Toilers of the East were former students of Mao.[10]

Besides the university and the Cultural Book Society, Mao took part in a number of other activities of the sort that one would expect from a liberal member of the Hunan literati. He participated in the debate over the provincial constitution, criticizing the document for failing to give women sufficient rights and for its lack of "stipulations about issues relating to labor."[11] He even taught Chinese at the First Hunan Normal School, the institution from which he had graduated.

At a meeting of the New People's Study Society devoted to discussing means of carrying out a Soviet-style revolution in China in the summer of 1921, Mao comes across more as an administratively minded do-gooder than someone who had just become a member of a Communist group allied with the Comintern: "I agree with the various methods for getting started you gentlemen have proposed: study, organization, propaganda, establishing links, fund raising, and business. I would merely add that 'self-cultivation' should be included under study." He encouraged his fellow members to engage in self-criticism as well as the constructive criticism of other members. Mao told the group that he was planning to stay in Changsha for only another year and a half or so and then would go to study in Russia—something he never did. He was reading books and newspapers, he said, to improve his life and teaching.[12]

In 1922 Mao became the head of the Hunan Office of the Secretariat of Chinese Labor Organizations as well as of the All-Hunan Federation of Labor Organizations. Even before becoming a Marxist he had been interested in improving the squalid condition of workers in the infant Hunan industries and had tried to help anarchist colleagues who were working with them. The conditions of the laboring poor appalled many members of the Hunanese upper echelon. Although he was not always happy about it, the new Hunan warlord, Zhao Hengti, briefly tolerated these efforts to help the working poor in his province.

Mao had rather inclusive ideas about the identity of the working class that he wished to help. In a May Day essay in 1922, he wrote: "Except for those who practice usury, those who live on an inheritance, and those who have investments in some business enterprise, most people are workers who work with their hands or their minds. From their bodies these workers produce 'labor power,' which alone makes it possible for them to support themselves on the one hand and, on the other hand, for the capitalists to make a profit."[13] This is a long way from Marx's idea of a revolutionary working class with a sophisticated understanding of its potential power, a result of its concentrated position in the highly organized factories developed in advanced capitalist societies. Marx distinguished this proletariat from other members of the working poor. China, of course, was not an advanced industrial society. Without a broad definition of the working class, there would have been few workers in Hunan for Mao to organize.

Some of the prime targets of the Communists throughout China were the railway workers. In February 1923 railway workers in North China called a strike. The Beijing warlord Wu Peifu had seemed sympathetic to Communist labor activities until the railway workers went on strike. In what became known as the February Seventh Massacre, Wu's forces killed and injured scores of workers. The Chinese labor movement ground to a halt in most parts of the country, though it took two months before all labor organizing was shut down in Hunan.

In April 1923, with labor organization now increasingly risky in Hunan, Mao took off for Shanghai where he was to begin working for the Central Committee of the Communist party. He came to Shanghai at a major transition point in Chinese Communist party (CCP) history.

For almost a year the Comintern had pressed the CCP to work with the Guomindang or Nationalist party of Sun Yatsen. Communist party members, however, were not enthusiastic: the Guomindang (KMT) was the party of the crass bourgeoisie. In the past Chen Duxiu and other senior members of the CCP had looked down on Sun Yatsen as a former Cantonese peasant with no literary education and unsophisticated revolutionary ideas.

But responding to Comintern pressure, the CCP reluctantly agreed to cooperate with the KMT. In September 1922, after being told it was a matter of Comintern policy, Chen Duxiu, Li Dazhao, Cai Hesen, and Zhang Tailei had joined the Guomindang, though there was still little real cooperation between the two parties.[14] The CCP's reluctance to work closely with the KMT changed in the wake of the February Seventh Massacre. In June 1923, a few months after Mao returned to Shanghai, the Third Congress of the Chinese Communist party, held in Canton, formally approved the United Front and voted to have Communist party members join the Guomindang.

Mao was more enthusiastic about the alliance with the KMT than many of his comrades. Unlike Chen Duxiu and many of the other CCP members, he had long shown an inclination to work with diverse groups. He argued to the Third Congress that as long as China held to a backward economic position, and warlords and foreigners dominated the country, the Guomindang was the only real revolutionary faction within the country. A broad-based alliance with them was needed to attack China's reactionary forces.[15]

His Hunanese colleague Zhang Guotao, who was to challenge Mao for the leadership of the party in the 1930s, was unalterably opposed to the structure of this alliance. As a result, Mao was selected to replace Zhang as a member of the CCP's Central Committee, something that still rankled Zhang years later.[16]

The alliance with the Guomindang forced Chen Duxiu, Li Dazhao, and the other Communist leaders to set aside some of the ideas that had initially attracted them to communism. These intellectuals had been excited that Russia, a backward, autocratic country like China, had overnight become the world's leading revolutionary nation. By forming a United Front, Chinese Communist party members conceded that China had to undergo an ordinary bourgeois revolution before it could participate in the more advanced international revolution begun by the Soviets.

Many of the early Chinese Communists had also liked the idea that an intellectual elite similar to themselves had led the Russian Revolution. In agreeing to a United Front with the Guomindang, the Communists now were obliged to support the leadership of the revolution by Sun Yatsen, a peasant who had emigrated to Hawaii and trained as a dentist before returning to China and becoming the leader of the 1911 Republican revolution and then the head of the KMT. Sun's support came from the very people whom many of the sophisticated patrician leaders of the early Chinese Communist party hoped the revolution would eliminate—the new Chinese bourgeoisie with their emphasis on business and money.

Mao, however, clung to the idea of an inclusive revolution. At the Third Congress he was one of only two delegates to speak in support of the Comintern's further proposal to bring peasants into the movement. He was ready to consider not only peasants but merchants. In the summer of 1923 Mao suggested that merchants should lead the next "bourgeois-democratic stage" of the Chinese revolution, and that warlord and foreign domination over China might soon be ended. He shortly abandoned this idea, but he continued to be interested in finding a broad-based coalition.[17]

Mao joined the Guomindang shortly after the Third Congress. He was once again working on the same side as his old ally Tan Yankai, the former Hunanese warlord. At the end of August 1923, Tan Yankai retook Changsha. As soon as he heard the news, Mao returned to his native province to help Tan establish a Guomindang organization there. By the time Mao arrived in Hunan, the situation had changed. Tan's old nemesis, Zhao Hengti, had recaptured Changsha. Forced to work under an assumed name, Mao tried to use anti-foreign sentiments to mobilize support for the idea of a KMT government (a tactic similar to one he later used to win acceptance of the Communist cause). He did not stay long. In December 1923 he returned to Shanghai, bringing with him an older Hunanese woman to do the cooking in the house he was sharing with Cai Hesen and other friends.[18]

Things did not go well for the Communists. While they made little progress of their own, right-wing anti-Communist elements in the Guomindang grew influential. To a disappointed Mao it began to seem that the Nationalist party had little commitment to its alliance with the Communists or to any real revolution. In July 1924 Mao and Chen Duxiu jointly wrote a memo warning Communist members to be alert to right-wing efforts to expel radical elements from the Guomindang: "Only in those places where the Guomindang is not an open party, and its local organizations are entirely created by us, can we work openly under the name of this association."[19]

In late 1924 a discouraged Mao took leave from his work to go home and rest. He remained at the family home throughout the winter and spring of 1924–1925. While others went abroad or immersed themselves in radical activities when the revolution was at low ebb, Mao returned to his roots, reinvolving himself in the life of the Hunan peasantry.

At a number of key junctures in his career, when things were not going well within the party, Mao took sick leave, causing later researchers to speculate about the psychological roots of these illnesses. But sick leave was a convention used by a number of CCP leaders well into the 1960s, when policies were implemented with which they did not agree. For instance, the economic planner Chen Yun retired from politics on "sick leave" at the start of the Great Leap Forward rather than clash with Mao.[20] Mao's use of this practice indicates his commitment throughout most of his career to avoid roiling the party even when he opposed it.

In this case his leave, which may have had some genuine roots, lasted less than a year. Prospects for the Communists improved dramatically on May 30, 1925, when British police in Shanghai killed thirteen labor demonstrators. Anti-foreign protests, boycotts, and strikes erupted throughout the country, drawing people of all classes and from every part of the nation. Overnight Communist party membership swelled from a few hundred to more than twenty thousand. The left wing of the KMT, which supported the alliance with the CCP, gained new influence. Energized by these events, Mao again became politically active, encouraging radical peasant activities in his native district. His actions so aroused the ire of the Hunan authorities that in October 1925 he fled the province.

Mao headed for Canton this time, deciding to work with the

Guomindang rather than with Chen Duxiu and the Central Committee of the CCP, who were still in Shanghai. In Canton the Guomindang left-wing leader Wang Jingwei, supported by Comintern officials and Canton party workers, had assumed the leadership of the KMT. Wang appointed Mao to the important post of acting head of the Guomindang propaganda department, a job Wang had become too busy to do himself. Mao also started and edited the official publication of the Guomindang executive committee, Political Weekly (Zhengzhi zhoubao). Overnight Mao became one of the most important CCP members in the KMT.

It was as an official of the Guomindang that Mao first published his later-to-be-famous ideas about the revolutionary potential of the peasantry that he had developed during his stay in the countryside. In an article, "An Analysis of the Different Classes of Chinese Society," issued in Canton in December 1925, Mao argued that the main force of the revolution was composed not only of urban workers but also of a group he called the rural proletariat—farm laborers. Also friendly to the revolution, in his view, were semi-owner tenant peasants, poor peasants, handicraftsmen, shop assistants, and street vendors, whom he called members of the semi-proletariat. The petty bourgeoisie—owner peasants, small merchants, master handicraftsmen, and the lower levels of the intellectual class—could also be drawn to the side of the revolution, he believed. The enemies of change were the warlords, large landlords, and wealthy merchants, whom Mao considered the big bourgeoisie. He thought the middle bourgeoisie would probably ultimately become enemies of the revolution, though some might be won over to its side. Finally, Mao suggested that the lumpenproletariat—thieves, soldiers, prostitutes, and the like—could, if properly led, fight for the revolution. This idea, developed further by Mao in other articles, was to lead to Mao's alliance in 1928 with two bandit leaders in the countryside.[21]

Mao's article was the beginning of what is often considered his original contribution to Chinese revolutionary thought. It is the first article in the official Chinese canon of his *Selected Works*. Yet in spite of what has been made of Mao's ideas in later years, the article issued in Canton was far from profound and not really all that radical. It showed Mao's acute powers of observation and his ability to assimilate vast quantities of data and organize it. But the basic idea he set forth was prosaic. Essentially Mao was arguing that if you wanted a revolution in China, you had to get the majority of the people on your side. The majority of the people were peasants and other rural workers. Attempts to relieve the poverty and suffering of the peasantry and other members of the downtrodden who lived in the countryside would attract their support and encourage them to help transform the existing Chinese political system.

Ever since at least the establishment of the Han dynasty in 206 B.C.E., it had been known that peasant rebellions were capable of toppling and transforming the governments of China. In 1922, three years before Mao wrote this article, the Princeton- and Yale-educated Chinese Y.M.C.A. director James Yen began to work with the Hunan warlord Zhao Hengti to develop a mass education program in rural Hunan. Within a few years he had developed a nationwide movement to improve agriculture and spread literacy among rural people. Also in the early 1920s, Peng Pai and radical reformers from Guangdong had begun to organize the peasants in their district to seize power.

Nor was the idea of a rural uprising foreign to the Soviets. Although Marx wrote about worker, not peasant, revolution, Lenin recognized the need to use the peasantry in carrying out the overthrow of the government. The Comintern had told the Chinese comrades that they needed to help carry out an "agrarian revolution" among the peasantry, a position that Mao supported at the Third Congress.

Chen Duxiu and other CCP leaders also recognized the need to get the peasants involved in the revolution. While working as Guangdong educational commissioner, Chen Duxiu supported

Peng Pai's peasant organizing activity. The Guangdong branch of the party was engaged in peasant organization before Mao published his article in Canton.[22]

A decade later, Mao told Edgar Snow that Chen Duxiu did not favor a radical land policy and had opposed Mao's article. Mao complained that he could not print the article in the central party organs and had to publish it in the *Canton Peasant Monthly* and *Chinese Youth Magazine*. His memory on this point seems to have been faulty. He first published the article in *Geming* (*Revolution*), the official organ of the Guomindang army.[23] There is no evidence that Chen Duxiu refused to publish the article.

A week before the article appeared, the right-wing Western Hills faction of the KMT broke with the party's left faction. Industrialists and warlords supported the Western Hills faction. Mao's article, which explained how to attract more people to the side of the revolution by reducing peasants' rent and other such policies, seems to have been an attempt to explain to the Guomindang military how they could carry out their mission without the support of the departed right wing.

Mao repeated many of these same points the next month, January 1926, at the Second Congress of the Guomindang.[24] Peasants, he suggested, hoped to eliminate warlords, bullies, and bad landlords. They wanted famine relief for the unemployed and better treatment of young farm laborers and women workers. They aimed to forbid usurious loans, reduce working hours, and abolish exorbitant taxes. Finally, they wanted adult education classes.

Mao wrote this analysis as a Guomindang official teaching at the Peasant Movement Training Institute of the KMT. In the spring he would be appointed principal of the institute. Over the next several months, Mao argued again and again that support for the KMT right wing came from big landlords, a group Mao called "the real deadly enemies of the Chinese peasantry, the true rulers of the countryside, the real foundation of imperialism and the warlords, the only secure bulwark of feudal and patriarchal society, the ultimate cause for the emergence of all counterrevolutionary forces." In article after article he classified the countryside, minutely describing the details of peasant life and suggesting that there were precisely 395 million people on the side of the revolution, only 1 million, or .25 percent, against the revolution, and about 4 million, or 1 percent, wavering in the middle. In a number of essays he was to write about the peasantry between 1925 and 1927, Mao, in his accountantlike fashion, placed these kinds of precise numbers on the friends and enemies of the revolution. In most of these essays, Mao used the figures to show that the Guomindang's left was strong enough to triumph without the departed right wing.[25]

But events did not occur exactly as Mao hoped. In March 1926 Jiang Kaishek, then identified as much with the left as with the right, launched a coup against his Communist allies in Canton, removing many of them from effective power within the KMT. Jiang drove Mao's boss Wang Jingwei out of the country and two months later appointed Gu Mengyu to replace Mao as head of the propaganda department. But Mao retained his job with the increasingly important Peasant Institute.

After the Comintern came to an understanding with Jiang, Soviet military advisers supported his Northern Expedition, the campaign to reunify the country by marching northward from Canton. When the expedition began in July 1926, Mao, as principal of the Peasant Institute, dispatched operatives into the field to organize the peasantry ahead of Jiang's advance. Peasant uprisings aided the army's mission. Warlord armies fearful of this fifth column threw in their lot with the KMT. Within a few months the greatly outnumbered but well-financed National Revolutionary Army of the Guomindang gained control of Hunan and Hubei. By the end of the year Jiang's forces had taken the provinces of Jiangxi and Fujian. In the early spring of 1927 revolutionary forces approached Nanjing and Shanghai. Most of the South was now at least nominally under the control of Jiang's armies.

While peasant organizers sought to consolidate their gains in the countryside, Jiang moved to the right to conciliate the growing number of warlord armies that had joined his ranks. In the countryside the principal supporters of the warlords were the large landlords. Thus Jiang distanced himself from the peasant movement, and in the process he terminated Mao's Peasant Training Institute. In November 1926 Mao moved to Shanghai to become head of a peasant commission that the CCP had established the previous year.

About this time Wang Jingwei returned from abroad and with the support of left-wing members of the KMT established a new KMT capital at Wuhan. Jiang Kaishek stayed away, ultimately establishing a separate headquarters in the old southern capital of Nanjing.

As this new rift developed between the left and right wings of the KMT, Mao continued to concentrate on the peasant movement. In February 1927 he published his famous essay "The Report on the Peasant Movement in Hunan," which he wrote in late 1926 and early 1927 as the result of an investigative trip to areas of his native province, where the peasant movement had surged. This passionately written essay expressed Mao's conviction that the peasantry had become an unstoppable force for change:

> What Mr. Sun Yatsen wanted, but failed, to accomplish in the forty years he devoted to the national revolution, the peasants have accomplished in a few months. The Revolution of 1911 did not bring about this change, hence its failure. Now a change is taking place, and this is an important factor for the completion of the revolution. Every revolutionary comrade must support this change or he will be a counterrevolutionary.[26]

Mao triumphantly proclaimed that those who had been at the bottom were now "giving orders and running things. They, who used to rank below everyone else, now rank above everybody else — that is what people mean by 'turning things upside down.' "[27]

For the first time in his revolutionary utterances, Mao did not shy away from terror and violence. He wrote his famous lines: "A revolution is not like inviting people to dinner, or writing an essay, or painting a picture, or doing embroidery; it cannot be so refined, so leisurely and gentle, so 'benign, upright, courteous, temperate, and complaisant.'" A few reactionaries in every country, he argued, had to be executed. Mao defended the excesses that peasants were committing against landlord and gentry groups, noting: "To right a wrong it is necessary to exceed the proper limits; the wrongs cannot be righted without doing so."[28]

Written in the middle of the KMT's war in which thousands of people were being killed daily, Mao's contention that the fighting could be resolved by killing reactionaries was not particularly extreme. Most of Mao's goals, in fact, seem reasonable and laudable by contemporary standards. He believed that the peasants were pursuing a democratic revolution in the countryside and creating "village self-rule." He argued that they sought to get rid of the old government and the police forces supporting it. They wanted to eliminate gambling, opium smoking, sedan chairs, banditry, vulgarity, and even liquor. Mao supported restrictions on the number of pigs, chickens, and ducks people could own—a proposal that may strike some today as radical—because, he explained, these animals consumed much grain at a time when there was little to go around and a need to prevent the price from rising too high. If "The Report" does not seem as provocative to modern readers as it did to Mao's contemporaries, it is nonetheless surprising that, as Benjamin Schwartz pointed out almost fifty years ago, it "is almost completely bare of Marxist trappings."[29]

But this isn't why the CCP—still trying to preserve the United Front—was leery of what Mao had written. CCP officials feared that sanctioning the executions of landlords would repel the warlord allies of Jiang Kaishek and his KMT officers from landlord backgrounds. Thus the party published only the first two parts of Mao's article in *Xiangdao (The Guide)*, the official organ of the

Chinese Communist party. The magazine refused to print the third section of the essay, in which Mao described peasant executions of landlords and attacked the left wing of the KMT for its fear of the masses. Mao, aided by Qu Qiubai (the Chinese Communist party leader who was then scheming to replace Chen Duxiu as the party leader), issued the essay in April as a pamphlet and distributed it in Wuhan. Qu and his backer, the Comintern agent Borodin, used the report to show that the party under Chen Duxiu was suppressing the mass movement.

Although some elements of the CCP worried about the radicalism of Mao's writing, the KMT left remained receptive to his ideas. Mao was a featured speaker at the Third Plenum of the Guomindang. He spoke at length about the results of his investigations in the countryside. On March 15, 1927, the KMT adopted Mao's suggestion that bad gentry and bullies needed to be dealt with through revolutionary means. The plenum also issued a manifesto proposed by Mao, calling on the peasants to form armed self-defense organizations—obviously a good way to gain new military recruits for the left wing of the Nationalist party, which was struggling to wrest power from Jiang Kaishek. After his speech at the party plenum, Mao once more settled into the life of a KMT party official.

But now Jiang Kaishek upended him. On April 12, 1927, Jiang's troops turned on their Communist allies in Shanghai. Aided by the notorious underworld group, the Green Gang, and by foreign forces in the city, Jiang's armies slaughtered thousands of Communists and their supporters, destroying the major stronghold of the Communist party. Over the next few months, while the Communists and the KMT left wing tended their own separate government in Wuhan, Jiang consolidated power throughout central China.

Talking to Edgar Snow in the 1930s, Mao believed that had Chen Duxiu sent him to Hunan at the time of Jiang's attack, he could have organized an independent Communist government in the countryside. Concerned about alienating the remaining party allies (other than Communists) among the KMT's left wing, the party turned Mao down. Party leaders also rejected his proposals to allow the widespread distribution of land. Concerned lest the leading classes in the countryside be turned prematurely against the party, the CCP deemed that only landlords owning "over 500 mou [82 acres] of land" should be subject to confiscation. Thus only very large landowners would be affected. Mao believed this policy blocked the success of the revolution.[30] During the CCP's Fifth Congress from April 27 to May 10, 1927, Mao played a much smaller role than he had at the Third Plenum. He was not even elected a full member of the Central Committee.

In late June 1927 the CCP finally began to realize the need for an independent army of its own. The party belatedly appointed Mao Hunan party secretary and sent him to the province to coordinate the peasant struggle there, hoping he would be able to use peasant militia groups to form a Communist army. It was too little and too late. In early July, as factional bickering continued between the left wing of the KMT and the CCP, Mao returned to Wuhan. He was still there on July 15, 1927, when Wang Jingwei decided to quit his independent initiative and link up once more with Jiang Kaishek, turning on his erstwhile Communist allies and ending the United Front. Like other Communist leaders, Mao was forced into hiding.

By the time the Communists convened an emergency conference on August 7, Mao Zedong was able to state forcefully for the first time the need for the CCP to mobilize its own independent military force. In an address to the meeting, Mao noted that the Communists should take a lesson from Jiang Kaishek's success in "grasping the gun." It was here that Mao made his famous and oftquoted statement: "Political power is obtained from the barrel of a gun."[31]

By 1927 Mao had traveled a political path from participation in the progressive Hunan establishment to membership in the Communist party and serious involvement with the Guomindang. In every organization he had shown himself to be quite willing to accept group sanctions and rules. His main goal was still to unify and develop China. He had recognized the natural revolutionary potential of the Chinese peasantry. He was one of the strongest defenders within the CCP of the need for the party to have an independent army. In the KMT, one of his most important audiences had been the left-wing military. One of the main points he had tried to make to this group was that in the process of helping the peasantry eliminate bullies, build schools, improve their livelihood, and create democracy, they would form armies to carry out a nationalist revolution that would unite the country and free it from tyranny. Although he was no longer a moderate, Mao hardly seemed like someone who would one day be considered one of the horrific tyrants of the twentieth century.

Rethinking Mao—
The Long March

🐾 WHILE I have been arguing that Mao's personality and actions differed greatly from Stalin's, I must also grudgingly acknowledge that it took a Stalin to appreciate Mao. It was the Soviet
leader who correctly foresaw that Mao's ability to connect with
everyday Chinese and his formidable organizational and strategic
skills would enable him to become an important player in the
Chinese revolution.[1]

Stalin began to take a strong interest in Mao beginning in the
1920s. This was especially fortunate for Mao, because in the twen-
ties and thirties he was not the original thinker or the brilliant
actor that many observers have later recognized. Many of his supposed accomplishments were more a testimony to Mao's after-the-
fact brilliance at self-promotion, or to the unsung help of the
Russians, than they were genuinely innovative thought and action.

The important role that Stalin played in Mao's career may
seem surprising, given that both Western and Chinese historians
have long argued that Mao's successes were achieved in spite of
hindrance by the Soviet leader. Yet at several key junctures Stalin
in fact furthered Mao's career. Mao himself acknowledged Stalin's
aid at the time of the Soviet leader's death: "We rallied around

him, ceaselessly asked his advice, and constantly drew ideological strength from his works."[2]

Several years after crediting Stalin, Mao began to change his views on Soviet communism and to claim retroactively that the Soviets had hindered the progress of the Chinese revolution. But although these ex post facto explanations have been widely accepted, it is undeniable that in August 1927 it was the new Comintern-dominated Chinese Communist party Central Committee that made Mao an alternate member of the Politburo, the first time he had risen to the top ranks of the leadership since 1924.

Stalin's representative in China, Besso Lomindaze, had determined Mao to be quite capable. But it turned out that Mao was not yet ready to meet Lomindaze's expectations. After Lomindaze authorized the new party leader, Qu Qiubai (1899–1935), to order revolts in Hubei, Jiangxi, and Hunan, Qu put Mao in charge of the Hunan insurrection. Mao formed a small army of coal miners, peasants, and soldiers who had defected from the Guomindang. On September 9, 1927, his troops began the uprising. The peasant movement of which Mao had written six months earlier had already collapsed. Within ten days the government crushed Mao's ragtag, inexperienced forces.

Mao himself was captured, but he broke away and hid in the grass, narrowly escaping with his life. As if this were not sufficiently humiliating, the party's Central Committee, which had previously registered its concern with Mao's "military opportunism," blamed him for deviating from the party's policy by not distributing land to the peasants and not "massacring the local bullies and bad gentry."[3] They relieved him of all party offices.

Mao took to the hills, leading the thousand or so survivors from his army to a remote stronghold in the Jinggang Mountains on the Hunan-Jiangxi border. There he linked up with what he later referred to as two former bandit groups whom he claimed to have converted to communism.[4]

In the spring of 1928 Zhu De, a military leader who nine

months earlier had helped lead an uprising in the Jiangxi provincial capital of Nanchang, brought his army to Jinggangshan. Zhu
became commander of what would be known as the Fourth Red
Army, and Mao became political commissar. But their positions
fluctuated based on orders from the Central Committee and their
own personal rivalries. Even on the remote hilltop of Jinggangshan, Mao not only remained attentive to the occasional commu-
niqués from Shanghai, but time after time he dutifully compared
the situation in China to that of Russia at the time of its revolution—a fact often not recognized because in the post-1949 official
edition of Mao's works, these comparisons were edited out.[5]

Mao did not write only about party issues. With the help of
Zhu he developed a few pithy, easily remembered military phrases
for the mostly illiterate and ill-trained soldiers they commanded:
"The enemy advances, we retreat; the enemy camps, we harass;
the enemy tires, we attack; the enemy retreats, we pursue."[6]

Mao wrote down these and other sayings a few months after
leaving Jinggangshan. By the 1960s they were being quoted in a
manner that suggested they were profound and original. But as
Mao made clear at the time, the sayings were simply vernacular
rewordings of Sun Zi's two-thousand-year-old Chinese military
classic.

Mao and Zhu combined the military tactics of Sun Zi with
land distribution among the peasants. But given the meager provi-
sions available to the Red Army on Jinggangshan, Mao's troops
often had to depend on expropriations from landlords and exac-
tions from merchants. In the winter of 1928–1929, warlord armies
allied with Jiang Kaishek gradually began to overwhelm Mao's
forces.

At about this time, in November 1928, the Fourth Red Army
was reinforced by the arrival of a ragged band of soldiers under the
command of Peng Dehuai, a Hunanese from the same county as
Mao. (This is the same Peng Dehuai with whom Mao was to have
a bitter confrontation in the 1950s.) On January 14, 1929, not long

after Peng arrived, Mao left the unhappy Peng in Jinggangshan to deal with Jiang. He and Zhu led their followers out of Jinggangshan, crossed Jiangxi province, and—after a terrible battle in which half their forces perished—established themselves in a new base near Ruijin in the Fujian-Jiangxi border region.

In his talks with Edgar Snow a few years later, Mao complained that while he was on Jinggangshan, the Central Committee wanted him to adopt a policy "of raiding, burning and killing of landlords in order to destroy their morale." Instead he instituted a moderate land-reform policy emphasizing "free trade, generous treatment of captured enemy troops, and, in general, democratic moderation."[7] Mao's policy was not as moderate as he later suggested to Snow, but it was more realistic than that of Qu Qiubai, whom the Comintern stripped of all his party posts in the summer of 1928. The party leadership passed to Zhou Enlai and Li Lisan. Li had been a rival of Mao's since their student days in Changsha.

At the Sixth Party Congress, held for reasons of security in Moscow in the summer of 1928, the CCP adopted a policy calling for a United Front with as many of the peasantry as possible. The approach was so moderate that in June 1929 Stalin criticized the "indulgent" attitude toward the rich peasants adopted in the Sixth Congress. Stalin's stance was close to the position of Mao, whose ideas coincidentally and eerily echoed the Soviet premier's throughout much of the 1930s.[8] Rich peasants were those who, working their own land, produced enough of a surplus that they were able to hire others to work for them. In spite of the debate that raged over the policy toward rich peasants, middle peasants, and even small landlords, the emphasis on the peasantry led to a surge in the soviet movement. By 1930 there were eight Chinese soviets. The largest one was Mao's in Jiangxi, but an important base also existed in west Hunan-Hubei (Xiang-Exi) under He Long, and in Hubei-Henan-Anhui (E-Yu-Wan) under Xu Xiangqian. These rural soviets contained almost a hundred thousand party members. Jiang Kaishek's conflict with the warlords

Feng Yuxiang and Yan Xishan provided the soviets a breathing space that lasted until October of that year, when Jiang launched the first of five "suppression" campaigns to annihilate these enclaves.

Mao was thirty-seven years old when he and Zhu De established the Jiangxi base. As he had done on Jinggangshan, he began a series of social surveys to gather information for a program of land reform and agrarian revolution. His eye for detail and organization served him once again. In his study of Xunwu, Mao compiled the name of every gentry and every merchant as well as every item produced and sold in the district.[9] This kind of information allowed him to write authoritatively on leadership, political training, military discipline, and territorial bases.

The program he offered was reasonable and levelheaded. In thinking about the military, for instance, he advocated the elimination of brutal practices like corporal punishment and urged soldiers and cadres to develop professional attitudes and discipline in their jobs.[10]

Driving him to consider these options realistically was Mao's sense of revolutionary optimism. Paradoxically it led him to embrace what others saw as Stalin's most absurd and coldly manipulative gestures toward the Chinese revolution. In July 1929, a few months after Mao arrived in Jiangxi, Chinese authorities arrested the manager and seized the telegraph operations of the Russian-operated Chinese Eastern Railway, which in 1924 the Soviets had promised to place under joint Chinese-Soviet control. Soviet troops then attacked and forced the Chinese to restore Russian control of the railroad. The Soviets called on the Chinese Communists to rally behind the slogan "Defend the Soviet Union with Arms." Chen Duxiu, the founder and first secretary general of the CCP, saw this as the last straw. He left the party and became a Trotskyist. Chen particularly mocked Soviet claims that China was about to enter a new high tide of revolution and that CCP uprisings would catch this new "revolutionary wave." But Mao de-

fended the Soviet Union against the Guomindang, truly believing
that the revolution was imminent.[11]

Even before word came from Stalin about "the beginning of
the revolutionary wave" in China, Mao in January 1930 advanced
similar feelings in a letter to Lin Biao, later his defense minister
during the Cultural Revolution. The purpose of the letter was to
refute Lin's pessimism about the possibility of a new revolutionary
tide. After liberation all references to Lin were deleted, and an edited version of the letter was published as the now-famous article
"A Single Spark Can Start a Prairie Fire." As revised, the article
showed Mao's prescience in describing how the slender Chinese
forces would soon grow and how the party's power could be developed in inland areas away from direct imperialist power. Although
Mao's prediction was ultimately realized, most readers have not
understood that Mao's assessment of the situation at the time was
wrong. It was Lin who was correct. Mao's plan to "take Jiangxi in
one year" did not happen. It was not, as he and Stalin believed,
the right time to mass troops for a revolutionary high tide.[12]

Yet Mao was not alone in his optimism. Party leader Li Lisan
believed this was a time for even more radical action. In June 1930
he ordered the Red Army to attack the major cities of central
China. On July 27, 1930, Peng Dehuai occupied Changsha, holding the city for ten days. At the end of July Mao and Zhu De's
forces marched on Nanchang. After discovering how heavily forti-
fied the city was, they made a symbolic show of force and then retreated. In late August, at the party's urging, Mao and Zhu joined
Peng in another attack on Changsha. By September 12 they were
forced to abandon this somewhat lackadaisical siege, though they
did manage to take the smaller Jiangxi provincial city of Jian and
hold it for six weeks.

Mao paid a terrible personal price for these foiled assaults. In
the summer of 1930 the vengeful warlord government of Hunan
executed Yang Kaihui, Mao's former wife. His adopted sister, Mao
Zejian, was also killed. Friends and relatives hid Mao's three sons

until they could be secreted in Shanghai, where the two older boys spent several years living on the streets. The party eventually rescued them and sent them to the Soviet Union. The middle son seems to have incurred brain damage, which hampered him for the rest of his life. The youngest son disappeared altogether. Although Mao was to mourn Yang Kaihui throughout his life, writing one of his most soulful poems in her memory, by the time she was killed he had already "married" an eighteen-year-old girl named He Zizhen, with whom he was to remain for many years and who bore him several children, most of whom had to be placed with peasant families. After 1949 several searches were mounted for the abandoned children, but they remained lost.[13]

Li Lisan also suffered for his temerity. On August 6, 1930, Qu Qiubai and Zhou Enlai, then in Moscow, were sent back to China to moderate Li's excesses. On January 16, 1931, the Fourth Plenum of the CCP sent Li Lisan to the Soviet Union for "study" and named Wang Ming the new head of the Chinese Communist party.

By this time Mao had begun some purges of his own. He had had to deal with tensions between the outsiders who had come from Hunan and older local party groups. The rich peasants and small landlords who rushed to join the party ranks once it became the new ruling structure in the area had weakened party discipline and diluted its ideology. As Guomindang forces bore down on the soviet, the resentment of the locals increased, as did Mao's urgency to build a strong, coherent party. In November 1930 Mao's forces arrested almost four thousand officers and men from the First Front Army, claiming they were members of a seditious AB corps (a reference to an older KMT group that had been in the area). About half were executed.

In December troops associated with the purged cadres rose against Mao in an event known as the Futian Incident. The rebellious army seized the prison, freed many of those imprisoned by Mao, and killed more than a hundred of Mao's supporters. These local cadres proclaimed themselves the legitimate government and appealed to Zhu De, Peng Dehuai, and other leaders for support against Mao's "despotism."[14] Since the government of the soviet was then defending itself against Jiang Kaishek's suppression campaign, the insurrection was for the moment ignored.

Mao and Zhu De resolved to deal with the KMT attacks by allowing the vastly larger and better equipped Guomindang army to enter deep into the soviet's territory, where the Communists could then use the advantages of better intelligence, terrain, and supply to launch a surprise counterattack. Early in 1931 they routed the KMT.

The victory did not mollify Mao's enemies within the party. Many members of the so-called AB corps were cadres from the soviet base area. They had wanted the Red Army to defend the soviet from the outside or at least to divert the enemy to other locations. Local cadres, even those not labeled as members of the AB corps, sympathized with this position. Victorious or not, they opposed Mao's tactics of luring the KMT into the soviet, bringing destruction to land and property and the deaths of many supporters, friends, and relatives.

When the Central Committee learned of this division within the ranks, a representative tried to mediate between Mao and the rebels. At the same time the party was also debating its tactics in opposing the huge 200,000-man army that Jiang had assembled. To many it seemed that the 30,000 soviet troops stood no chance against Jiang's new force and that the Communists should either disperse their troops into small, scattered units or relocate to a new site, sparing the soviet the hazards of further battle. It was not until early April that a delegation sent by the new CCP leader, Wang Ming, brought word of the Central Committee's support for Mao. This tipped the scales. Mao and Zhu De won a majority of votes for the strategy they had used successfully in the first campaign.

Consolidating his support, Mao quickly moved against the rebels, executing several thousand. Over the next few months

Mao's forces continued to arrest and kill officers and cadres from the AB corps. Ultimately, as one historian has noted, "the purges became so widespread, decentralized, and paranoid that for a time they were beyond the control of any of the top leaders."[15] One reason for this behavior is that Mao and Zhu were distracted by other concerns. They were in the midst of successfully repelling the second encirclement campaign and winning an important military victory.

Mao's purge of the AB corps was not a precursor to the Cultural Revolution. While reprehensible, the purge took place under conditions of war. During the same period Jiang Kaishek and his supporters were ruthlessly assaulting villagers suspected of supporting Communist infiltration. In Shanghai, Zhou Enlai and the Central Committee were ordering the deaths of the families of those who defected from the Communist cause. Although I will later show in more detail why Mao was not the kind of villain that his mentor Stalin was, he certainly could be draconian and authoritarian when the situation demanded it and when his interests were at stake. In this case at least, Mao's killings served a viable though not a defensible purpose. As Stephen Averill and Stuart Schram have noted:

> Whatever else may be said about the purges, they assisted Mao's efforts to centralize and consolidate power within the base area. . . . The fact that by autumn 1931 a very high percentage — in many places the vast majority — of the founders and leading cadres of local bases throughout southern Jiangxi and western Fujian had been either killed or cowed by the purges did much to facilitate these processes of centralization and consolidation of power into the hands of higher-level regional Party and army organs and their leaders.[16]

What the killings did not accomplish was to prevent a new Guomindang assault. By July 1931, just a month after the second campaign ended, Jiang began a third encirclement campaign, this time assembling a massive army of 300,000 troops commanded by some of his leading generals. Mao's tired and ill-equipped troops somehow succeeded in holding off the huge force until early September, when Jiang was forced to withdraw his army to deal with threats from political rivals in Hunan, giving Mao a third victory.

Although Mao had proved his value as a military strategist, other Communist military leaders were thought to have a much better understanding of theoretical matters. In November 1931, at two back-to-back party congresses, Mao's party positions were downgraded somewhat. He was appointed to the more visible though less important role of chairman of the soviet government. He was now the formal head of a government with some five million people under its control.

If Mao was happy with his new role, he did not remain so for long. Even before the Jiangxi party congresses, the Central Committee had begun to criticize him for being too lenient with rich peasants and landlords and not sufficiently diligent against counterrevolutionaries, and for promoting "guerrillaism."[17] A month after the congresses ended, Zhou Enlai arrived in Jiangxi, signaling Mao's political decline. As the highest-ranking member of the Central Committee in Jiangxi, Zhou took over from Mao the position he had held as acting secretary of the Central Bureau. Zhou also looked into Mao's harsh actions against the AB corps, issuing a report critical of Mao. Zhou was an experienced military leader who had served on the Northern Expedition. In January 1932 the Central Committee relieved Mao of his military duties for "health reasons," and he and his wife retired to an old temple.

Shortly thereafter Mao was called back to duty, and for almost six months he again helped plan military affairs. In March 1932 he suggested a march into Fujian. Although his proposal was rejected, Mao used his influence over the military leaders Lin Biao and Nie Rongzhen to lead part of the army into Fujian anyway, more or less in defiance of the soviet government.[18] The successful raid proved once again Mao's brilliance as a military strategist.

But in October 1932 incensed party leaders removed all of Mao's remaining military responsibilities, and Zhou Enlai took charge of military operations. Soon after, Mao was diagnosed with tuberculosis and spent three or four months recuperating.

For the next two years, until the start of the Long March, Mao remained removed from military affairs. In his absence, Zhu De and Zhou Enlai faced the fourth encirclement campaign launched by Jiang Kaishek. In the first few months of 1933, ignoring advice from the Central Committee, they returned to the tactics of mobile warfare used earlier by Mao and Zhu. They succeeded without the strategy of drawing the Guomindang troops into the soviet area that had been used by Mao in the three earlier campaigns.[19]

Meanwhile Mao, as chairman of the soviet, immersed himself in the rules and regulations of government. He involved himself in a myriad of details, from suggesting the type of newsprint to be used in newsletters to deciding the precise punishments for various crimes. He worked out the details of new tax policies and wrote a marriage law that granted women, except those married to soldiers, complete freedom of divorce. He made suggestions about crop plantings. He objected to the prevailing policy of rubber-stamping candidates for local elections, insisting that voters should at least be allowed to reject the candidates selected by the party. He also wanted to make sure that "at least 25 percent of those elected are working women."[20] He remained vitally concerned about improving education and developing the economy.

He also was interested in minority affairs, continually reminding his fellow Communists that according to the 1931 constitution of the new soviet, Tibetans and other nationalities not only had the full right of self-determination if they remained within the Chinese federation, but if they so chose could secede from China and establish their own states. Mao emphasized these concerns throughout the mid-1930s, telling Edgar Snow in 1936 that the Communists opposed the "Pan-Hanism" of the KMT policy toward minorities. Mao maintained that "minorities can of their own will unite with the Han to oppose Japanese imperialism, but force will never be used against them." In December 1935, when the party looked to establish itself in the North, Mao proclaimed his support for the Mongol struggle to "preserve the epoch of Genghis Khan," and acknowledged Inner Mongolia's right "to remain completely separate." In May 1936, in a statement to the Muslim nationalities of China, he not only insisted that the party wanted all Muslims (and other minorities) to handle their own affairs, but he called on them to "unite with Turkey, Outer Mongolia, the Soviet Union, and other nationalities and countries."[21]

In early 1933, while Mao was involved with administrative matters, the German Comintern officer Otto Braun, a six-foot blue-eyed blond whose Chinese name was Li De, took control of military policy. Years later Braun would reminisce about the seven years he lived with the Red Army, remembering Mao as a "slender, almost willowy man, more a philosopher and poet than a politician and soldier." Mao, Braun noted, "maintained a solemn reserve," encouraging others to "drinking, story-telling, and singing," but not joining in himself. Like a revolutionary Charlie Chan, Braun's Mao had an aphorism for every occasion. When the Communists were debating whether to try to break out of the encirclement by Jiang's forces, Mao "commented noncommittally: A bad butcher splits the bones with a cleaver; a good butcher severs them with a blunt knife." Braun believed that Mao developed sayings such as these "into catchy slogans of revolutionary pathos" so that he could "sweep away his audience of peasants and soldiers with his words."[22]

While Mao was yielding to Braun's advice, Jiang Kaishek was using his own German military advisers lent him by the Nazis. In October 1933 Jiang assembled a new force of more than 500,000 for the fifth encirclement campaign. This time he pursued a slow, methodical advance against the soviet, building a series of block-houses connected by modern roads that drew an ever-tighter ring around the enclave.

After initial attempts to defend the base areas from within, Braun switched to a strategy he called "short, swift thrusts," engaging the Guomindang through attacks in areas that attempted to divert Jiang's troops away from the encirclement of the Soviet. It is uncertain that any strategy could have succeeded against the huge force that Jiang and his Nazi advisers had this time arrayed so efficiently, but in any event Jiang's tactics bested Braun's. In October, after it became clear that they could no longer hold off the KMT's forces, soviet leaders decided to relocate, setting off on what became known as the Long March.

On October 10 an army of 86,000 broke out of the base area. According to one account, "All but a handful of those who left were able-bodied men. There were almost no women among the eighty-six thousand marchers; about thirty-five women went with the First Front Army, together with some female nurses."[23] Most of the money and supplies went with them; those left behind had to fend for themselves. Among those whom Braun and Zhou Enlai decided to leave behind was Mao's youngest brother, Mao Zetan, who was killed by Nationalist troops in 1935.

Originally the intent of the marchers was to head into neighboring Hunan to link up with Communist forces in the northwestern part of that province. Blocked from this direction, they headed further westward, suffering huge losses as they moved. In the first month and a half of the march, Jiang's forces continued ground and air assaults on the heavily weighted army. In late November the crossing of the Xiang River in northern Guangxi resulted in devastating losses. By early December fewer than thirty thousand troops remained.

On December 12 the struggling army stopped in the small southwestern Hunan town of Tongdao, and on December 18 they rested in the town of Liping in Guizhou. At meetings in these towns, the majority of the Politburo agreed with Mao that the best strategy was for the army to forget about fighting its way through Guomindang lines in order to link up with nearby Communist base areas. They decided to head westward toward the lightly defended town of Zunyi in Guizhou, and planned to move on from there to establish a new base in southern Sichuan.

At the Zunyi Conference of January 15–17, 1935, Mao again became a member of the Standing Committee of the Politburo, gaining the right to be involved in all party and army decisions. Zhang Wentian, who had supported Mao, became the new party leader. In yet another meeting two months later, Mao was named political commissar of the army and Zhu De its commander-in-chief. By the end of March, Mao had become one of three military leaders of the party, along with Wang Jiaxiang, who was severely wounded on the Long March, and Zhou Enlai, whose authority had been diminished by defeat in the fifth encirclement campaign. By default Mao soon came to exercise primary responsibility for military decisions, which were to be the key decisions for the rest of the Long March. Zhou was the chief decision-maker, but Mao was now his primary assistant, removing from Braun his control of military affairs.[24]

Mao's promotion was largely due to the failure of Braun's military strategy as well as Mao's own lobbying, but it was also a result of powerful outside help. In November Moscow had signaled the beleaguered Communist forces that it considered Mao an important leader. For years Stalin had looked favorably on Mao, no doubt noting that he was one of the few leaders whose views on the Chinese situation most often paralleled his own. Now, as the party meandered through the remote recesses of the Chinese interior, cut off from most contact with the outside world, one of the last words they would hear from Moscow in many months was that Stalin supported Mao.[25]

Because of Stalin's endorsement, fortunate circumstances, and his own good judgment and personality, Mao would emerge from the Long March as one of the few leaders viewed as not responsible for the mistakes made in the fifth encirclement campaign and in the initial stages of the Long March. He was one of only two Politburo members who "survived the Long March without committing major errors or suffering serious setbacks."[26] The other was Liu Shaoqi, but Liu had no military experience. Mao's growing responsibility for military matters greatly enhanced his overall position in the party during the course of the Long March, especially after he helped maneuver the army out of several seemingly impossible situations.

He Zizhen, Mao's wife, did not fare as well. One of the few women on the journey, she became pregnant at the beginning of the Long March. After giving birth she was forced to abandon the baby to the care of peasants along the way. Throwing herself back into the struggle, she was in a convalescent unit caring for the wounded when a Nationalist plane strafed the area. She threw herself over one of the soldiers to protect him from the bombs and was struck in the head with shrapnel. For days she was unconscious and near death. Somehow she recovered and continued the march, though she was carried much of the way on litters. She gave birth to another daughter not long after she and Mao settled into the new Communist base area at the end of the Long March. The daughter survived, but a son she subsequently gave birth to in Moscow, where she lived after separating from Mao, died while in a Soviet nursing school. The baby boy had been her sixth child.[27]

As Mao had advocated, the Communist army proceeded into Sichuan. After making a difficult journey through territory inhabited by unfriendly Tibetan and Yi minorities who harassed them, they made a dangerous crossing of the Dadu (Tatu) River, which in Edgar Snow's later description was presented as the heroic focus of the epic of the Long March.[28] Although the troops were now in Sichuan, this was really the Tibetan borderland, an area with a large Tibetan population and many Tibetan place names, a territory beyond the pale of the Guomindang.

In mid-June they met up with Zhang Guotao. Zhang, like Mao, had been a leading member of the party since its formal founding in 1921. He had studied in Russia and had shown himself at least as adept as Mao in military matters and probably more so in theoretical concerns. He commanded a larger army. "According to recent accounts," Stuart Schram writes, "Zhang Guotao's forces numbered 70,000 to 80,000, while only 7,000 to 10,000 remained of the First Front Army after the losses caused by enemy action and the many perils of the journey from Jiangxi to Sichuan."[29] Had Zhang's forces merged permanently with Mao's, Zhang might very well have become the supreme leader. Now, unable to contact the Comintern, the two sides jockeyed for power, differing on which direction to head.

Although they agreed to work together, in early September 1935 Zhang's main forces balked at traveling through the almost impossible terrain of the Tibetan grasslands and turned back. Zhu De, who might also have been a contender with Mao for supreme power, stayed with Zhang.[30] Fearing Zhang might still try to resolve this internal conflict militarily, Mao pushed his forces toward the border with the Soviet Union, where his exhausted and understaffed army could get help from their Communist brethren.

Mao later claimed that he took his troops north to fight the Japanese invasion. Ever since the 1931 Manchurian Incident, when Japanese forces conquered Northeast China and began to clash with Chinese forces around Shanghai, Japan's growing occupation of Chinese territory had disturbed Chinese nationalists. Throughout the early 1930s Mao and the CCP had made a number of statements opposing these incursions, which aroused ever greater Chinese sentiment as the Japanese maintained their military pressure and added to their territory in North China by occupying much of Inner Mongolia. Nonetheless Mao's primary concern had been fighting the Guomindang and linking up with the Soviet Union. At no time did Mao mention to Zhang or any-

one else that he wanted to head north primarily to help repel the
Japanese invasion.

But Mao's plans to head toward the Soviet border changed
when Mao and his colleagues discovered from Guomindang papers that a Communist base area existed in Shaanbei, in northern
Shaanxi province near the base of the Great Wall. Mao now determined to head there, pledging to unite the Chinese people against
the invading Japanese in the North. So while Zhang Guotao
headed south, Mao's forces went north, making their way across
the Tibetan grasslands in another grueling phase of an already
harrowing journey. Toward the end of October 1935, Mao's greatly
diminished armies arrived in Shaanxi, ending the Long March.

By any ordinary analysis the Long March had been a colossal
military failure, resulting in the almost total destruction of the Red
Army and the loss of an important base area. But one of Mao's key
attributes was his ability to see the positive aspects of what many
would view as horrifying and crippling events. Eight months later,
when Edgar Snow arrived in Mao's base area, invited because of
Stalin's instructions that the CCP develop international connec-
tions, Mao in his interviews with Snow used his power with words
to cast the march in an epic light. It mesmerized Snow, just as it
later would Chinese audiences. As a result of Mao's narration and
Snow's reporting, the Long March came to be considered an epic
of human endurance that put the Communist forces into fighting
form. As one mocking writer has noted:

> Snow chose to skim quickly over the early stages of confusion and
> hardship and focus on the battle he had first learned about in
> Sian, the battle to cross the Tatu River in the remote mountains
> of Szechuan. His story of that pivotal event blended revealing his-
> tory with agitprop drama more effectively than anything he had
> observed at the outdoor theater in Pao-an.

When Snow's reports of his northwest journey began to reach

readers in China even before *Red Star over China* was published
in English, this story would stir the passionate idealism of a generation of young people hungry for an authentic national political
force to believe in. And for generations after the Communists
came to power, songs, films, and endless political rhetoric would
celebrate the battle over the Tatu. Edgar Snow gave the crossing
of the Tatu a giant push into the same realm of legendary history
as the Battle of Valley Forge occupies in American history.[31]

It was not just that Snow overemphasized the famous battle to
cross the Dadu, where a detachment of Communists, after making
a nearly impossible forced march along almost impassable mountain trails, crept across a half-destroyed iron suspension bridge
straight into Nationalist machine-gun fire. Snow also exaggerated
the extent to which "the Reds themselves declared, and apparently
believed, that they were advancing towards the anti-Japanese front,
and this was a psychological factor of great importance. It helped
them turn what might have been a demoralized retreat into a spir-
ited march of victory." Although Mao had "declared war" on
Japan as early as 1932, and although he had claimed that his army
was heading north in order to fight the Japanese, these statements
were made without much conviction. They probably would have
been just one more rhetorical cry if Stalin had not found a way to
make Mao's nationalist agenda more than just empty rhetoric.[32]
While the CCP was on the Long March, Stalin's Comintern,
concerned about events in Germany and Japan, called for a
United Front in China of all elements, classes, and nations in the
fight against fascism. In an effort to make it look as though their
Chinese comrades had originated this change in Chinese Communist policy, the Soviets had Wang Ming issue from Moscow
(where Wang resided at the time) an "August First Declaration"
(1935) in the name of the CCP and the Chinese Soviet Republic.
Wang Ming declared that it was the "sacred duty of everyone to resist Japan and save the nation." While the document criticized the

actions of "scum" and "traitors" such as Jiang Kaishek, Yan Xishan, and Zhang Xueliang who had not adopted a policy of resistance to Japan, it declared the willingness of the CCP to cooperate with all those prepared to join a government of national defense.[33]

Sometime after Mao and his group were shown this document in November 1935, they issued a new manifesto saying they were willing to align with any group against the Japanese. But Mao's primary aim was still to move to the Soviet border and become "one with the Soviet Union and the People's Republic of Mongolia." It was not until December 1935 that an enlarged CCP Politburo meeting endorsed the idea of creating the widest political front to oppose Japanese imperialism *and* Jiang Kaishek, and agreed to combine the civil war with the national war against Japan. Reflecting this conciliatory approach, the party changed the name of its government from the Worker and Peasant Soviet Republic into the People's Soviet Republic, hoping to create a broader alliance of social and political groups. Mao began to concentrate on how to carry out the campaign to resist Japan. He did not, however, abandon his attempt to link up with Soviet troops, though his efforts to push through to the border were continually frustrated by Guomindang troops.[34]

As part of the United Front strategy, the Comintern directed the CCP to moderate its social policy by distributing land to rich peasants and to welcome industrial and commercial entrepreneurs to invest in the Chinese soviet. The Chinese Politburo complied, with only minor modifications.[35] Criteria for party membership were relaxed. Businessmen and other patriots were told that their rights would be protected. These policies of inclusiveness would bring increased public support for the CCP.

The Soviets even helped heal the split within the CCP. After he separated from Mao, Zhang Guotao had formed his own Central Committee, eliminating Zhou and Mao from power. Now that all groups were again in touch with Moscow, the Comintern threw its support behind Mao and his colleagues. It ordered

Zhang to drop his pretense at standing for the Communist party as a whole and to join together with Mao's forces. Although Zhang did not immediately comply, approximately a year later, in December 1936, after his forces had been battered and greatly reduced, Zhang Guotao brought his troops to Shaanxi, eliminating one of Mao's major foes within the party. In December 1938 Zhang, who had been marginalized within the CCP, joined the KMT. After 1949 he moved to Canada, where he wrote his memoirs.

On December 9, 1935, even before Zhang rejoined the party, Beijing students mounted street demonstrations against the Guomindang's so-called policies of appeasement toward the Japanese. Nationwide protests ensued. The sentiment motivating the December 9th Movement, as it came to be called, struck a particular chord with the leaders of the KMT's Northeastern Army under Zhang Xueliang's command. Four years earlier Zhang's army had been pushed out of Manchuria by the Japanese invasion. They were receptive to the appeal that Zhang's forces and the Communists join together in resisting the Japanese.

By February 1936 Zhang's forces had entered into talks with the Communists. The Guomindang itself also began tentative discussions with the CCP. Zhang Xueliang insisted that in order for the United Front to succeed, Mao had to stop calling for the overthrow of Jiang Kaishek and instead join the generalissimo in the war against the Japanese.[36] On July 13, 1936—the same day that Edgar Snow arrived at Mao's headquarters—Jiang Kaishek took a stand against Japan's puppet regime in China, and Mao responded positively. Increasingly he began to talk about the need for a United Front.

These steps helped, but again Stalin had to push Mao into making further concessions to the Guomindang. The Soviet leader had now begun to funnel badly needed money to the Chinese forces while promoting his United Front ideas. In August

1936 the Soviet Union, with whom Mao was now in telegraphic contact, demanded that the CCP move closer to Jiang Kaishek and establish even firmer ties with Zhang Xueliang. Mao, of course, realized all this was in his interest, and he agreed to Zhang Xueliang's demand that the Communists work to get Jiang to join together with them to resist Japan. In September 1936 the CCP and Zhang Xueliang, who by this time had been given reason to believe that he too would receive Soviet military aid, reached a secret agreement to cooperate.[37]

On December 12, 1936, Zhang Xueliang arrested Jiang Kaishek after Jiang flew into Xian to prosecute the war against the Communists. The jubilant CCP initially wished to try Jiang before a People's Court. The Soviets, however, called Jiang a patriot who had shown his willingness to lead the defense against Japan. They worried that the kidnapping would result in Jiang's replacement with someone in the KMT government more acceptable to Japan—a not unrealistic concern. Stalin demanded that the CCP seek a peaceful resolution of the situation and that the two sides work together for a democratic China. He telegraphed Mao telling him to "take a resolute stand in favor of a peaceful solution to this conflict" and to use the opportunity to create a broad anti-Japanese movement. Edgar Snow was sent a postcard from a friend, which described how when Mao received the telegram he "flew into a rage, swore and stamped his feet."[38] Whether or not this is true, Mao complied, agreeing that if Jiang approved of the coalition against Japan he should be freed. Despite his feelings, Mao understood that this was probably greatly in his interest.

On December 25 Jiang Kaishek agreed to the United Front. Feeling personally obliged, Zhang Xueliang naively accompanied the generalissimo to Nanjing, where he was promptly arrested by Jiang Kaishek. He was not released by the Nationalists until the 1990s. The Northeastern Army evacuated the city of Yan'an, and the CCP was able to move its headquarters there. They were to remain in Yan'an for the duration of the war. Negotiations between the CCP and the KMT continued for the next several months, not aided by the ill will created by Zhang's arrest.

On July 7, 1937, when Japanese troops crossed the Marco Polo Bridge near Beijing and began to move farther into Chinese territory, Jiang at last agreed to the Second United Front. In August the Guomindang accepted Communist troops as part of the Nationalist army. The Red Army was renamed the Eighth Route Army of the National Revolutionary Army. In November the remaining Communist guerrilla forces in central China were renamed the New Fourth Army.

Under the Second United Front the Communists radically expanded their army and their following. By the end of the war Mao had become the undisputed leader of the CCP, and his forces had grown so large that they were in a position to challenge Jiang for the supreme leadership of China. Mao reached this stage by being a durable and crafty politician and a clever military tactician with an eye for administrative detail and a common touch. But he was given a kick-start by Stalin, who often favored Mao over his opponents within the party and who pushed him to accept the United Front strategy.

By 1937 Mao was not yet the supreme leader of the party, but thanks to the public relations brilliance that would later serve him so well, he was already seen by the world as an up-and-coming Communist star. Later Mao's shrewdness with propaganda allowed him to understate his debt to Stalin, who not only aided his career but regarded him as the one Chinese Communist leader whose ideas were closest to those of the Russians. It is therefore ironic—though consistent with the distorted view of Mao—that he is often credited as being independent from the Soviets during the 1930s, whereas in the 1960s and 1970s, when Mao actually broke with the Russians, he is considered to have become a Stalinist.

FIVE

Becoming the Chairman

❧ IT WAS an American, Edgar Snow, who shaped the way the world first looked at Mao. Snow's seminal portrait of Mao has since been retouched—indeed, painted over—by others so thoroughly as to resemble the attic picture of a haggard Dorian Gray, but the force of the original remains. Snow transformed Mao's life into a captivating tale of a poor child of the soil who triumphed over evil and adversity to save himself and those he held dear.

In *Red Star over China*, which sold twelve thousand copies in its first month of publication in 1937, Snow depicted Mao as a pragmatic man still close to his humble roots. Robert Farnsworth, Snow's biographer, notes that in *Red Star over China* "the personality of Mao is put vividly before the reader early and dominates all four parts concerned with soviet life in the capital." Snow refers to Mao as a "cross-section of a whole generation" and suggests that "whatever there was extraordinary in this man grew out of the uncanny degree to which he synthesized and expressed the urgent demands of millions of Chinese, and especially the peasantry."[1]

The reporter filled his book with telling, humanizing details and with tales of Mao's devotion to his people, his shrewdness, hard work, and stamina. In this regard Snow's story of Mao had much in common with *The Good Earth*, by the Nobel Prize–winner Pearl Buck, who was Snow's friend and contemporary. That story transposed American Horatio Alger myths to Asia while evoking the Western archetype of the good Asian—the hardwork-ing, practical peasant.

Snow portrayed Mao as having "no ritual of hero worship built up around him." He described a "gaunt, rather Lincolnesque fig-ure, above average height for a Chinese, somewhat stooping, with a head of thick black hair grown very long." He "had a lively sense of humor and a love of rustic laughter." He enjoyed eating hot peppers so much, he "even had pepper cooked into his bread." Snow admired the way "Mao spoke to his followers in their own terms and seemed to possess a native shrewdness. Iron-willed, he worked for hours on end and during the Long March walked nearly as far as his men; his reputation for a charmed life, an American image of heroes, seemed well-deserved." Snow also ad-mired Mao's casual informality: "Once while talking with Snow," Farnsworth records, "Mao rolled down the waistband of his trousers to hunt for lice; on a hot day, while Snow was interview-ing Lin Biao, Mao nonchalantly pulled off his trousers."

> An individualist, Mao shunned the close-cropped haircuts com-monly worn in the Soviet for his own long, awkward locks and smoked cigarettes inveterately, though the Communists consid-ered the vice a sign of personal corruption. Like a good citizen soldier he rendered the most feeble salute Snow had ever seen. During a picture session, Snow had to loan his Red Army cap to Mao, who did not have one.[2]

Almost all of Mao's visitors in the late 1930s, even the most cynical, proved similarly pliant in helping promote Mao and his causes. Agnes Smedley, the tough, notoriously outspoken left-wing writer and novelist, initially felt repelled by Mao's faintly feminine characteristics. Soon she decided that "the sinister quality I had at first felt so strongly in him proved to be a spiritual isolation." He was "stubborn as a mule, and a steel rod of pride and determina-tion ran through his nature. I had the impression he would wait and watch for years, but eventually have his way." In the end

Smedley was won over. She tried to teach Mao how to dance and later acted as a go-between for the chairman's love interests.[3]

The image of Mao that Snow and Smedley publicized in the 1930s intrigued Americans and captivated young Chinese intellectuals, who saw in Mao someone who could give both their country and themselves a place in world history. University students in Beijing invited Snow to speak and then listened enthralled while he recounted his experiences with Mao and the Communists. When the *China Weekly Review*, a prominent English-language journal edited by *Chicago Tribune* correspondent J. B. Powell, published Snow's interviews with Mao, the Chinese read them eagerly. As soon as the manuscript for *Red Star* was finished, a group of Chinese professors and writers translated it under the title *Travels in the West*. The picture that Snow took of Mao with Snow's hat on the chairman's head became a Chinese icon.[4]

Attracted by the seeming purity and sincerity of the Communists, young Chinese intellectuals flocked to Mao's cause and helped to turn the urban population in favor of the Communists. As the Japanese seized ever larger portions of China, many patriots traveled to Yan'an rather than live under the Japanese puppet regimes. Even more went to the new Nationalist capital at Nanjing.

Mao, however, was not as important a leader as Snow made him out to be. If Snow had come to the Communist base camp at any other time than "in the summer of 1936, [when] most Politburo members were absent, [he] would have talked to other politicians and would have got a different impression." During the Long March, Mao had gradually achieved military predominance in the party, but he had not become the supreme party head. He shared power with several others.[5]

Mao's key rival was Wang Ming, a Politburo member who not only enjoyed the prestigious support of the Comintern but also was the former leader of the party. During the Long March, Wang resided in Russia. But on November 29, 1937, not long after the conclusion of the United Front, he returned to China where, as Zhang Guotao later put it, he seemed like "an 'imperial envoy' from Moscow." Overnight Wang became a member of the Chinese Politburo and a contender for the top leadership. Mao later complained that after Wang Ming's return, "my authority didn't extend beyond my cave."[6]

While in Russia, Wang had drafted the paper that led the CCP to push for the establishment of the United Front. Now back in China, he continued to promote the alliance. He called for a massive mobilization under KMT leadership to prevent Japanese forces from reaching Wuhan, the temporary KMT capital after the Japanese captured Nanjing in December 1937. He proposed using the Communist Eighth Route Army in the enemy's rear to destroy supply lines, which would have deemphasized Mao's guerrilla warfare. He also advocated the establishment of a national assembly that would legalize and encourage the development of mass organizations. Wang even suggested the consolidation of the United Front into a political confederation with a "united army, united assignment, united command, united combat."[7]

Mao tried to argue that the victory over Japan would have to be won slowly, by gradually mobilizing China's vast human resources against the enemy. But Wang garnered substantial support for his ideas. He assumed responsibility for negotiating with the KMT and moved to Jiang's new headquarters in Wuhan. Several prominent CCP officials accompanied him there, most notably Zhou Enlai. Articulate and talented, Wang quickly became something of a political celebrity. For a while it seemed that Wuhan would become the center of Communist activities and that Mao would be relegated to a secondary position in the Politburo.[8]

Not surprisingly, the KMT grew alarmed by Wang's popularity. Jiang Kaishek knew his soviet history. He worried that the Communists might mobilize the urban population to bring down the Nationalist government. On August 5, 1938, the KMT closed a number of mass organizations associated with the CCP, and the Guomindang secret police placed Communist activities under closer scrutiny, undermining Wang's position. On October 25, 1938, when Wuhan fell to the Japanese, Wang's United Front strategy was dealt a fatal blow.

Several of Mao's supporters now went to Moscow to lobby for Mao. Wang was not worried; he assumed he had Stalin's support. It was a blow when the Soviet premier gave his nod to Mao. Georgi Dimitrov, the Comintern official responsible for Chinese affairs, sent a message that arrived in Yan'an sometime in August 1938: Mao Zedong was to be the party's senior leader, and Wang Ming was not to compete with him. Many supporters of Wang Ming came over to Mao's side.[9]

In late 1938 Mao gained the chief position in the Secretariat and took over control of the day-to-day operations of the party. Wang's position slipped to fifth and last in the Politburo.[10] The CCP centralized its authority, forbidding individuals from speaking on behalf of the party or distributing documents in its name unless entrusted to do so by the Central Committee or some other leading organ. Mao now had his finger on the flow of information coming into the Politburo. He decided the agenda for its meetings and played a major role in emergency decisions that were made in the name of the Central Committee. More and more, Mao—who thanks in part to Snow and his associates was already the public voice of the party—became its internal voice as well.

Still, Mao needed to demonstrate that he could be a credible Marxist theorist. Wang Ming's theoretical depth was a major factor in his ability to challenge Mao's leadership. Both in and out of the CCP, Wang was considered a brilliant theoretician. His intellectual reputation appealed to the same student and intellectual audiences with whom Snow had made Mao so popular. Yet Mao had barely looked at Marx and had written little of theoretical note. After the party came to Shaanxi, he began to make up for this deficit by systematically reading Marxist literature. When Snow first visited, Mao interrupted their discussions so that he could read new translations of Soviet works on Marxism.[11]

In 1937 Mao began a series of talks on Marxist theory, eventually compiled into a book called *Lecture Notes on Dialectical Materialism*. It was a derivative work, much of it plagiarized from the Soviet writers he had been reading. But Mao's choice of topics was telling. As Nick Knight has noted: "It is significant that Mao regarded the philosophy contained in these [the Soviet] reference materials as reflecting the orthodox response to problems of philosophy within the Marxist tradition." These works "contributed significantly to the construction of the theoretical framework from within which Mao observed and interpreted the world."[12]

The Soviet works touched a chord in Mao. He did not attribute his sources, but Chinese culture does not attach the same opprobrium to this failure as the West does. Chinese scholars have published the pages of comments and annotations that Mao wrote in the margins of the texts; the notes became the basis for his lectures.[13] He may have been technically guilty of plagiarism, but he was really assimilating the new ideas he was reading and putting them in a form that would make them appealing to his audience.

Mao never developed his lectures into a polished, sophisticated study. He later tried to disavow his *Lecture Notes*, implying in a 1965 discussion with Edgar Snow that he had never written it. (The writings were in fact published in limited editions for selected audiences several times during Mao's lifetime.) Whatever his feelings about the main body of the work, which was after all intended to be his lecture notes, he was proud to acknowledge the two essays he wrote as part of this same enterprise, "On Practice" and "On Contradictions," though they too were largely derived from Soviet sources.[14]

After Mao later polished and edited these two essays, they came to be considered seminal parts of his efforts to "Sinify Marxism," helping enhance his reputation within the Communist world. Mao argued in "On Practice" that "man's social practice alone is the criterion of truth."[15] The truth for the Chinese revolution would be determined by the country's concrete reality. Mao thus implied that unlike Wang Ming, his Marxist theory was not only Sinified but independent, a point he was to repeat in a number of essays written over the next few years. He was not one of those who knew only what he had learned in Moscow.

In truth Mao was indebted to Stalin both for his position and for the ideas in the essays he wrote. He had at best an ambivalent attitude toward Chinese culture. In the main body of *Lecture Notes*, Mao argued that "because of the backwardness of the evolution of Chinese society" it was necessary "to expose and criticize the philosophical legacy of China."[16]

Although Mao was hypocritical in trumpeting his apparent independence from Stalin, the contradictory feelings he expressed toward China's past culture resonated powerfully within Chinese society. Many modern Chinese political philosophers felt that China could advance only if its past thought were eliminated or at least radically revised; at the same time they recognized that China's culture and traditions were an important part of Chinese identity with which they had to work.[17] Proposals during the New Culture movement to abolish all of China's Confucian thinking and bring in foreign ideas went hand-in-hand with patriotic suggestions to protect the Chinese nation. One of the initial attractions of Marxism to many Chinese intellectuals was that it explained China's Confucian past as simply a "feudal" stage through which all countries had to pass and then move beyond, not something the Chinese must expunge.

Mao showed that he had found in the Soviet texts an even better explanation for the ambiguous angst of modern Chinese thinkers, when he declared in the opening sentence of "On Contradictions": "The law of contradictions in things, that is, the law of the unity of opposites, is the basic law."[18] In seeming to contradict himself, Mao could now say that he was simply practicing what he preached.

Marx had argued that ideas were derived from the material world. Many of the twists and turns in Mao's strategies were thus ascribed to China's ever-changing material conditions. Mao synthesized his experience of revolutionary struggle and his vision of how the revolution should be carried forward in the context of the United Front. On military matters there was first "Strategic Problem of China's Revolutionary War," written in December 1936, which summed up the lessons of the Red Army's experiences and justified the correctness of Mao's own military line. This was followed in 1938 by "On Protracted War" and other writings, which dealt with the tactics of the anti-Japanese war. Now that Mao understood more of Marx, all these writings could be said (sometimes in retrospect) to have adapted Marxism to the Chinese environment.

In "On Contradictions," his most profound essay, Mao explained that while contradictions existed in any situation, it was always necessary to determine the "primary contradiction." This elevated to the level of philosophical discourse a justification for the CCP's alliance with the KMT against what Mao called the primary contradiction—the Japanese.

As this example shows, Mao's genius lay in his ability to weave philosophical ideas into practical notions about the Chinese revolution in a way that made them understandable to a large audience of his countrymen. In his various essays, Mao interpreted Marxist ideas through the prism he knew well—traditional Chinese philosophy—and by so doing he adapted Marxism to Chinese circumstances.

Mao claimed that even democracy, which Stalin had instructed the party to set forth as a goal when he initially urged the CCP to establish a new United Front, needed to be adjusted to the material conditions of the Chinese revolution. Here he again followed the Soviets. In *On Imperialism* Lenin had argued that in countries suffering from imperialistic domination, the proletariat would have to help a weak bourgeoisie carry out their capitalist revolution before the world would be ready for a Communist revolution. In his January 1940 essay "On New Democracy," Mao explained that in China the proletariat had to assume leadership of the struggle against imperialism and feudalism. He assured the bourgeoisie that they would be welcome to join this revolutionary struggle and help establish a "revolutionary democratic dictatorship" of several classes. In the 1940 version of this essay, which Mao altered after 1949, he even suggested that if the bourgeoisie did a good job they might continue to lead the revolution. In both forms, writes Stuart Schram, "Mao, following Stalin (who himself was following Lenin), declared China's New-Democratic revolution to be an integral part of the proletarian-socialist world revolution."[19]

Contemporary Americans would not find a Leninist-style "dictatorship" terribly appealing, but many middle-class Chinese found "New Democracy" reassuring. They welcomed Mao's declaration that during the lengthy presocialist stage, the new government would allow private capitalist production so long as it did not dominate the "livelihood of the people on a national scale." Although banks and some industry would be nationalized, the Communists would tolerate most small capitalists.

During the "New Democratic" period, Mao claimed, the party's policies toward the peasantry would be those of Guomindang founder Sun Yatsen: "The republic will take certain necessary steps to confiscate the land of the landlords and distribute it to those peasants having little or no land, carry out Dr. Sun Yat-sen's slogan of 'land to the tiller,' abolish feudal relations in the rural areas, and turn the land over to the private ownership of the peasants. A rich peasant economy will be allowed in the rural areas."[20]

As Stalin had suggested, the CCP agreed to tolerate small land-lords in order to win a greatly expanded following in the country-side.

CCP policies brought artists, intellectuals, and actors to Yan'an, including a number of attractive young women who doted on the new Communist elite. Mao began to dally with Lily Wu, Agnes Smedley's flirtatious translator.

In an article that Edgar Snow published in Japanese in 1954, he related a story that Smedley had told him in confidence before she died. "Smedley, who took the side of the men at Yan'an and thought the women conservative pansies," told Snow how one night when Mao was flirting with Lily Wu, who was living in the cave next to Smedley, Mao's pregnant wife, He Zizhen, burst in and began hitting Mao with her flashlight. She then took out after Lily Wu, scratching her face and pulling her hair. Lily tried to hide behind Smedley, who had been awakened by all the noise and had gone next door to see what was happening. An angry He Zizhen then struck Smedley too. Whereupon the former cowgirl decked her "with a single punch." When He Zizhen appealed to Mao for help, he criticized her for attacking Smedley and tried to persuade her to leave. When she refused to cooperate, he ordered his bodyguards to drag her back to their home while he shame-facedly followed in their wake.[21]

Mao's flirtation with Lily Wu prompted He Zizhen to leave him. Mao tried to win her back, sending her gifts and expelling Lily Wu from Yan'an, but the infuriated He Zizhen left for the So-viet Union.[22]

Mao did not remain on his own for long. He set up house with Jiang Qing, a twenty-four-year-old former Shanghai actress with a dubious reputation. Not long afterward the two had their only child, a daughter. The relationship was tempestuous, and by the 1950s it had developed into what might be called an open mar-riage.

He Zizhen meanwhile fared poorly. After her last child died in

Russia, she grew unbalanced and had to be placed in a mental institution. Mao arranged for her to return to China in 1947, where she continued to receive psychiatric treatments, but she never fully recovered. Mao's doctor, Li Zhisui, described how shaken Mao was when late in life He Zizhen came to Beijing to visit him. Mao still remembered her as a high-spirited twenty-seven-year-old. He saw before him a confused old woman, who warned him to watch out for the long vanquished Wang Ming.[23]

Years before He Zizhen returned to visit Mao, Wang Ming had gone into exile in the Soviet Union, where he wrote a book claiming, among other things, that Mao had tried to poison him.[24] He could not admit, of course, that the person who had really undermined him was Stalin. But although Stalin had chosen Mao, Mao recognized that the Soviet leader's interest in China was far from altruistic. Stalin hoped the United Front would prevent the KMT from surrendering, thereby ensuring that Japanese troops would remain occupied with a ground war in China and leaving them fewer resources to attack the Soviet Union.

However much he suspected Stalin's motives, Mao listened to him, even when the Soviet leader's henchmen tried to censor Mao's public pronouncements. This occurred most notably in October 1939, after Mao, in an interview with Edgar Snow during Snow's return to Yan'an, admitted that Communist-controlled areas were administratively independent of the KMT. Mao further criticized the effectiveness of the United Front by acknowledging that China would not be fully unified until it had a government representing all the parties. Georgi Dimitrov immediately telegraphed Mao, warning him that such statements were "provocative" and likely to undermine the United Front.[25]

Although he may have spoken too frankly to Snow, Mao, like Stalin, wished to retain the United Front policy because it benefited the CCP. It gave the party the opportunity to expand behind Japanese lines to become the main national force in defense of the peasantry. By 1941 the Red Army had become half a million strong, and the CCP had gained financial stability. The Soviets had sent them money, and Jiang had not only dropped his economic blockade of the soviet area but was paying a substantial stipend to the CCP government.

But in order to maintain the United Front in 1940, Mao had to walk a tightrope. The KMT worried about increasing CCP strength. Mao knew that if he continued to expand his forces he risked provoking the Nationalists. The situation was particularly tense in the Yangzi Delta of central China, where the Communist New Fourth Army operated with great success. By 1940 the two groups increasingly faced off against each other. Mao knew that if he allowed his troops to remain in the area, he might provoke the KMT; but the temptation was great. After analyzing the radio messages Mao sent to these forces, Gregor Benton noted: "Mao's view on how to treat the Guomindang moved, between late October and early November 1940, from a position of extreme caution, generated by a fear that Chiang Kai-shek was on the point of surrendering to Japan, to one of optimism and relief, when it seemed to Mao that Chiang's relationship with Britain and the United States would hold the Guomindang to an anti-Japanese course." Mao overestimated his troop strength in the KMT-controlled areas, holding them there until it was too late.[26]

In early January 1941 KMT forces ambushed the southern wing of the New Fourth Army, killing thousands and arresting and executing many more. This so-called South Anhui Incident destroyed the United Front in all but name. It was a great blow to the Red Army but also a major propaganda victory for the CCP, creating widespread indignation against the Nationalists and increasing support for the Communists.[27]

Mao considered ending even the fiction of the United Front. But Zhou Enlai soothed him, pointing out that Jiang Kaishek had distanced himself from the attack. Stalin, alarmed by Mao's aggressive posture, pushed him to reconsider. Mao began to realize that Japanese pressure on Jiang would force him to come to terms with the Communists, and he backed down.[28]

Nonetheless the Guomindang set up new economic blockades against the CCP in the North and halted its stipend to the Chinese Communist government. Complicating matters, in June 1941 the Soviet Union went to war with Germany, forcing a reduction in aid to the Chinese; and the Japanese became more aggressive toward CCP bases in the North. In the face of this economic and military pressure, Mao attempted to gain funds by authorizing the Red Army to engage in the opium trade.[29] At the same time he instituted a number of increasingly radical campaigns in North China to cement the relationship between the CCP and the peasantry.

As pressure on the Communists intensified, Mao felt a need to consolidate the party and unify his leadership. He easily found a model for a way of shaping party views toward its past so as to emphasize the wisdom of its own leaders. In 1938, Stalin had supervised the writing of the *History of the Communist Party of the Soviet Union (Bolshevik), Short Course*, which presented the history of the Bolshevik Revolution from Stalin's point of view. Mao had the book translated into Chinese, and by March 1941 some 100,000 copies were circulating. Mao referred to this hack job as "the highest synthesis of the world communist movement in the last 100 years." Party members were convened into study groups to pore over the official packet of documents on Chinese party history and theory that Mao assembled to go with the study of the book, reinterpreting the history of the Chinese Communist party in such a way as to justify his own actions.[30]

In September 1941 this effort to ensure the triumph of Mao's version of party history broadened into a Rectification Movement. The primary target of this first stage of the campaign was Wang Ming. Many of Wang Ming's previous associates understood the exercise and engaged in self-criticism for what Mao referred to as the "subjectivism" of their past policies — though Wang Ming himself refused to confess any errors.[31]

Mao employed Kang Sheng as his hatchet man in the Rectification Movement. Kang was so taken with his role that he costumed himself for the part. "He dressed in black leather, rode a black horse (Mao's horse was white), and was followed by a ferocious black police dog. Kang symbolized that social and intellectual 'cauterizing' was necessary to change rectification into purification. He was the necessary evil to enable the good."[32]

Kang Sheng had learned at the source how to conduct a purge, having studied in Moscow along with Wang Ming. Kang became a supporter of Mao's in 1938 while Wang Ming was off in Wuhan. He was from the same town as Mao's new wife, Jiang Qing, and played a key role in helping "clear" her name. By 1939 he had taken over many of the party's secret service duties. In 1941 Kang also took charge of cadre screening. In the spring of 1942 Kang transformed the Rectification Movement, moving it from a behind-the-scenes attack on Wang Ming and his supporters into a public effort to bring discipline and regulation to the party.[33]

The CCP had a problem with order. Party membership had expanded exponentially in the late 1930s and early 1940s, from around 40,000 in 1937 to more than 800,000 by 1940, straining the unity of purpose forged among the survivors of the Long March. No longer were party members ideologically attuned; carping and whining persisted among intellectuals who had flooded into Yan'an. The party sought to convert these people "into effective revolutionary cadres" by employing "small group learning rituals." Mao told the writers and artists who had joined the party that they must forget their cultural heritage and become spokesmen for the masses, extolling their struggle. They were told to create literature and art that would "fit well into the whole revolutionary machine as a component part." They needed to "operate as powerful weapons for uniting and educating the people and for attacking and destroying the enemy, and . . . help the people fight the enemy with one heart and one mind."[34]

Mao and Kang Sheng were not the types to leave things to chance. To ensure that their message was taken seriously, they initiated a Stalinist crackdown on dissent that victimized people such as Wang Shiwei, a left-wing novelist and translator of Western literature who had moved from Shanghai to Yan'an in 1936. Wang's sin was to criticize the arrogance, self-indulgence, and special privilege he saw among the top leadership at Yan'an. He was remorselessly denounced and his supporters intimidated. When Wang refused to admit his mistakes, in 1942 he was expelled from the party, jailed, and later executed—an action that Mao eventually denounced as a mistake.[35]

In mid-1943 the Rectification Movement turned into a hunt for spies that weeded out dissidents, tightened party controls, and crushed dissent.[36] This stage of the campaign lasted only three months, but it was a grueling, Stalinesque three months in which people were forced to confess their subversive thoughts. In all, some forty thousand people were expelled from the party, and many of them were arrested, tortured, and even executed, though generally those who were willing to engage in self-criticism were—unlike in Stalinist Russia—treated more leniently.

In March 1943 the CCP promoted Mao, giving him final authority over the day-to-day decisions of the Secretariat and the new title of Chairman of the Politburo and of the Secretariat. For the first time the party formally excluded Wang Ming from the Secretariat, blaming him for adherence to foreign ideas—that is, dependency on the Comintern—but also contradictorily criticizing him for "betraying the Comintern line."[37] In July 1943 the term "Mao Zedong Thought" began to be used for the first time. Mao's portrait and words began to appear throughout Yan'an.

In early 1944 Mao, sensing that the Rectification Movement had gone too far, apologized. Kang Sheng's standing was reduced, and he was not to reemerge in a position of power until 1955.[38]

In attacking intellectuals, Mao wished to emphasize that his party did not have the same deference for elitist ideas and ways that had existed in the old China. He aimed to create a government based on the common folk, the people whom he said artists had a duty to represent. This was a central notion of "New Democracy, proclaimed to be the most distinctive feature of Mao Zedong Thought. . . ."[39] It was vital to the driving concept of the Yan'an era, the mass line. Mao summarized his idea of the mass line as "from the masses, to the masses."

> This means: take the ideas of the masses (scattered and unsystematic ideas) and concentrate them (through study turn them into concentrated and systematic ideas), then go to the masses and propagate and explain these ideas until the masses embrace them as their own, hold fast to them, and translate them into action, and test the correctness of these ideas in such action. Then once again concentrate ideas from the masses and once again go to the masses so that the ideas are persevered in and carried through. And so on, over and over again in an endless spiral, with the ideas becoming more correct, more vital, and richer each time. Such is the Marxist theory of knowledge.[40]

The mass line was democratic in the sense that it represented a real effort to find out what the masses wanted. But it also emphasized that the party must "concentrate" and "propagate" the ideas of the masses. Mao saw the party as the ultimate arbiter, and he wanted a Stalinist political structure in order to make sure that the ideas of the Chinese people were implemented. Mao made his debt to Stalin explicit in June 1943, when he attempted to sum up the lessons of the Rectification Movement:

> In every organization, school, army unit, factory, or village, whether large or small, we should give effect to the ninth of Stalin's twelve conditions for the bolshevization of the Party, namely, that on the establishment of a nucleus of leadership. The

criteria for such a leading group should be the four which Dimitrov enumerated in his discussion of cadres policy—absolute devotion to the cause, contact with the masses, ability independently to find one's bearings, and observance of discipline. Whether in carrying out the central tasks—war, production, education (including rectification)—or in checking up on work, examining the cadres' histories, or in other activities, it is necessary to adopt the method of linking the leading group with the masses, in addition to that of linking the general call with particular guidance.[41]

Where Mao differed radically from Stalin was in his attitude toward his associates. Stalin "had a penchant for obedient subordinates." Not Mao. Mao "remained broadly consultative" in his political style and highly "democratic" in his dealings with other party leaders. In finally assembling his new Politburo in 1945, Mao went out of his way to embrace people who had earlier opposed him. Over half the people he included were those who "had stood on different sides of important issues from the Party's newly confirmed Chairman."[42]

More than past loyalty, Mao valued talent and a broad constituency. He could have included close followers—specifically Lin Biao and Li Fuchun—but he refrained in order to make room for representatives of wider sections of the party.[43] He even retained Zhou Enlai in the Politburo, though Zhou not only had supported Wang Ming but had taken part in the decision to leave Mao's youngest brother in Jiangxi, where he was killed. Mao made Zhou Enlai an important deputy and allowed him to continue in place even through the 1960s Cultural Revolution.

Mao's loyalty to the team may explain why, as Frederick Teiwes has noted, he "never openly challenged the Comintern before the 1940s, and even then his independence in deed was mitigated by continued deference in word." When Mao was finally made chairman in March 1943, "the matter was not reported to Moscow in advance but rather was presented to the Comintern as a *fait accompli*. To have done otherwise, a party historian observed, would have invited Stalin's veto on the ironic grounds that the changes violated inner-Party democracy."[44] Mao would have had to take the veto seriously.

On May 15, 1943, shortly after Mao consolidated his power, the Soviet Union dissolved the Comintern. Even so, Mao remained deferential toward Stalin. On December 22 Dimitrov wrote to Mao defending Wang Ming and expressing doubts about the tactics of Kang Sheng. Mao did not return Wang Ming to power, but he did keep him in the Central Committee. Dimitrov also expressed concern for Zhou Enlai. Although Zhou's clear talents, his willingness to admit his past errors, and his declarations of loyalty to Mao probably had more to do with Mao's moving him into the number three position within the government than Dimitrov's expressions of concern, Moscow's efforts may have helped influence Mao.[45]

On August 10, 1945, Soviet forces entered the war in the Pacific, invading Manchuria just four days after the United States had dropped the atomic bomb on Hiroshima. The Soviets had to stay in the war for only a few days before the Japanese surrendered. As soon as the cease-fire was announced, the Nationalists and the Communists began a mad scramble to seize Chinese territory that had been occupied by Japan. As the rush began, Mao seemed to believe that with Soviet support the revolution could be won immediately. He ordered the CCP military to seize such major cities as Shanghai.

But while Mao planned for the coming war against Jiang Kaishek, Stalin, in the closing hours of the conflict with Japan, was signing a treaty of alliance with the Nationalist leader that cut much of the ground out from under the CCP. The pact gave the Soviets privileges that even after the Communists won control of China, the Russians would remain loath to abandon. After signing the treaty with Jiang, Stalin cabled Mao, arguing that a civil war would be ruinous for China. Mao was angry, but he canceled the

Shanghai uprising. At a Politburo meeting on August 23, Mao tried to put Stalin's approach into a global perspective: "It is certain that a third world war should be avoided. If the USSR were to support us, the U.S. would certainly support Jiang, and a third world war would erupt."[46] Mao formulated a new political slogan: "For peace, for democracy, for unity."

In spite of his bluster about wanting to push ahead to victory, Mao recognized that his army and his constituents numbered fewer than half of Jiang Kaishek's. After "Stalin sent Mao a second cable in which he said that because the international community and the Chinese people desired peace, Mao should go to Chongqing to negotiation with Jiang and the U.S.," Mao agreed—an act that took considerable personal courage.[47] He stayed there from August until October 1945, trying to gain at the negotiating table what he could not then win on the battlefield.

Mao knew that in spite of Stalin's double-dealing, the Soviets were sending great amounts of critical aid to the CCP. The Soviets advised the CCP to pour as many troops as possible into Manchuria to "hold the gate," and even delayed their withdrawal so as to deny U.S. and KMT forces quick and easy entrance to the rich northeastern region. They made trains available to speed the first CCP forces into the area to key locations and even helped them subdue recalcitrant Japanese troops. The Soviets also turned over to their Communist allies the huge Japanese weapons caches in Manchuria. The arms and vehicles in these supply dumps were of enormous help to the poorly equipped CCP armies, who then had enough weapons to fight the Guomindang throughout the remainder of the civil war.[48]

By helping the CCP, the Soviets risked the wrath of the United States, which was aiding the Nationalists. When the war ended, U.S. Pacific Commander Douglas MacArthur ordered the Japanese to surrender to the KMT. The United States sent fifty thousand American troops to occupy key ports and urban centers in North China to wait for occupying Nationalist forces. This gave the Nationalists control of most of the key cities of North China, though the Communists retained a hold over the countryside in North China and Manchuria.[49]

In all, Mao not only participated in negotiations in Chongqing but also authorized numerous other attempts at talks, including those brokered by the United States. The Communists and the Nationalists came to no agreements about troop size or the autonomy of Communist-controlled areas. In July 1946 Jiang, believing he had the advantage, decided to solve the problem militarily. His troops went on the offensive, meeting with swift and easy victories. From July to December 1946, Jiang's army seized more than a hundred thousand square miles of Communist territory. For nine months the Communist army retreated, losing almost all the major urban strongholds they had seized at the end of the war, with the exception of Harbin, near the Soviet border. In March 1947 the Communists were forced to abandon Yan'an. In June 1947 Jiang declared "absolute superiority."

Using the same strategy that he had practiced in Jiangxi a decade and a half earlier, Mao had lured the enemy into an overconfident, overextended situation. Always cool under fire, he now made himself a personal target. Knowing how anxious the KMT troops were to capture him, day after day he waited until his intelligence forces let him know that the Nationalist forces were within a half-hour of his camp; then he would saddle his pony and ride away.[50] By the summer of 1947 the trap had been set. The CCP was ready to stop retreating and begin a counterattack.

In the fall and winter of 1947 the Communists won important victories in Hunan, Hubei, and Manchuria. Momentum shifted. The Nationalist army suffered staggering losses and in mid-1948 began to disintegrate. By late 1948 the CCP had liberated much of northern China. In his New Year's speech of 1949, Jiang Kaishek called for a truce. But Communist victories continued to mount. Tianjin fell on January 15. A week later, in time for the Chinese New Year celebrations, Beijing surrendered.

Stalin telegrammed Mao, advising him to go easy and not to

forgo the CCP's image as the party of peace by rejecting Jiang's offer. Although an incredulous Mao was at first unwilling to consider negotiating with the KMT, Stalin eventually persuaded him of the tactical benefits of accepting the Guomindang peace proposal. But, Stalin added, it was to be agreed before the negotiations that the CCP should dominate any United Front government, should occupy the majority of seats in the Consultative Council, and should hold the majority of cabinet posts as well as the premiership, commander-in-chief of the army, and, if possible, the presidency.[51] Mao did not need Stalin to tell him how to reply to proposals from Jiang Kaishek. But even as he grasped victory, he continued to respect his mentor. As it turned out, there was no need for concern. After Mao attached the conditions that Stalin suggested, Jiang rejected the negotiations and fled to Taiwan.

Even at this point Mao listened carefully when Stalin warned him not to alienate the United States, lest it intervene in the civil war. Stalin told a disappointed Mao to put off his visit to Moscow for a while, suggesting that it might alarm the Americans by fostering the idea of CCP dependency on the Soviets. Mao began working hard to court Washington, making a number of comments to U.S. journalists and diplomats, like the one he related in 1945 to John Service, an American Foreign Service officer who was later purged from the State Department during the McCarthy period for the realistic reports he had written about the Chinese Communists:

> America is not only the most suitable country to assist the economic development of China, she is also the only country fully able to participate.
>
> For all these reasons there must not and cannot be any conflict, estrangement, or misunderstanding between the Chinese people and America.[52]

By the time Mao emerged victorious in the Chinese civil war on October 1, 1949, it was clear that in spite of his approaches to the United States he owed a great debt to Moscow. A decade later, after Khrushchev's 1955 denunciation of Stalin, Mao, who had learned from Stalin how to rewrite party history, advanced the idea that he not only had "Sinified" Marxism but had also won the revolution independent of the Soviets. In May 1956, during a lengthy conversation with the Soviet ambassador to Beijing, Mao claimed that during the anti-Japanese war Stalin had supported Wang Ming's "defeatist program," which was "against the CCP's independent policy, the strengthening of the CCP's armed forces and revolutionary bases." By 1965, in his *Talk on Questions of Philosophy*, Mao was even arguing that Stalin had "opposed our revolution, and our seizure of power."[53] None of this was true. The proposition that Mao had independently carried out the Chinese revolution should never have been accepted in China, let alone in the United States.

Mao was a good strategist, a skillful popularizer, and a great propagandist. His personality and his treatment of his underlings were very different from Stalin's, but Mao never would have achieved what he did without Stalin. Later he would do a thorough job of trying to destroy Stalinism in China—only after he first helped establish it. The paradoxical consequence of Mao's love-hate relationship with Stalin and Stalinism is that in the end, Mao's image was confused with the very person to whom he owed so much but from whom he had tried so hard to distance himself.

SIX

The People's Republic of China

❧ UNTIL RECENTLY most historians have viewed Mao as someone who, in adapting Marxism to Chinese conditions, accomplished a revolution independent of and different from that of the Russians. This explains why historians who have chronicled the aftermath of Mao's 1949 triumph have often seemed perplexed by his decision to establish a Soviet-style government in China. When looked at in this way, the decision seems an anomaly, as if after gaining power Mao somehow decided to forget everything he had learned in the course of the revolutionary struggle and instead return to a more conventional, urban-oriented Communist path.

But Mao's decision is eminently logical when the facts are examined dispassionately. As I have tried to demonstrate, in the years leading up to the Communist victory Mao depended much more on the Soviets than has usually been acknowledged. He had played by the rules of the international Communist party and was rewarded for his actions. He found Soviet Marxist theoreticians so convincing that he incorporated their ideas into his own writing. He believed that Soviet methods had helped Russia develop from a backward, semi-colonial country like China into an advanced socialist state. In light of these facts, his decision in 1949 to turn to the Soviet model is not surprising.

Mao once noted in a casual conversation with a Russian artist (dispatched to do an official portrait) that because of the cruel life to which the Chinese people had been subjected, their best hope was to depend on the Soviet model. "As for culture, we, the Chinese people, consider ourselves to be the most backward, because in the past there has not been in China an organized force or thought which has been able to unite the whole people and to direct their energy towards the correct path [of development]. The Chinese people, learning from the people of the Soviet Union, have finally discovered a correct path for themselves."[1]

Certainly at the beginning of the new government there was no question that Mao looked to the Soviet model. One of his first steps in imitating the Soviets was his choice of living and working quarters. Just as Lenin had established his government in the Kremlin, the former seat of the Russian tsars, Mao and most of the other high Chinese Communist officials moved from their Shaanxi caves into Zhongnanhai, the locus of power of the former emperors. But imitating the Soviets in this regard proved to be an unwise move. Several observers have argued that this cut Mao off from the world around him and led to his gradual estrangement from the common people, whom he had previously seemed to understand so well. From this perspective, Mao seemed to have stopped being a peasant revolutionary and become a combination of Chinese imperial leader and Soviet chieftain, surrounded by retainers like his doctor Li Zhisui, who fussed over his leader's refusal to brush his teeth and adhere to other "scientific" hygienic practices.[2]

Still, many Chinese both in and out of the party believed that Mao deserved special treatment because of his achievement in reuniting the country. Even today there is great pride in Mao's proclamation in late September 1949 that the Chinese people "have now stood up." On October 1 he presided over Tiananmen Square and in his high-pitched, Hunan-accented speech officially declared the establishment of the People's Republic of China.[3]

But even if Mao may have implied in this declaration that China was somehow gaining independence from a colonial master—nonexistent in China's case—he clearly did not wish to cut off all contact with the West. "The government is willing to establish diplomatic relations with any foreign government," proclaimed Mao, "that is willing to observe the principles of equality, mutual benefit, and mutual respect of territorial integrity and sovereignty."[4]

He had made this clear months earlier when he instructed Huang Hua, who would become China's foreign minister in the 1980s, to meet in Nanjing with the American ambassador to China, John Leighton Stuart. Meanwhile Zhou Enlai and Chen Yi contacted American and British diplomats and separately suggested that the new regime was not terribly excited about the prospect of aligning itself with the Soviet Union and would welcome aid from the West. Zhou let slip that there was a split within the Chinese leadership over the country's alignment. According to Zhou, Liu Shaoqi led the group championing the Soviets.[5]

In late June 1949 the American ambassador agreed to go to Beijing (then still Beiping) to negotiate the establishment of relations with the Chinese Communists. But on June 30, 1949, before Stuart was to leave on his trip, Mao announced that China would be "leaning towards the Soviet Union." The U.S. government ordered Stuart to cancel his visit to Beijing and to return instead to Washington. Mao stoked the fires further with his August 18 statement, "Farewell, Leighton Stuart," in which he not only called Stuart "a symbol of the complete failure of the aggressive policy of the United States towards China" but also attacked Secretary of State Dean Acheson and the Truman administration.[6]

Even today there is debate over whether Mao was sincere in his approaches to the United States or whether he simply dangled the possibility of closer relations to prevent Washington from intervening in the Chinese civil war at the last minute. His repeated requests to Stalin to visit Moscow, which began years earlier, make it evident that Mao had long intended to establish close relations with his sometime mentor. Nevertheless he probably did want a connection with the United States. Had Washington been less caught up in the new mentality of the cold war, Mao might have had more and earlier contact with the Americans than occurred, and relations between the two countries in the 1950s probably would not have been as strained.

If Mao's feelings about the United States were ambiguous in these years, his admiration for the Soviets was clear. He demonstrated this reverence at one of his first meetings with Stalin, when he asked the surprised Soviet leader for Russian help to make sure that he did a proper job of "editing the Chinese" version of his own (that is, Mao's) works. Mao also seemed willing to countenance Soviet troops in the northern Manchurian treaty city of Port Arthur, presumably so that the Russians would prevent imperialist incursions into the area. When Stalin told Mao that the Russians would eventually surrender all rights to Port Arthur, Mao asked if the city could then become a free port. Stalin explained that since the Soviets were giving up all their rights to the port, "China must decide on its own."[7]

After two months of talks, Stalin agreed to a "Sino-Soviet Treaty of Friendship, Alliance and Mutual Assistance." The Russians decided not to end their extraterritorial rights in China immediately. They hung on to the Changchun Railway until 1952, at which time they at last pulled out of Port Arthur (now part of the Chinese city of Dalian). In return for relinquishing extraterritorial privileges that other powers had long since abandoned, the Russians received the right to set up joint Sino-Soviet stock companies to drill for oil and to mine nonferrous metals in the northwestern Chinese province of Xinjiang, a concession that later particularly annoyed Mao. The Soviets gave China an interest-bearing loan of $300 million, a paltry sum that was even less than the $450 million the Soviets had guaranteed Poland the year before.

On June 25, 1950, not long after Mao returned from the Soviet

Union, North Korean troops poured across the 38th Parallel into South Korea, igniting civil war in Korea just as China was in the midst of its land-reform campaign and was preparing to invade Taiwan. Two days after the invasion, President Truman ordered the Seventh Fleet into the Taiwan Straits, preventing China from fully "standing up." By the fall, as North Korean troops fell back toward the Chinese border in the wake of a U.S.-led counterattack, the Chinese leadership considered whether or not to enter the war. Although the U.S. commander, Douglas MacArthur, threatened to pursue the war across the border and into China, the majority of the Politburo seemed reluctant to become involved in the conflict. Only Mao, Zhu De, and Peng Dehuai favored China's entrance into the war, fearing that a U.S. victory in North Korea might make it impossible to halt American forces at the border in the event of an invasion. Mao also believed it was important to show Stalin that he was a loyal member of the Communist team, and he convinced his colleagues of the need for war. But Stalin refused to provide air cover for Chinese ground forces as he had earlier promised, making it necessary for China to enter the conflict on its own.

U.S. troops ignored China's warnings not to continue their advance. On October 8, 1950, Mao ordered the "Chinese People's Volunteers" to "move immediately into the territory of Korea, to join our Korean comrades in their fight against the invaders."[8] The night of October 19, Chinese forces began to enter Korea. Soon the Chinese troops had pushed the stunned U.S. forces back to the 38th Parallel. There, after some give and take on both sides, U.S. troops stood their ground, and the conflict bogged down. It was almost three years before the two Koreas agreed to a truce.

China did not need a victory: Mao gained respect for having fought the greatest power in the world to a standstill. He felt that China had "dealt United States imperialism a severe blow and made them quite scared."[9] But his success came at a great price. China lost some 900,000 soldiers in the conflict, including Mao's eldest and dearest son, Anying. The boy had survived the death of his mother, life on his own on the streets of Shanghai, and exile in the Soviet Union before happily reuniting with his father. Now, with the family together again and not long after Anying had married, he was killed.

China also expended great amounts of badly needed funds. Mao tried to claim that it was "not that much," because it amounted to "less than a year's [revenue from] commercial and industrial taxes." But he did admit that the expenditures not only took money away from other projects but made agricultural taxes "slightly heavy."[10] Moreover, because of the war the United States blocked China's admission into the United Nations until 1971 and ended Chinese hopes for the absorption of Taiwan. The Korean War further isolated China from the West and made the country even more dependent on the Soviet Union.

The war also changed Mao's internal priorities. In September 1950, shortly before Chinese troops entered the war, he had demanded that the government not execute "a single secret agent" and not even arrest "the majority of them." He hoped to induce them by peaceful means "to make a clean breast of things" and to prevent the courts from being overwhelmed. After the war began, Mao, worried about the dangers of facing internal and external enemies at the same time, emphasized the need to consolidate power, noting, "It is absolutely essential that suspicious elements be dealt with so that these organs may be placed in the hands of reliable personnel." Instead of talking about not executing secret agents, Mao now warned: "In suppressing counterrevolutionaries, please make sure that you strike firmly, accurately, and relentlessly, so that nothing [detrimental] can be said about it among the various circles in society."[11] The government summarily executed those it considered bandits, spies, or secret agents. In less than six months more than 700,000 counterrevolutionaries were put to death.

Mao, who had studied Stalin's methods, knew the value of

ruthlessness. But he was not bloodthirsty. In his correspondence he was clearly worried that lower-level officials were sometimes being overzealous, and he made a number of efforts to restrain them. Again and again he sent memos cautioning cadres to act with care. "No matter where the place is, we must have planning, pay attention to strategy, do propaganda, and not execute anyone by mistake." In February 1951 he felt compelled to justify his tough policies to Huang Yanpei, the former chairman of the Democratic National Construction association, who after 1949 became one of the non-Communist ministers in the new government.[12]

In the countryside Mao had focused on establishing capitalism, not communism, before the war. The party had won in large part by addressing the great economic imbalances endured by the Chinese peasantry. Land reform, which ensured that even lowest-level peasants had a piece of property to call their own, was not a "communist policy." By carrying out a land-reform policy, Mao had seemed intent on turning China into a nation of bourgeois property owners with a stake in the new society—which is why the United States pressed Jiang Kaishek to carry out land reform after he occupied the island of Taiwan.

By 1949 land reform had been completed in less than one-third of Chinese villages. Mao favored slow reform in the vast area remaining. He worried that, given the huge scale of what had to be accomplished, in hasty action it would be "easy for ultra-Left deviations to occur." He wanted to confiscate only the land of "the landlords but not the rich peasants," so as to "protect the middle peasants, and prevent indiscriminate beatings and executions. In the past, land reform in the north was carried out during wartime, and the atmosphere of war had overwhelmed the atmosphere of land reform." Mao worried that now, without a war, land reform "will be particularly conspicuous; its impact on society will appear particularly great, and the clamors of the landlords will also be particularly shrill."

He pointed out that "our united front with the national bourgeoisie is closely tied to the question of land. In order to stabilize the national bourgeoisie, it seems more appropriate not to touch the semi-feudal rich peasants for the moment." He called for the preservation of "a rich peasant economy, in order to facilitate the early restoration of production in the rural areas." He not only seemed to favor allowing rich peasants to keep their disproportionate shares of land, but also permitted them to employ tenant farmers who would lease "small plots of land." It would be impossible, he noted, "to eliminate capitalism and implement socialism at an early date." As late as June 1950 Mao was demanding that the party "earnestly unite with democratic personages from all circles" and not try to exclude people who came from "bad" class backgrounds.[13]

After the Korean War broke out, the government moved rapidly to extend land reform to every part of the country. To carry out the program, the Chinese government was forced to press into service young, poorly trained party workers, who exercised little restraint. By 1952 they had extended land reform throughout the countryside, but in the process somewhere between two and five million landlords had been killed. This staggering carnage occurred despite Mao's exhortations to have lower-level cadres follow rules and even to have "democratic personages and university professors who wish to go and see land reform [in action]" do so, not just "the good parts" but also "the bad things."[14]

In the wake of the Korean War the new government also took a much harder stand toward intellectuals, businessmen, and bureaucrats. From 1951 to 1952 Mao's "Three-Anti Campaign" (against corruption, waste, and bureaucratism) attacked urban cadres involved in corruption. He wanted "a big clean up throughout the Party in order to expose thoroughly all cases of corruption, whether of major consequence or of mild or even minor significance, and to emphasize dealing heavy blows to those who have committed major offenses of corruption, while adopting a policy of education and reform toward those who have committed medium or minor offenses." Mao claimed that his Three-Anti Campaign was "equal in importance to that of suppressing counterrevolutionaries." His Five-Anti Campaign (against bribery, tax evasion, stealing state property, cheating on government contracts, and theft of government economic data) followed, in pursuit of former capitalists who were still holding money from the government. He hoped the Five-Anti Campaign would "eliminate hidden accounts, make the economic [picture of enterprises] public, and gradually establish the system in which workers and shop personnel supervise production and management."[15] Mao saw the two campaigns as part of a concerted effort.

Although Mao wanted these two campaigns enforced, he tried to prevent them from getting out of hand, calling for leniency for past offenses and for the great majority of wrongdoers. He refused to allow the campaigns to be extended to the countryside and scolded those in smaller cities who failed to respect the restrictions that were attached to the campaigns.

But his efforts proved inadequate. The government forced suspected offenders to be humiliated at mass meetings, apparently choosing some victims at random to fill the quotas that various groups and organizations had been apportioned. Family members denounced one another. Nor were intellectuals excused; they were forced to disclose impure thoughts in small group discussions, a process that supposedly cleansed them of pro-Americanism, individualism, and bourgeois ideology. By the time these campaigns ended, Mao's government had exacted a huge toll on many individuals, fattening government payrolls and bringing the urban populations under control.

However draconian and unpardonable, Mao's Stalinist methods succeeded in restoring order to a country that had been laid low by civil conflict and was now in the midst of a war with the most powerful country in the world. Mao inherited a China crippled by more than a dozen years of economic stagnation, hyperinflation, massive poverty, and lawlessness. Inflation had been so onerous that "just prior to the collapse of the domestic currency in August 1948, the wholesale price index in Shanghai reached a level 6,600,000 times that of 1937."[16] The new government quickly balanced the budget and brought inflation under control. It reorganized the educational system and restored social stability.

Mao brought the peasantry, the petty bourgeoisie, and the national bourgeoisie together into a "national united front" officially led by the working class. He allowed non-Communist democrats to be appointed heads of eleven of the twenty-four government ministries, though few enjoyed much real power. He regularly sought the advice of prestigious non-Communist figures. Among his letters there are probably more addressed to the well-known and highly respected democrat and government minister Huang Yanpei than to any other single person. At one point he even chided Huang for being too radical, suggesting that socialism had to be implemented slowly. As he had promised in "On the People's Democratic Dictatorship," Mao also permitted most capitalists and managers to retain control of their businesses.[17]

By 1952, in spite of the Korean War, Mao's government had restored China's agricultural and industrial production to their highest prewar levels. He had expelled almost all Westerners from the country and confiscated most of their property. He had virtually wiped out crime, prostitution, and infanticide. Nevertheless the hardest job remained—building the future China.

Mao's blueprint for that job was the old Soviet Union. Gradually he began to turn China into a replica of Russia. As Roderick MacFarquhar has put it:

> The Soviet constitution was examined and copied when the PRC's was being written. A vast central economic and planning apparatus was created on the Soviet model. The educational system aped the Soviet one. Simple PLA uniforms were redesigned to give Chinese marshals and generals something of the heavy gilt appearance of the Soviet counterparts. Even Soviet dietary strictures were faithfully adhered to.[18]

The Chinese went so far as to copy Soviet architecture — in spite of climatic differences and the disparity in traditional building styles between the two countries.

In 1953, having consolidated his government, Mao urged his countrymen: "We must whip up a high tide of learning from the Soviet Union throughout the whole country [in order] to build our country."[19] Chinese schools began to teach Russian, and Russian advisers flocked to China. Thousands of Chinese students went to study in the Soviet Union, including both Li Peng and Jiang Zemin, the two most important leaders of China in the 1990s.

The Chinese put in place an urban-oriented, Soviet-style technical education system. They neglected the rural schools, which had developed during the revolutionary period and in the first few years after the 1949 Liberation. Primary school enrollments in fact declined from 55 million in 1952 to 51.2 million in 1954. After 1953 an elitist urban education became almost a necessity for anyone who wanted higher education. "At the college level," Suzanne Pepper noted, "more than 80 percent of the 93,785 new students enrolled for the 1954–55 academic year came directly from the accelerated middle schools for worker-peasant cadres." Mao worried that these schools were causing students to spend too much time reading and studying, and not allowing enough time for sleep.[20]

He was also concerned that cadre schools were not integrated with "people's schools."[21] As in the Soviet Union, party members had become the rulers of the new society. A government bureaucracy existed separate from the party, but party members became the principal leaders in factories, schools, villages, offices, mass organizations, and the military. Every citizen had to belong to a party-controlled unit, or *danwei*. The unit determined one's housing, ration coupons, vacations, and even marriage. The units organized political study classes, meetings, and criticism and self-criticism sessions. Between 1945 and 1952 party rolls quadrupled. As in the Soviet Union, party members gained special privileges and powers.

Also as in the Soviet Union, the system produced factional problems. In late 1953, when Mao hinted he might want a respite from his responsibilities, Gao Gang, the leader of the Northeast region, plotted to push Zhou Enlai and Liu Shaoqi aside and insert himself as Mao's successor. Thinking Mao was behind Gao's moves, several prominent leaders, including the military chiefs Peng Dehuai and Lin Biao, apparently went along with Gao's plans. But after talking with Gao, Deng Xiaoping and Chen Yun reported the plot to Mao, who put an end to Gao's efforts. The disgraced Gao eventually committed suicide.[22]

The area in which Mao most strictly adhered to Soviet principles was the economy. In January 1953 he announced China's first Five-Year Plan, modeled on the Soviet idea. As in the Soviet Union, targets and quotas for the entire country were to be monitored by the central government. The plan called for industrial production to double and agricultural production to grow by one-fourth over five years. Twenty percent of the nation's income was to be used for investment. Like the Soviets, Mao planned to devote the overwhelming majority of investment income to so-called heavy industries — steel, chemicals, machine tools, and electric power.

For a price the Soviets supplied detailed blueprints and technical information for virtually all of China's major construction projects. They also sold the Chinese 156 giant industrial units that served as the core of the system. Many of these new industries even required imported raw materials.

Nevertheless the economy grew at a spectacular rate. While the Five-Year Plan called for an industrial growth rate of 14.7 percent annually, the actual increase was approximately 3 percent higher. In five years China's industrial output more than doubled. It was an impressive performance. Still, it should not be forgotten that the country had started from a narrow base. China in 1949 had less than half the heavy industrial base and grain output that the Soviet Union recorded on the eve of its first Five-Year Plan in 1928.[23]

The Chinese peasantry who had helped create the Chinese revolution reaped few if any benefits from the new industrial growth. The peasants received low prices, fixed by the state, for their agricultural products and encountered high prices for the few manufactured goods they bought. As in the Soviet Union, purchases of grain from the peasantry at below-market prices financed the industrialization.

To increase agricultural production, Mao's government encouraged the peasants to form mutual aid teams in which five or six families pooled their tools and helped one another through the growing season. The hope was that gradually, as the peasantry began to see the value in joint labor, the teams would become more integrated and several mutual aid teams would join together to form Agricultural Producer Cooperatives which pooled labor and land. In these lower-level APCs the land would still be individually owned. The proceeds would be divided based on the contributions of labor and property. The first Five-Year Plan foresaw that only about a third of the peasantry would form lower-level APCs by the end of 1957. Mao saw this as "a gradual transition to socialism. By gradual we mean dividing [the process into] fifteen years and each year again into twelve months."[24]

Mao and most of the members of the new government believed that the peasants would not truly become part of the new society until they formed cooperatives, thereby creating a more efficient form of agriculture. Initially Mao believed that China would not see this development until after the widespread dissemination of tractors and other tools made the benefits of cooperatives obvious, and when the improved educational level of the peasantry allowed them to understand the benefit of joining with others to purchase these tools.

The Soviet Union had forced collective agriculture on its peasants at horrific cost. Mao knew it would be problematic for the Chinese: "The fact that the Chinese people are culturally backward and do not have a tradition of cooperativization makes expanding and developing the cooperativization campaign quite difficult for us. Nevertheless, it can still be organized, and must be organized; it must be expanded and developed." By the end of 1953, in spite of the problems he knew it would engender, Mao had begun to call on the party to speed up the pace of cooperativization, suggesting that though there were "six thousand cooperatives in North China," the figure could easily be doubled. Instead of establishing only small cooperatives, "Wherever it is possible to set up medium-sized cooperatives, it ought to be done, and wherever it is possible to set up large ones, we ought to do so. We mustn't be unhappy to see large cooperatives with one or two hundred households, even some with three or four hundred households."[25]

Mao wished to speed cooperativization not only to advance socialism, but also because he believed that without benefits of scale, agriculture would continue to be a problem for China. The first Five-Year Plan assumed that even without any investment in agriculture, the greater efficiency gained by having peasants pool tools and holdings, work ever larger plots of land in tandem, improve irrigation, reclaim land, and plant trees would increase agricultural production by some 23 percent over five years. Instead, in 1953 and 1954 grain output increased by only 1 or 2 percent. Industrial crops such as cotton and oilseeds grew by less.

This slow agricultural growth, Mao realized, jeopardized China's ability to pay for continued industrial growth and the purchase of technological imports from the Soviet Union. The formation of the lower-level APCs was moving too slowly. Poorly educated cadres responded to the growing need to collect more grain by extracting it from the few APCs that had formed. It was much easier to take grain from a large organization like an APC than to collect it from individual producers. But this pattern made those who did join APCs resentful, and those who had not joined were even more reluctant to do so.

In the summer of 1955 Mao changed course after meeting with local officials who were eager to continue the campaign for cooperatives: "We must guide the movement boldly and must not fear dragons ahead and tigers behind."[26] As we shall see, this was to be Mao's Achilles heel: a firm belief that lower-level officials were somehow more in tune with the masses than officials in the upper reaches of government.

In this case, local officials with a vested interest in the APCs — because the cooperatives gave them more power — responded quickly to cues from the center. Mao grew more enthusiastic. Although most high-level officials were still inclined to go slowly, at a gathering of provincial and subprovincial party secretaries at the end of July 1955, Mao called for a "High Tide" of socialist transformation in the countryside. He sarcastically complained that those who wanted to go slow were "tottering along like a woman with bound feet, complaining all the time about others saying: '[You're] going too fast, [you're] going too fast.' [They are given to] excessive nitpicking, unwarranted complaints, endless worries, and countless taboos, and take this to be the correct policy for guiding the socialist mass movement in the rural areas." Mao, now sure that cooperativization was necessary for industrialization, pointed out that "this policy has been proven to be a correct one in the Soviet Union," where experience showed that "socialist industrialization cannot proceed in isolation from the cooperativization of agriculture." A few months later he made this point even more clearly when he told the Central Committee that the idea that agricultural machinery was essential in establishing cooperatives was a "superstition that can be completely destroyed."[27]

Although his rhetoric was bold, Mao's plan was not overly radical. As Frederick Teiwes describes it:

It called for careful preparations for new APCs, allowed peasants to withdraw or even dissolve unsatisfactory cooperatives, and warned against rashness as well as timidity in cooperativization. Moreover, even though Mao's targets substantially raised those earlier decided on by the rural work department, the rate of increase was less than that achieved in the year from early 1954 to early 1955, and the absolute numbers involved were only slightly larger.[28]

But China's Soviet-style system was not geared to subtleties. Local officials asked to produce more tax revenue for the country's heavy industrial policy knew that the easiest way to carry out their jobs and the best way to increase their power was to push the peasants into APCs as fast as possible. They sped the campaign along. As the pace of cooperativization accelerated, concerned state officials reduced procurements in order to lighten pressure on the APCs. This forced Mao to imitate Stalin in another area. In the summer of 1955 the party began large-scale rationing of grain in urban areas in an effort to reduce grain consumption.

By the end of 1955 nearly two-thirds of the countryside had formed APCs. The first cooperatives averaged twenty-six households. By 1956 the typical lower-level APC had forty households. A bumper crop was produced in 1955, and this success spurred the collectivization campaign. In December of that year the Politburo called for lower-level APCs to be established throughout the countryside by the close of 1956. In a speech in late 1955, Mao implied that socialism and prosperity were just around the corner, and that they would be led by the agricultural sector. He triumphantly proclaimed that "we underestimated our own capacity. In the past, agriculture lagged behind industry." As a result of the success of the initial cooperativization drive, Mao declared that "agriculture caught up with industry and forced industry to make progress."

The lower-level APCs were considered by the government to be semi-socialist. Seeing how quickly they had been established,

Mao pushed ahead with the upper-level APCs, noting that "it is possible that socialism will be realized in 1959." Soon he talked about his goals more specifically: "We must strive to fundamentally achieve the higher-stage form of cooperativization by 1960. Is it possible to shorten the time by one year and strive to achieve [this goal] fundamentally by 1959? To this end, it is necessary for one or several large-size (over 100 households) higher-stage cooperatives to be established in 1956 in each xian or each district. . . ." His troops heard the message. Cadres throughout rural China concluded that it was "better to err to the left than the right."[29] In early 1956 the Politburo speeded up the timetable even further, calling for the creation of upper-level APCs throughout the country by the end of 1958.

These new higher-level APCs were far more complicated than their lower-level counterparts, and more than six times larger. They averaged approximately 246 households per collective, or about 1,200 people, generally encompassing an entire village. The lower-level APCs had paid people for the property they contributed. In the higher-level APCs, except for small private plots, private land ceased to exist. In accordance with socialist principles, people were paid for the amount of labor they contributed, not for their property. The old lower-level APCs became production brigades.

A new Mao now began to emerge. He thought he saw a way of transforming China outside the tedious bureaucratized manner of the Soviet-style five-year plans. In what became known as the "Little Leap"—to distinguish it from the Great Leap Forward carried out after 1958—in late 1955 Mao called for "the transformation of handicraft industries" and for more rapid "nationalization of industry and commerce." He urged the development of plans to mobilize peasant labor and rural financial resources to boost grain yields, breed more animals, end "more than a dozen insect pests and disease," eliminate wastelands, and produce more fertilizer. He wanted evening schools in every district. He urged equal work and equal pay for men and women in the cooperatives. He told his party audience: "We must accelerate and achieve faster, greater, and better results in all aspects of our work. We must obtain better results in a shorter period of time."[30]

For the first time Mao began to suggest that China could do better than the Soviet Union, that the country could move faster than the Russians had because "we had more than twenty years' experience in the base areas and the practice of the three revolutionary wars. We are extremely rich in experience." China had "the help of the Soviet Union and other democratic countries," and "our population is large and our location is good." He thought he and his fellow Chinese "should not always compare ourselves with the Soviet Union. After three five-year plans we shall be able to produce twenty-four million tons of steel. This is faster than the Soviet Union."[31] Once again Mao's wish was taken as a command. Ministries and local officials raised their quotas from one month to the next, producing dislocations and other problems. When the economy threatened to career into chaos, Mao agreed that the "Little Leap" had to be ended and the pace of change slowed.

Although Mao had reason to be happy that collectivization in China had occurred with much less violence than in the Soviet Union, the movement was not a success. In 1956 and 1957 the growth in food grain production was well below the levels called for by the Five-Year Plan. Poorly educated cadres had difficulties managing new, larger, more sophisticated organizations. A lack of incentives caused the well-off peasants, usually the best producers, to slack off. Some deserted the collectives altogether.

These problems did not prevent Mao from extending the collectivization program to urban areas. In December 1955 he began meeting with businessmen in Shanghai to talk about speeding up the socialization of commerce and industry. He warned the businessmen not to go too fast, but those who met with him had already been bruised by the Five-Anti Campaign and were not about to resist a program that Mao considered a priority. Although the official date for the transformation was set for 1957, by early 1956 most privately owned and managed enterprises in China's largest industrial cities had become government organizations.[32] In March Mao called for the transformation of handicraft industries from individual to cooperative production. Within a short time virtually all private businesses, big and small, had been socialized and reorganized into cooperatives. Owners received bonds for the property that had been confiscated from them. Most became salaried managers in their old concerns.

In spite of the problems he faced, by the end of 1956 Mao had unified China, created an impressive rate of growth, restructured the education system, improved living standards at least modestly, and fought the greatest power in the world to a standstill in Korea. During the first Five-Year Plan, according to Nicholas Lardy, "national income grew at an average annual rate of 8.9 percent (measured in constant prices), with agriculture and industrial output expanding annually by about 3.8 and 18.7 percent, respectively." On top of the large increase recorded from 1949 to 1953, this was a stunning rise. Since population growth was 2.4 percent and output grew at 6.5 percent per person, the growth rate, if sustained, would double national income every eleven years. Peasant income rose, worker income rose, the percent of children in primary school doubled, and "life expectancy, the single best indicator of a country's health status, rose from 36 years in 1950 to 57 years by 1957, fifteen years longer than the average life expectancy of low-income countries at the time."[33]

Yet in spite of Mao's talk of having China "stand up" for itself, what he had instituted in China was Stalinism. He later explained, "Because we didn't understand these things and had absolutely no experience, all we could do in our ignorance was to import foreign methods." He complained that he could not eat eggs or chicken soup "just because an article appeared in the Soviet Union which said that one should not eat them."[34]

Mao was most unlike Stalin in the way he ruled by consensus.

He was the supreme leader, but he did not act without the concurrence of other officials. Yet the system that Mao established was one in which it became increasingly difficult to distinguish consensus agreement from his personal will. This was not because, as with Stalin, officials feared they would be imprisoned or executed. Rather it was because they genuinely believed in the party's consensus politics, preferring to take sick leave rather than disagree.[35]

Whether working collectively or by himself, Mao had allowed the state to take almost complete control of the economy. The state planned the production process; it collectivized the peasantry and made them state employees; it transformed private firms into state-owned companies. Mao had pushed China so far into the Soviet camp that, as he later explained: "When Chinese artists painted pictures of me together with Stalin, they always made me a little shorter than Stalin."[36] After Stalin died in 1953, it took Mao several years to realize that China would not advance further until he radically revamped much of the system he had helped put in place after 1949. In 1955 he began to make small efforts in that direction. The big push, the one that turned Mao into a Maoist, was yet to come.

The Great Leap into Cataclysm

❧ . IN EARLY 1956 Mao turned sixty-two. He was pudgier than in the austere days of Yan'an but still physically fit enough to swim the Yangzi River three times, a feat he celebrated with a poem:

> A swim cuts across the Long River;
> A glance gauges the sky's width.
> Let the wind blow and waves strike,
> This surpasses an aimless stroll in the country.[1]

He was approaching a turning point in his life. Within two years he would launch an all-out assault on the Soviet economic model, breaking with the Stalinist policies he had admired for decades. Mao's "Great Leap Forward" initiated the remaking of China's political and economic system—at the cost of thrusting China into disaster.

Even in the early 1950s it was already apparent that Mao's style of governing was radically at odds with the Soviet style. Stalin ruled by fiat, Mao by consensus. Stalin had no strong number-two man while Mao had long entrusted Liu Shaoqi with enormous power and autonomy. Stalin kept to regular work routines and was a slave to bureaucratic norms. Mao did not even go to his office, preferring to operate from his home, usually his bedroom. He often lolled in an enormous bed, aides entering and exiting as he carried out his everyday bodily functions. The bed was filled with books and papers the chairman was reading or poems he was writing.[2]

From his bed Mao carried out policies, plotted the downfall of real and imagined enemies, and read pornographic novels and sex manuals to stimulate his performance for the nubile young women sent in to service him. Even in his vacation home in Hangzhou or in stops in some provincial city or on his special train, he did most of his work in his bed. In a scene that would become famous, a furious Mao summoned the editor of the *People's Daily* and a group of his aides to his bedside one afternoon in 1957. Awaiting the astonished journalists was a chain-smoking Mao, clad in a towel and a pajama top, his fat belly protruding. Totally unself-conscious about his appearance, Mao berated the group for almost four hours on their failure to cover his efforts to open the party to outside criticism.[3]

This style of living isolated Mao from the rhythms of everyday Chinese life. Yet he had come to understand that the Soviet system, so radically different from his own approach, was also not ideal for Chinese conditions. Ever since Stalin's death in 1953, Mao had been looking at new paths for China. But he might never have moved to alter his increasingly rigid and unresponsive government if Stalin's successor, Nikita Khrushchev, had not himself first begun to question the Soviet system. In February 1956 Khrushchev unexpectedly denounced Stalin's despotism and paranoia, attacking the mass arrests, murders, and tortures that Stalin had made commonplace. Stalin's central fault, Khrushchev charged, was his "cult of personality."

For Mao it was a little like learning that the emperor wore no clothes. While he continued to insist that "Stalin's merits outweigh his faults," Khrushchev's speech forced Mao to rethink the Soviet model and begin to give vent to some of the personal frustrations he had sometimes had with Stalin. Mao soon claimed that the Soviet leader had tried to undermine the Chinese revolution at several key moments.[4]

Unlike Stalin, Mao "had proven he could work with former rivals and antagonists."[5] But after listening to Khrushchev's attacks on Stalin's "cult of personality," Mao knew that without changes in the Chinese state his own political leadership and legacy could ultimately be called into question. He began to consider seriously the effects of Soviet-style centralized authoritarian bureaucracy in China.

In April 1956, in a carefully worded speech entitled "The Ten Great Relationships," Mao suggested that he was interested in modifying many of the fundamental economic and political principles of the Soviet model. Although he still recognized the importance of emphasizing heavy industry, he now suggested that agriculture and light industry needed more attention. Too many resources had been directed to coastal areas. More investment was necessary in inland regions. Mao wanted less emphasis on the center and more on the localities. He insisted that "We must learn the good points of all countries and all nationalities. Every nation has its strong points; otherwise how could it exist, how could it develop?"[6] He called for better relationships with minorities and respect for nonparty groups. He even suggested trimming military expenditures.

Sounding like an American-style anti-Washington politician, he noted disapprovingly: "At present there are dozens of hands meddling in regional affairs, making them difficult to manage. Every day various ministries issue orders to the offices of provincial and municipal governments." Mao wanted more than simply eliminating a few federal offices. He proposed that "the Party and government be streamlined and that two-thirds of their numbers should be axed." In a separate talk to the Central Committee, he insisted that "The localities have the right to resist all impracticable, unrealistic, and subjectivist orders, directives, instructions, and forms which the various ministries of the Central Government may send down to them."[7]

A few months later Mao began complaining publicly about how some officials thought that everything Soviet should be copied: "Some people say that no matter what, even the farts of the Russians smell good; that too is subjectivism. Even the Russians themselves would admit that they stink!" In a judgment identical to what was later applied to himself, Mao claimed that Stalin was 30 percent bad and 70 percent good.[8]

To avoid the political and economic problems that had plagued Stalinist Russia, Mao hit on the idea of combining his campaign against bureaucracy with the need to allow intellectuals more freedom. That would allow them to help more effectively with education, propaganda, and the technical requirements needed for more rapid economic development. In a talk before the Politburo in April 1956, Mao used a classical allusion—one he would repeat in a better-known May 2 speech—to encourage those outside the party to speak out and criticize the party. "Let a hundred flowers bloom," he proclaimed, and "let a hundred schools contend."[9] His urging recalled a famous period when China's great philosophical schools—notably Confucianism and Taoism—sprouted during a time of contention and debate.

By giving scientists and engineers the freedom to express their ideas, Mao sought to prevent party bureaucrats from interfering with technical decisions. He wanted intellectuals to expose and attack corruption and bureaucracy. He also wanted peasants, students, and workers to speak out and even demonstrate to prevent government bureaucrats from running roughshod over their rights. "When the masses have a reasonable petition to make, they should be permitted [to make it], absolutely. In the future we can give some thought to adding an article in the Constitution permitting the workers to strike. This would be of beneficial influence to correcting the bureaucratic work style of the factory leadership. . . ." Admitting that "nationality issues in the Tibetan region have not been fully resolved," Mao called on the party to "oppose Han chauvinism."[10]

Even with this encouragement, it took several months for the discouraged and beleaguered intelligentsia to believe that Mao meant what he said, and to begin complaining about cadre interference in their work. By the summer of 1956, writers and artists were attacking the social realist style. Scientists were debating Soviet-adopted concepts like the genetic theories of Lysenko, and previously banned ideas like birth control. Social scientists were criticizing Marx and Engels's ideas of historical periodization, the role of Marxism-Leninism, and even the relevance of Marxist economic theories. Government employees were pointing to the arrogance and incompetence of party bureaucrats and noting the party's failure to observe Marx's humanitarian principles.[11]

Even more radical changes were occurring elsewhere in the Communist world, especially in Hungary, where the political and intellectual climate was shifting so remarkably that in the fall of 1956 the Soviets sent in troops and tanks to restore the Communist government. Mao backed the Soviets, but he argued that the same thing could not happen in China. "When there is a sore, things will be resolved when the pus breaks out. The Chinese Party, China's government, and the armed forces will not be toppled by these kids. If we allow students to topple us, then we would be good for nothing idiots."[12]

In making this statement, Mao was attempting to quiet the fears of officials such as Peng Zhen, the mayor of Beijing, who were uneasy over the mounting attacks on the Chinese Communist party's power and role, especially in light of the Hungarian situation. Mao's efforts did not work at first. By early 1957 his underlings had succeeded in stopping the Hundred Flowers campaign in spite of Mao's assurances that it would expose "poisonous weeds" that the party could later dig out.[13]

The resistance of officials like Peng illustrates an important point about Mao. Although he may have feared that his cult of personality could be compared with Stalin's, the fact is that he did not act like Stalin. Throughout the 1950s, officials were free to criticize Mao's policies, and he was careful to obtain consensus on issues before acting.[14]

Of course, Mao usually got his way. He did so at this time by cajoling audiences of party members, repeating his "hundred flowers" statement and reminding them how he had expanded the circulation of the newspaper *Reference News* (*Cankao xiaoxi*) from 2,000 copies to 400,000 copies. *Reference News* was a compilation of articles from the non-Chinese press. Most copies went not to individuals but to work units, where it was passed around. By increasing the circulation of the paper so radically (in the 1970s it was expanded even more), Mao made sure that the uncensored news of the outside world was available even in rural districts throughout China. He explained, "The purpose of this is to put non-Marxist things and poisonous weeds in front of the comrades and the non-Party people so as to temper everyone. Otherwise they will only know Marxism and nothing else, and that wouldn't be good. It is like a smallpox vaccination which causes struggle inside the human body and produces immunity."[15]

Mao insisted to party officials that even bourgeois and imperialist thinkers should be allowed to express themselves: "If they have to fart, let them fart; otherwise it will be harmful to us. If it's out, then one can decide if it smells good or bad."[16]

In late February 1957 Mao gave a four-hour talk "On the Correct Handling of Contradictions Among the People." In this speech, which was not distributed until June and then only in a revised form, Mao suggested that there could be "nonantagonistic contradictions" between leaders and their followers even in Communist societies. The party, he told his startled listeners, held no monopoly on the truth. On certain questions the people might be right and the party wrong. Different opinions were needed. Intellectuals performed an especially important task when they exposed the party's bureaucratic tendencies. Mao even suggested that criticism by non-Communist democratic parties could help prevent the CCP from growing too rigid. Disparagement of Marxism was all right too.[17]

The speech outraged many Chinese officials. Pointedly, Liu Shaoqi, the second highest-ranking official in China, did not appear in any of the photographs of officials at Mao's "Contradictions" talk. Some enraged officials who did appear walked out.[18] The idea that those outside the party should be encouraged to criticize those within it was not easily tolerated.

For the next several months Mao gave speech after speech on the need for those at the local level to speak out about "bureaucratism," suggesting that in factories, schools, and cooperatives, if criticism did not work, strikes and boycotts should be used.[19] Again and again he repeated his point that democracy was a way of vaccinating society against problems and that bad ideas would harm few people. Only those with the worst ideas should be kicked out of the Communist party, but such people should not be expelled from the schools. Dissent was necessary for scientific progress. As he continued to reiterate, it was the only way to "inoculate" the party.

Not until April 1957 did Mao win Politburo approval for his Hundred Flowers campaign. The movement slowly revived. By the late spring Chinese intellectuals were again lambasting almost every aspect of Chinese life. Some denounced the petty party interferences in their lives. Others questioned the monopoly of power exercised by the Communist party. A few doubted the legality of the way the party maintained its power. They criticized the special privileges and facilities bestowed on party officials and cadres and the oppressive burdens under which the peasants and workers toiled, condemning the entire social and political order that had developed since 1949.[20]

At Beijing University hundreds of posters appeared at a location known as the "Democratic Wall." In these posters and in speeches the students denounced the government's educational policy, questioned the failure to raise China's living standard since 1949, and attacked the suppression of freedom of speech and publication. Angry students fanned out across the country, and campuses throughout China joined the protests. On June 12 and 13, 1957, student riots broke out in the North China town of Hanyang in Hubei province.[21]

Not only intellectuals had joined the protests. Workers, to Mao's approval, began to demonstrate for better conditions. As Elizabeth Perry has shown, Mao's encouragement produced a strike wave of "massive proportions."[22]

In the face of these events Mao at first appeared unconcerned. His secretary, Chen Boda, visited the Beijing University campus and told him that reports of uncontrolled dissent were exaggerated. Mao welcomed the strikes as good for the party.[23] But party members grew increasingly frightened that China was being threatened with a Hungarian-style uprising.

By early June, as attacks on the party mounted, Mao faced a growing rebellion among government officials and party bureaucrats. He decided to halt the campaign. On June 8 he authorized a *People's Daily* editorial signaling that criticism of the party would no longer be tolerated. Ten days later he published his "Contradictions" speech for the first time, adding a new section in which he distinguished "poisonous weeds" from "fragrant flowers." He had used the "poisonous weeds" before, but now he made it ominously clear that the weeds were those who criticized socialism and the party. The new version of the speech also omitted Mao's acknowledgment that the party had made major mistakes in Tibet and thus needed to postpone further reforms there for several years. With this silence on the issue of Tibet, party officials ended Mao's effort to offer better treatment of minorities. Also, with his support for more openness under attack, Mao now excised from the speech the figures he had admitted about the number of "counterrevolutionaries" killed following the establishment of the People's Republic of China.

As late as July 1, even as he backed away from his efforts to change the political climate in China, Mao was still arguing that "We should be lenient and not mete out punishment" to rightists, and was maintaining that "we need not call them reactionaries." Although a week or so later he acknowledged that it might be "necessary to hit them with a few blows," he still believed that most "rightists" could be won over.[24]

By this time an anti-rightist campaign had been launched to "cut off the heads of the poisonous weeds" that had sprouted amidst the flowers of revolutionary debate. By mid-July even Mao was using the word "reactionaries" to describe the worst offenders, in spite of his earlier caution that it would not be necessary to use this highly charged word.[25] He allowed official criticism of many students and prominent intellectuals. A number were arrested. In Hanyang, in an ominous portent, three middle-school leaders of the student riots were executed.

This anti-rightist movement was prosecuted by Deng Xiao-ping, the man who, after his mentor's death, was credited with turning China away from the oppressiveness of the Maoist system. Despite his later reputation as a moderate foil to Mao, Deng is said to have showed "far more enthusiasm for squashing non-party dissidents than he had for rectifying party bureaucrats." Instead of the more open political system Mao had hoped to create, Deng's anti-rightist campaign "exacerbated the CCP's intolerance," writes David Bachman. "Instead of playing a larger role in economic construction and in the political sphere, intellectuals and non-CCP personnel suffered severe persecution."[26]

A man who had been a minor party official during this unsettled period once told me how the campaign worked. Each work unit was given a quota of names to be reported to the government as "rightists." My friend was told to send the authorities three names. After searching the ranks of his organization, he reported that he found only two people who could be labeled rightists. Fine, came the response, then you will serve as number three. They imprisoned my friend for three years.

This dismal end to Mao's effort to stimulate innovation and

initiative by opening up the Chinese system did not stop the search for a new economic agenda. By the end of 1957 it was clear that, contrary to Mao's expectations, the rate of agricultural growth had actually declined after collectivization. In 1957 the increase in grain was a paltry 1 percent, less than the population increase.[27] Without greater agricultural growth, the country might soon face food shortages. Certainly China would not be able to pay for its Soviet-style heavy industrial program.

During the first Five-Year Plan, Mao and his colleagues had been such good students of the Soviets that "the Chinese managed to devote nearly 48 percent of their public capital investment to industrial development, whereas the comparable Soviet figure was under 42 percent."[28] The problem was that per capita agricultural productivity in the Soviet Union was twice as high as in China. Even if the Chinese chose to bleed their peasants dry to pay for this kind of industrial expansion, as the Soviets did, it was not certain they could do so.

One solution to this problem was to get the people to work harder and produce more by reversing the policy of gradualism that had been adopted since the ending of the Little Leap. Mao was apparently convinced to move in this direction as a result of prompting from local leaders and support from the government's "planning coalition," especially Bo Yibo and Li Fuchun. By October Mao had revived the Little Leap program of "greater, faster, better, and more economical" and was pushing labor to increase production.[29]

In Moscow in November 1957, Mao listened to Khrushchev's plans for the decentralization of the Soviet economy. The Soviet premier optimistically announced that within fifteen years the USSR would match the United States in the production of important heavy products.[30] An eager Mao decided that if the Soviets were abandoning their centralist economic model, so would China, and they too would ramp up their steel production.

Other Chinese leaders fell in line. When Mao returned from

Moscow and began to talk about increasing steel production as the Russians were doing, members of the planning coalition produced new statistics on the possibilities of growth in steel that surpassed even Mao's expectations.[31] The party also approved. Liu Shaoqi and Deng Xiaoping were enthusiastic advocates of the program.

The Great Leap Forward became both a production drive and a continuation of Mao's attack on bureaucracy and elitism that had been curtailed by the start of the anti-rightist campaign. Agricultural and political decisions were decentralized. China's surplus labor force was put to work increasing agricultural production by developing new irrigation and water conservancy projects. Thousands of simple small-scale factories were built with the hope that China's vast manpower could replace the machines used in other countries, eliminating the need for expensive, large-scale industrial plants. The most notorious examples were the backyard furnaces built in every village to smelt steel in small, low-tech operations. In the larger factories, workers put in longer hours and developed new homegrown innovative techniques to increase output.

Using a slightly modified version of the old Little Leap slogan, Liu Shaoqi called on the country "to achieve greater, faster, better, and more economical results." Mao's declaration that China would "catch up with Britain in about fifteen years"—now often derided—was made after consultation with and the approval of his colleagues. The Secretariat, headed by Deng Xiaoping, was the key central organ that promoted and carried out this Great Leap Forward. Deng's identification with Mao and his policies at the time of the Great Leap was so strong that Mao referred to him to "as boss number two."[32] In 1958 Deng accompanied Mao on several of his Great Leap tours of the provinces.

Only the economic administrators, Chen Yun and Zhou Enlai, were unenthusiastic about the plan, but they did not protest vociferously or extensively, even when given the opportunity to do so.[33] Zhou, in fact, soon fell in line.

With this kind of backing, Mao enthused to the country that the program would not only boost the economy but would bear "magnificent ideological and political flowers," developing new communal and cooperative organizations that would lead to the development not just of socialism but of communism.[34] By late spring 1958 this ideological goal had become as important as having China produce more steel and grain.

Confirming Mao's enthusiasm, the program at first seemed to work. In the first months industrial production was greater than anticipated. An excited Mao solicited new, higher targets from lower levels. Given Mao's old belief in "from the masses to the masses," this attention to the people's estimate of the situation seemed to confirm his growing disenchantment with the central bureaucracy and heighten his expectations that through the masses he would reinvigorate the country.

He was, of course, smart enough to understand that the lower levels might simply be following the newest political line; but reports from experts and Mao's own information gleaned from visits to factories confirmed everything he was hearing. The technicians at the Ministry of Metallurgy declared that, on the basis of their investigations, China could overtake Great Britain not in fifteen years but in ten. On a visit to a steel plant in Sichuan, Mao was shown how the workers had radically increased production by rebuilding the old machinery. A provincial leader excitedly told a skeptical Mao that the peasants were so enthusiastic about the new program that by overhauling irrigation works and changing production methods, they were achieving yields as much as seventy times higher. Soon stories even more preposterous began to pour in from around the country, many endorsed by reputable scientific organizations.[35]

During his tour of Baoding prefecture in Hebei, Mao was told that the area "expected a fantastic harvest of 550,000 tons of grain." These numbers were so extraordinary that an excited Mao asked, "How can you consume all this food? What are you going to do with the surplus?" He advised shifting land from grain to oil-bearing crops and a variety of vegetables to upgrade the diet. "Plant a little less and do half a day's work. Use the other half of the day for culture; study science, promote culture and recreation, run a college and middle school."[36]

Mao may have been naive to believe these reports, but as Li Zhisui, his doctor, has confirmed, local officials went to elaborate lengths during Mao's visits to show him what he hoped to see. When Mao traveled extensively to inspect progress in the country-side, as he did at the beginning of the Great Leap, he used a special train and was accompanied by a large entourage. Local officials were alerted to his visit well in advance. They deliberately kept Mao away from real people and went out of their way to sugar-coat their situations. On one trip during the Great Leap:

> The party secretaries had ordered furnaces constructed every-where along the rail route, stretching out for ten li on either side, and the women were dressed so colorfully, in reds and greens, be-cause they had been ordered to dress that way. In Hubei, party secretary Wang Renzhong had ordered the peasants to remove rice plants from faraway fields and transplant them along Mao's route, to give the impression of a wildly abundant crop. The rice was planted so closely together that electric fans had to be set up around the fields to circulate air in order to prevent the plants from rotting.[37]

High-level officials such as Liu Shaoqi and Deng Xiaoping—for whom local officials offered less showboating—were equally enthusiastic. So Mao's excitement at the party's achievements with un-Stalinist methods, while misguided, is at least understandable. He himself said that though his enthusiasm might sound "madly arrogant," he did not think that he and his colleagues were "mad-men" but "revolutionaries who seek the truth from facts . . . unit-ing the Russian revolutionary zeal with the American spirit of realism!" He began to feel that if China's huge population went to work, the country could "catch up with the United States in fifteen years."[38]

In at least one respect Mao really did achieve what many Americans would consider a political miracle—he emptied most administrative offices. Ministries in charge of consumer goods handed over their enterprises to local governments. The central government reassigned great numbers of officials to local and regional ministries. Innovation was encouraged. Bureaucratic controls were loosened.

More than two million party cadres were sent down to join in production work. Even Mao went out to dig gravel, staying until his face turned bright red and sweat beaded from his forehead.[39] Later he sent his entire staff out for a few weeks to continue the work. Others spent far longer. The social gap between the countryside and the city, between mental and manual labor, between officials and workers was to be closed. Laborers began to participate in management. A million students were sent to do manual labor, as were large numbers of People's Liberation Army soldiers, many of whom were assigned to be cadres. In Beijing, professors and students joined to help build some of the massive monuments that still stand in the nation's capital. China's huge population, previously a problem, now appeared an advantage as new buildings and irrigation projects began to surface throughout the country, the result of Mao's mobilization of China's vast manpower.

The essential idea of the Great Leap was to put most of the excess population to work in new labor-intensive industries that required little or no capital investment. Everywhere an effort was made to develop small and medium-scale industries that could supplement the large, expensive modern factories already in the cities.

Since steel was a focus of the campaign, ingenious local efforts to increase steel production received much attention. Soon every village in China was constructing a small backyard steel furnace. Instead of creating giant new steel plants requiring great technical expertise and enormous investment, local leaders built tens of thousands of small steel furnaces in which previously unemployed rural workers made steel by hand. The Secretariat was particularly involved in this effort.

In addition to backyard steel furnaces, many areas built small chemical and fertilizer plants. In some places peasants mined small coal deposits as a way of increasing the local fuel supply. The party mobilized armies of peasants to reclaim land, improve soil, and develop irrigation and water-control projects. In cities and towns throughout China, millions screamed and shook trees to confuse and tire sparrows so that they could be easily killed when they alighted on the ground. Everywhere people swatted flies and mosquitoes and exterminated rats and other vermin. Some visitors reported seeing no flies or sparrows for days. (Mao mistakenly believed that sparrows ate grain. When he was finally persuaded that in fact they ate insects, he substituted bedbugs for sparrows.) By early 1958 the campaign had been extended against the major diseases plaguing China, including schistosomiasis, or liver flukes. In June 1958 Mao composed a poem noting that the disease "had been washed away by the tide." He was, it turned out, too optimistic.[40]

Massive peasant projects stimulated by the Great Leap demanded a large administrative unit. As Roderick MacFarquhar notes, "Liu Shao-ch'i had been talking of the need to combine industry, commerce, education, and military affairs with agriculture as early as mid-July [1957]." In the early summer of 1958 a super collective appeared in Henan province. In a July issue of the theoretical journal *Red Flag*, Mao's secretary, Chen Boda, gave it the name "people's commune."[41] Touring Henan in August, Mao praised the productivity of the communes and called for their extension to the whole country. In effect Mao was decentralizing the countryside through these massive new political and social organizations.

Mao's endorsement of the communes swept the country like a

storm. Within two months virtually the entire countryside had been organized into some 24,000 communes. The initial ones were huge, the equivalent of several American counties, an enormous area for an organization that became the lowest unit of government and was supposed to supervise not just agriculture but industry, education, police, and even the militia. Later the size of the communes was reduced to what in the United States would be considered a county.

The commune system encouraged the building of rural mess halls and nurseries to assume many of the tasks of cooking and childcare, freeing many women from household tasks and drawing them into the labor market. With the men engaged in large irrigation and water projects, the women took over men's ordinary tasks. Others went to work in nearby cities. Between 1957 and 1960 the number of clerical and industrial workers increased by more than 20 million. A similar growth occurred among the workers in the small industrial plants that the communes created.

With communism as the goal, worker-run factories abandoned piece-rate payments and created a more equalitarian system. More communes socialized property and provided free food and other goods and services according to the Marxist principle, "From each according to his abilities, to each according to his needs."

In his "Contradictions" speech, Mao had acknowledged that among children of school age, 40 percent had no school to attend. He now resolved to do something about this, noting, "The technological revolution is designed to make everyone learn science and technology." Beginning in January 1958 Mao encouraged the creation of thousands of work-study schools, night schools, and other part-time institutions so that millions of peasants and workers could continue their education. He gave local districts control over their own educational curriculums, believing they could best adapt them to local conditions. In turn they emphasized the kind of vocational education that would be most useful to peasants and workers. Local committees of party members, teachers, and students prepared educational materials in the new schools, including the rewriting of textbooks copied from the Soviet Union. Some of the results were ridiculous, like that of the chemistry students who wrote their own textbook.[42] But to put such mistakes in perspective, local school boards in the United States have also been known to make foolish decisions.

Before the Great Leap, various Beijing ministries controlled some fifty institutions of higher education. Because of Mao's prodding, these bureaus were merged into the Ministry of Education, which itself was so decentralized that it lost control of all but fourteen schools. Secondary schools and universities were directed to prepare for new peasant students. "Primary schools also 'sprouted like bamboo shoots after a spring rain' in 1958," Suzanne Pepper writes.[43]

The burgeoning of universal mass education, masterminded by Liu Shaoqi, was accompanied by a reported surge in agricultural and industrial production. In late October the harvest was estimated to be almost double that of the year before. The steel output of backyard furnaces also appeared prodigious. Other commodities showed similar increases.

But the Great Leap now became a victim of its apparent early success. Until late in the summer of 1958, as MacFarquhar writes, "the leap was still basically a highly successful production drive, with a summer harvest 59 percent up on 1957 already assured." News of success encouraged ever more ambitious projects. At an enlarged Politburo conference at the end of August 1958, China's leaders raised production levels for grain and steel to unrealistic levels while extending the commune movement throughout the country.[44] Lower-level officials anxious to show results exaggerated their figures, fueling the enthusiasm of higher-level officials who raised targets still higher in a vicious cycle. In this overheated atmosphere, even the reported increases in college and secondary school enrollment were padded.

Organizational chaos ensued. Inexperienced and undereducated managers mishandled fiscal affairs as they struggled to set up and manage the large, complex new structures. Local cadres became petty dictators. Richer peasants who resented amalgamating with poorer peasants destroyed livestock and supplies. Embittered and undermotivated peasants worked indifferently. Displeased with communal dining rooms and presented with a policy of free food, peasants in many areas ate themselves out of supplies. Even when there was enough to eat, canteens were often so far from people's homes that they wasted enormous time and energy getting there. The old and the lame often could not make it.[45]

The hours spent on iron and steel production kept the peasants from the harvest. Bumper crops withered in the fields as overworked peasants struggled at their backyard furnaces or on waterworks projects. At the last minute people were sent into the fields to work day and night to bring in the harvest. In many areas it was too little and too late.

Deep plowing, a Maoist idea for greater productivity, worked well in some farm areas, but when applied universally it often retarded and sometimes even prevented crop growth. Deep plowing and close planting required great additional labor and exhausted the soil. Mao, who had seen incredible results from test plantings in a few selected areas, had called for a one-third reduction in the amount of acreage devoted to crops in order to implement deep plowing. Few provinces reduced their plantings this much, but in 1958 reductions took their toll.[46] The huge increase in grain yields reported that year led officials to cut the land allocated to grain in 1959 and devote more acreage to industrial crops like cotton. The 1958 harvest—later stated to be 200 million tons—was indeed a record, but it was far less than the government's estimate of 375 million tons.

The higher steel quotas championed by Mao are often viewed as the greatest culprit in dragging down the Chinese economy. The backyard furnaces produced massive quantities of steel—some 3 million tons—but most of it was of poor quality. In order to fuel the backyard furnaces whole forests of wood were cut, creating long-term environmental problems and near-term fuel short-ages. Local cadres rode roughshod over complaints. Eager to produce results, they forced peasants to melt down badly needed farm implements to make new steel. Mao later admitted that he had not realized how much iron and coal would have to be moved around the country to produce this steel and how taxing it would be to China's transportation system.[47]

Meanwhile the increase in harvest projections led cadres to increase grain extractions in order to meet their quotas. Suddenly the till was empty. Communes ran out of food. Grain rations in the city had to be reduced.

In the midst of these economic problems, tension developed with the United States over Quemoy and Matsu, two tiny offshore islands that were controlled by the government of Taiwan. In late August 1958 Mao authorized the shelling of Quemoy (Jinmen), apparently believing that the United States would not come to Jiang Kaishek's aid over these islands. He hoped to force a KMT withdrawal from the islands that would demoralize the Nationalists and possibly lead to the ultimate surrender of Taiwan. But the United States did choose to defend the islands, precipitating an international crisis. After it was defused, Mao called for the establishment of militias in the communes as a way of militarizing the country and preventing attack. Dealing with the crisis exacerbated the internal situation and focused the attention of the leaders elsewhere.

In October, word of some of the Great Leap's problems reached Mao, who responded by trying to slow the campaign. He acknowledged that the transition to state ownership by the communes might not happen "that quickly" after all, but might need twelve years. He abandoned the idea of immediately establishing communism and suggested that, "After the establishment of the Communes, distribution should still primarily be remuneration according to work." By late November Mao took the lead in urging the party to readjust its production figures, acknowledging that many of them appeared to have been falsified. Although he worried about pouring "cold water" on the enthusiasm of the masses, he admitted that "people must eat their fill" and that the party "should adopt a low-keyed approach and pipe down a bit." He even suggested that "the people's communes have to be overhauled for four months" or else they might collapse altogether.[48]

Over the next few months Mao reduced steel targets and called for the government to publicize lower grain production statistics. As it became clear that the situation was worse than originally thought, he stated that he opposed "leftism." This was an attempt to rein in the lower-level cadres who had gained new power in the decentralization and were now resisting a retreat. Realizing how confused the party had become over the issue of establishing communism, Mao looked to his old mentor, Stalin, to justify a new, gradual approach. He told his followers "to reread Stalin's *Economic Problems of Socialism in the USSR* and look at the *Collection of Articles on the Problem of Bourgeois Right*," calling Stalin's work "extremely useful."[49]

In February 1959 Mao attempted to end the transfer of property from peasants to the collectives without compensation, and criticized efforts to equalize poor and rich brigades. In the months following he continued to urge provincial secretaries to moderate the Great Leap. During visits to the countryside in the spring, he upbraided local cadres who told him the peasants were hiding grain from the state.[50]

In late spring Mao called for help from the conservative economic planner Chen Yun, who had effectively left office at the beginning of the Great Leap. When Chen Yun recommended gutting the communes, Mao agreed.[51] The brigade (essentially the old collective) was again to be the basic unit of accounting. Common mess halls began to be disbanded. Private plots and markets reappeared. Steel targets were reassessed and inefficient small operations closed. Mao announced that he would step down as formal head of state at the end of 1959, retaining only his post as chairman of the Communist party.

Complicating Mao's problems was a worsening situation in

Tibet. In 1957, during the Hundred Flowers campaign, Mao had attempted to repair relations with minorities, urging tolerance toward what had already become a festering Tibetan rebellion. This stance did not sit well with other leaders, and with the end of the Hundred Flowers campaign Mao's efforts at moderation were ignored. Han chauvinism returned, and the situation in Tibet disintegrated. In March 1959 a frustrated and beleaguered Tibetan population rebelled. The Dalai Lama fled to India, as Mao had predicted in 1957 he might do. Still hoping to restore order, Mao personally gave the order not to pursue and capture him.

In late July 1959 the Politburo met at the mountaintop retreat of Lushan to review the Great Leap situation. During the first few days of discussion, Mao indicated that he favored further moderation. What changed his position was a letter from Peng Dehuai, the minister of defense, attacking Mao and the Great Leap. In the ensuing political struggle, Mao restarted the Great Leap, with disastrous consequences for China.

Although in the post-Mao world Peng has come to be viewed as a truth-telling hero unfairly persecuted by Mao, in reality Peng was a cantankerous man who had crossed swords with Mao on several key occasions in the 1930s and 1940s. Each time the two men had reconciled. But well before the 1959 summer plenum, they were already edging toward a new confrontation.

The new tension reportedly began over Mao's unhappiness with Peng's generalship in Korea. Mao also was reputed to have blamed Peng for the death of his beloved elder son during the conflict. And in 1956 Peng was the lone voice who attempted unsuccessfully to block Mao's desire to cut military spending, announced in his "Ten Great Relationships" speech. Peng argued that greater military expenditures were needed because of "the aggressive schemes" of the "imperialist aggressive bloc." Peng also successfully moved to omit Mao Zedong Thought from the constitution in the debate over the acceptance of this document during the 1956 Eighth Party Congress.[52]

In turn, Mao lowered Peng's ranking in the Politburo below

that of Lin Biao, who like Peng was a veteran military leader. Peng remained defense minister, but Lin Biao was now over him. Still, Peng's demotion was not that serious; his career had fluctuated before. Willing to allow dissent from his top officials, Mao had not dismissed Peng altogether but allowed him to retain a powerful place within the government.

On the eve of the Lushan plenum, Peng led a delegation on a tour of the Soviet bloc, advocating much closer relations than Mao preferred. In June 1959, immediately after Peng's return, the Soviets abrogated their agreement to supply China with nuclear military technology and began to criticize the Great Leap. Since Peng had talked at length with Khrushchev, Mao blamed him for the Soviet actions.[53]

After he returned from the Soviet Union, Peng attended the Lushan meeting at Mao's urging. He complained about the Great Leap in a series of small group discussions, as did many of the other leaders. Reinforced by Zhang Wentian, a Politburo colleague who in the 1930s had been secretary general of the party but whose star, like Peng's, was in eclipse, Peng wrote a private letter to Mao summing up his thoughts. In the letter Peng blamed the problems of the Great Leap on Mao. He complained about Mao's "petty bourgeois fanaticism" and implied that Mao did not even know what was going on in his own village. Peng came from the same county as Mao. His description of Mao's lack of knowledge, even of his own village, to which Mao had returned for a visit shortly before the conference, appears to have struck a nerve with Mao, who was already irritated and concerned over the criticism he was receiving at the conference.[54] Mao apparently feared that Peng's criticisms were the beginning of a campaign to undermine his position among the leadership, perhaps with help from the Soviets.

Peng's letter also seems to have forced Mao to rethink the trustworthiness of his subordinates' accounts in light of the disparity between the positive results of the Great Leap he had seen with his own eyes (not realizing that much of it was a deceptive display) and the problems reported by the high-level officials around him. While Peng was accusing Mao of not knowing what was happening in his own hometown, Mao had just been there to see a harvest whose "thousand waves of growing rice and beans" he had celebrated in a poem. Yes, he had been told about problems there, but nothing like what Peng was relating. In spite of his constant efforts to send his secretaries and bodyguards and even his doctor out to check on the pulse of the country for him, Mao simply failed to understand how isolated he had become. Shortly before the Lushan plenum, "in an episode that highlights how Mao—who had grown up in a farming family—had lost touch with reality, he wondered why the working class did not have meat, chicken, duck, or eggs to eat."[55]

On July 16, dressed in a white robe and slippers without socks, Mao spoke before the standing committee of the Politburo and defended the Great Leap. A livid chairman faced down his audience, threatening to "go to the countryside to lead the peasants to overthrow the government. If those of you in the Liberation Army won't follow me, then I will go and find a Red Army, and organize another Liberation Army."[56] This threat supposedly terrified his audience and helped cow them into going along with him.

There is no question that Mao's speech at the Lushan plenum marks a turning point, one in which he plunged China into disaster. But having read and reread the speech numerous times in both Chinese and English (admittedly without experiencing the force that would have come from being at the actual event), I do not believe it to be nearly as threatening as it has sometimes been made out to be. Certainly Mao was angry and disturbed, sometimes even a little incoherent, starting out by telling his audience that in spite of taking sleeping pills "three times" he had not been able to sleep. At one point he ranted that he knew what it was like to be heirless because "one son was killed, one went mad."[57]

In his speech Mao affirmed that the right course of action was to adhere to the Great Leap in spite of criticisms. He admitted its problems, some of which he caused. He took responsibility for what he termed his "crime" of calling for 10.7 million tons of steel and for mass smelting. He also acknowledged that he had been responsible for establishing the commune system and incautious in predicting a transition to "communist ownership by the whole people," which he now admitted might take quite a long time to achieve. But he insisted on maintaining other features of the Great Leap. He endorsed the idea of communal mess halls—an institution that later turned out to have had an almost direct correlation with the level of starvation in any given area—but he wanted them to be "voluntary."[58]

Mao's threat of another revolution came in the middle of the rambling speech. While it clearly upset his audience and no doubt reflected Mao's fears of Peng's influence with the army, it is also difficult to believe that his seasoned listeners could have taken it very seriously. For the aging and portly Mao it was a remote possibility at best, and the threat was preceded by his admission that "I am exaggerating." Moreover, he did not tell the audience he would try to "overthrow the government" if they failed to go along with him (though obviously some people took it this way). Instead he said he would have to find a new army if "we do ten things, and nine are bad, and they are all published in the press, then we will certainly perish, and we will deserve to perish." Only under these somewhat nebulous circumstances did Mao threaten to recruit a new army. And he immediately backed down, noting, "But I think the Liberation Army would follow me."[59]

Mao's listeners had little reason to fear what would happen to them if they disagreed with him. In fact those who opposed Mao at the meeting suffered no consequences, at least not until the onset of the Cultural Revolution. The worst punishment was that meted out to Peng, who threw oil on the fire when he angrily refused a face-to-face meeting with Mao. He was charged with heading an "anti-party clique" and was replaced as minister of defense by Lin Biao. Stalin would almost certainly have thrown someone like Peng in jail, or worse, but Mao allowed him to remain a member of the Politburo and to keep his title of vice premier. After a few years Peng was given a new government job, albeit at a greatly reduced rank. Zhang Wentian, who was part of Peng's clique and helped him draft his controversial letter, lost his job as deputy foreign minister, but he remained an alternative member of the Politburo and was allowed to take a research and academic position at the influential Academy of Sciences. Zhu De, who stood up for Peng even after Mao denounced him, was forced only to make a self-criticism. Even during the Cultural Revolution he was not punished.[60]

Mao's threats and tongue-lashings may have carried the day, but the fact is that no one besides Zhu De chose to stand up for Peng. Liu Shaoqi was probably as hostile to Peng as Mao was and equally defensive about criticisms of the Great Leap.[61] Given the Stalinist mind-set that prevailed within the party—even at a time when no Stalinist-type punishments were being meted out to dissenters within the leadership—no one felt he had a right to speak up and disagree with Mao on an issue on which he felt strongly. This group of revolutionary yes-men had not liked it when Mao wanted people to attack the party from the outside during the Hundred Flowers campaign, and they did not now wish to criticize it from the inside.

Peng had told the emperor he had no clothes. When Mao insisted that he was, metaphorically, well clothed—as others had been telling him on his tours of the countryside—few besides Peng cared to contradict him. This despite Mao having told his listeners at Lushan (some might say disingenuously) that they should criticize him if they wished.[62] Chen Yun's behavior was considered commendable by both sides, because he did not even bother to show up at Lushan to argue for his economic principles. Someone like Zhou Enlai is considered a clever party loyalist because, though he saw the reality of the situation, he went along with Mao.

Given this devotion to party principles, Mao's Lushan speech created an atmosphere in which no one would step forward to moderate the excesses of the Great Leap, and local officials again pushed the campaign to excess. Dali Yang has written, "The worst consequences of the Great Leap Famine, especially the disastrous population loss that occurred in 1960, could have been avoided had the Lushan conference turned out as originally intended by Mao. There should be little doubt that neither Mao nor Peng Dehuai wanted the famine to intensify, but their confrontation led to that, making the Great Leap a result of contingency and all the more senseless and tragic."[63]

The attack on opportunism that swept the country in the wake of the Peng Dehuai affair turned into a reaffirmation of the Great Leap. As Mao put it: "If you want others to stand firm, you must stand firm yourself." Private plots were again eliminated and the basic structure of the commune reinstated. Local-level cadres, terrified lest they be labeled as rightists in the wake of the attacks on Peng Dehuai, clung to leftist policies. Although at Lushan Mao had admitted his unrealistic targets for steel, because no one had told him how bad things really were, he soon again turned to the idea of raising steel production, telling the party, "We'll do 100 million tons in ten years, and then we'll be in heaven."[64]

By early 1960, with the Great Leap once again driving ahead full bore, agricultural production declined precipitously. According to later government figures, the harvest that year was off by more than 25 percent. Some think it was worse. A massive famine set in. The three years beginning in 1959 are now officially referred to as the "three bitter years." China's death rate increased from 12 per 1,000 in 1958 to 25.4 per 1,000 in 1960.[65] In that year China's population actually declined by more than 10 million people. Between 1958 and 1961 at least 30 million starved to death, a staggering number.

During these years China's relations with the Soviet Union fell apart. Although Mao had initially welcomed Khrushchev's leadership, his feelings cooled after Khrushchev's denunciation of Stalin and worsened during the Great Leap. In mid-1958, when Khrushchev traveled to Beijing, Mao continuously smoked in his presence, though he knew that Khrushchev hated cigarette smoking. When Khrushchev explained his hope of building "a common fleet," Mao "banged his large hands against the sofa, and stood up angrily." He accused the Soviet leader of wanting to take over the Chinese seacoast. Later Mao insisted on meeting with Khrushchev—who did not swim—in the pool. While Khrushchev clung to an inner tube, Mao swam circles around him and then swam over and tried to talk. Later Mao supposedly told Dr. Li that what he was doing to Khrushchev was "sticking a needle up his ass."[66]

In the late summer of 1959 Khrushchev made his third and last trip to Beijing. He requested that the Chinese release two imprisoned American pilots and that they reach an accommodation with India. The talks ended abruptly and unhappily. In July 1960 Khrushchev recalled all Soviet technical advisers in China, exacerbating the problems of the Great Leap.[67] The two countries began to clash in border incidents and at international meetings.

Mao became so preoccupied with relations with the Soviet Union that, according to MacFarquhar, the "only detailed directive on rural policy he appears to have issued in the 12 months following Khrushchev's visit to Peking was a letter on pig-breeding, dated 11 October 1959." Other Chinese leaders were similarly engaged. Deng Xiaoping and Peng Zhen, two key members of the leadership, spent almost half the year abroad at meetings of international Communist parties. At one point a fourth of the Politburo spent a month in Moscow for a party conference.[68]

Not until the summer of 1960 did the extent of the tragedy he had created with the Great Leap pull Mao away from his concentration on Sino-Soviet affairs. By the time he began to call for retrenchment, many of the provinces probably had already begun to take such measures on their own.[69]

At a January 1961 plenum, Mao, clearly shocked over the enormity of events, endorsed the end of the Great Leap. In the spring of 1961 he decreed that the team be made the basic accounting unit—in effect the old lower-level commune. The 24,000 communes became administrative units of the central bureaucracy. The government approved work point systems, paying people for the amount of labor they actually produced. Private plots were reintroduced and free markets established. The freedom of the provinces was again severely restricted, ending the competition over quotas that had brought economic chaos to China. The government abandoned work-study schools. In 1961, according to MacFarquhar, "decisions were taken to reduce the number of students in higher institutions by 22 per cent during 1961–63, upper middle-school students by 16 per cent, and lower middle-school students by 18 per cent. The actual reduction in college students was by almost 21 per cent."[70]

In spite of these measures, an economic depression set in on top of the famine. Millions of people were thrown out of work. In 1961 authorities transferred 10 million rural people back to the countryside, and millions more the next year. The action probably made matters worse, throwing millions of people back into a starving countryside, which they were not permitted to leave.

In early 1962 Mao turned the day-to-day operations of the party over to Liu Shaoqi. At the Seven Thousand Cadres conference, he made a self-criticism, admitting—though not with much conviction—responsibility for the excesses of the Great Leap. He called for more discussion within the party and more criticism of himself. In his earthy way, Mao summarized what had gone wrong: "The first Lushan Conference of 1959 was originally concerned with work. Then up jumped Peng Dehuai and said: 'You fucked my mother for forty days, can't I fuck your mother for twenty days?' All this fucking messed up the conference and the work was affected."[71]

Inadvertently the Great Leap accomplished one of Mao's cherished goals: greater regional independence. As early as 1959, because of their dislike of Great Leap policies, some localities began to ignore the dictates of the central government. Peasants refused to abandon their private plots and return to the communal mess halls. Following the Great Leap, members of some communities divided up the land and restored private farming, sometimes on their own, sometimes with the connivance of local and even provincial leaders. Cooperatives were effectively eliminated. As Dali Yang has shown, "Those areas that suffered more during the famine or were farther from Beijing, the political center, were also more likely to spearhead the introduction of household farming. . . . Contemporary documents circulated internally indicate that, in the immediate aftermath of the Great Leap Forward, nearly 30 percent of all rural units adopted some form of household responsibility—the essence of the post-Mao rural reforms— without central authorization."[72] The household responsibility system created the basis for the economic development of China during the 1980s and 1990s.

Mao, of course, sought to implement, not end, the collective system of agriculture, so he should not be given credit for its destruction. But he also sought to destroy the authoritarian bureaucratic culture. His success in weakening this culture therefore remains his positive legacy from this period, though one achieved at horrific costs. As Roderick MacFarquhar has pointed out, "Decentralization was not seriously implemented until the control of the planners was drastically reduced and the provincial secretaries given their heads during the great leap forward." The authors of *Chinese Village, Socialist State* have confirmed that in the area they studied, "the Great Leap undercut legitimacy."[73]

Although the costs were enormous, with the Great Leap Mao began the destruction of the Soviet system in China. Later he understood that the only way to do this effectively was by simultaneously decentralizing the state and weakening the centralist party structure. In the mid-1960s, when Mao began a new upheaval in China, he attacked the party and its leading officials, something he had tentatively attempted to do in the Hundred Flowers campaign that preceded the Great Leap. He wanted to get rid of the culture of yes-men who catered to his fancies better than he realized, preventing him and those at the top from clearly understanding what was wanted and needed at the local levels.

Anyone who dislikes authoritarian bureaucracy must at least sympathize with Mao's distrust of it. But many of the complaints against Mao are as much a reaction to his use of personal power against the Chinese bureaucracy as they are to the appalling consequences of the Great Leap, for which he deserved criticism. The assumption—put forth in the writings and memoirs of the bureaucratic survivors with whom Mao clashed—that the Stalinist bureaucratic structure was ultimately a good and rational one, is not one that I can accept in principle. I must acknowledge, however, that the results of Mao's anti-bureaucratic efforts were so iniquitous that almost any alternative plan would have been better.

Even those who, like myself, believe that Mao should be applauded for his role in attempting to weaken the bureaucratic structure in China—the same structure he had helped build—cannot justify Mao's actions in the Great Leap. By prolonging it, Mao was responsible for the single worst disaster in recorded history, one in which more than 30 million people may have lost their lives. Even Mao's good intentions may be questioned. By allowing his dispute with Peng to ravage China, Mao cast doubt on his own motives. However great Mao's historical figure may turn out to be, the Great Leap will always stand against him.

The Cultural Revolution Revisited

❧ NOTHING HAS DAMAGED Mao's image as much as his role in initiating the Cultural Revolution, yet few of Mao's actions deserve as much praise. From today's perspective it is hard to understand why many still condemn a movement that not only battled corruption and streamlined bureaucracy but also strengthened the economy and promoted artistic and educational reform. Far from being the wasted decade, as it is usually called, the movement inaugurated a period of cultural and economic growth which set the stage for the celebrated transformation of China's financial system that has been much ballyhooed since Mao's death. The decade dominated by the Cultural Revolution left an enduring legacy of social justice, feminist ideals, and even democratic principles which today still resonate with many Chinese.

The positive impact of Mao's exercise in political engineering cannot be underestimated. Not only did he succeed in ousting more than 70 percent of the Chinese Communist party's Central Committee, he also reduced and decentralized the Soviet-style bureaucracy that was threatening to choke China, pruning it to one-sixth its former size.[1] The impact of this bureaucratic cleanup was far-reaching, with especially salubrious effects on China's economy. By managing to remove the central government from much of the day-to-day functioning of the economy, Mao, contrary to popular views, not only spiked the growth of Chinese industry during the Cultural Revolution period but also made it impossible for his successors to reestablish a Soviet-style economy in China after his death.

Almost everyone agrees that during the Cultural Revolution Mao shattered the unity of the Communist party by attacking the system of consensus under which the party had built its rule during the previous decades. If you believe that the destruction of a bureaucratized Communist state is desirable, it is hard to understand why this assault on the party's traditions is not applauded — unless you believe that Mao's purpose was simply to build a new and more efficient party. I do not believe this was Mao's intent. Even if it was, the fact is that the party bureaucracy emerged from the Cultural Revolution more resilient than Mao had hoped but still a shattered remnant of its former self. That, I argue, cannot be a bad thing.

One of Mao's most important reasons for attacking the bureaucracy was the corruption he felt it engendered. As he put it: "At present you can buy a branch secretary for a few packs of cigarettes, not to mention marrying a daughter to him."[2] His belief that corruption wastes valuable resources and erodes the relationship between government and the people was an area where he found immediate support. His desire to rid his country of mindless bureaucrats who epitomized the problems of the Communist system was a goal with which almost everyone sympathized. Sadly, after Mao's agenda was overturned following his death, corruption returned, and so did the fear of popular participation in the government. It is no coincidence that many of the people whom Mao purged were the same bureaucrats who, when they returned to their jobs after the chairman's death, carried out the bloody massacre of Tiananmen demonstrators in 1989.

Of course, not everyone who was attacked during the Cultural

Revolution was a Communist thug. Far from it. Mao must bear responsibility for the innocent victims of the campaign. But much of the collateral violence was a result of efforts to sidetrack the Cultural Revolution by the bureaucrats that were being purged, many of whom are now falsely considered innocent victims; and some violence was the consequence of the oppressive political culture that Mao was trying to renovate.

The real question is whether Mao's actions during the Cultural Revolution represented an authentic break with his past Stalinist ideas or were simply a continuation of Stalinism. Were Mao's opposition to bureaucratism and corruption, his championing of the right to rebel, and his encouragement of mass participation in the government genuine? Or is this a 1960s Western view of Mao, resulting from a culling of his actions and words that ignores, as one observer put it, his "paranoid world view and treatment of 'enemies' as non-humans subjectable to any form of humiliation or torture"?[3]

Certainly there is much that Mao said and wrote to support the view that the Cultural Revolution was simply a continuation of Stalinism in another form. Although I believe that by the late 1950s Mao had begun to make a radical break with his Stalinist past, there is no question that remnants of his old ideas continued to influence him long after this time. Mao's idea that class struggle can continue under socialism—one of the main justifications for the Cultural Revolution—was derived from Stalin's development of the concept as a way of justifying his police-state terror. While Mao worked to decentralize the Chinese state during the Cultural Revolution, he did not totally abandon "central planning and the suppression of markets, proletarian dictatorship and democratic centralism." He continued to dislike "private plots, petty trade, profit motives, and individual bonuses" and to want to "radically rectify and enforce discipline and ideological conformity."[4]

Because after the mid-1960s Mao gave no lengthy speeches or wrote any systematic works on any subject, his thoughts must be derived from snippets of conversations or the occasional notes he made in books he was reading. His basic Marxist vocabulary since at least the 1930s had been derived from Stalinist ideas, so it should not be surprising that he occasionally lapsed into what might be called "Stalinist talk." When we look at his writings, it appears, as Graham Young has noted, that whatever theories Mao had during this time were "incoherent" at best.[5]

But if we accept Mao's belief that ideology is derived from practice, the best way to understand his growing anti-Stalinism is to examine his actions. By attacking bureaucracy and corruption, he helped reorient the Chinese political system in a non-Stalinist direction.

Mao's way of dealing with bloated bureaucracy certainly differed from Stalin's. Mao's nemesis during this period of Cultural Revolution was what he referred to as "high and overbearing bureaucrats."[6] Perhaps there were nicer ways to purge the bureaucracy than those he devised, but contemporary experiences indicate how difficult it has been for China to pare the country's bureaucracy gradually. Most of Mao's attacks on bureaucracy were not executed from above, like Stalin's; rather, they allowed largely unsupervised and unchecked Red Guards to act more or less on their own. While Stalin's purges ended up strengthening the bureaucracy, Mao's decentralized the government.

But the most important way to judge Mao's Cultural Revolution is not only to examine why and how he decentralized his bureaucracy but to look at what he attempted to do with the government he was transforming, beginning first with education. The Cultural Revolution is usually thought of as a period in which Mao closed the schools and ended all learning. In fact it was a time when the number of schools increased exponentially and learning was extended to huge areas of previously neglected parts of the country. Although urban schools closed for a time, Mao used the Cultural Revolution to dismantle the elitist and formalistic Soviet-style educational system that the country had returned to in the early 1960s. He shifted resources to rural education, in the process radically expanding China's educational system.[7] Since Mao's death, his successors have gutted the rural education system he put in place—once again discriminating against people from poor rural backgrounds. This despite the fact that almost everywhere resources devoted to rural education remain the most efficient way to promote economic development.

Mao first attacked this problem indirectly in 1962, when he launched the Socialist Education campaign. Although this was a movement to eliminate corrupt cadres and restore revolutionary idealism, it had the word "education" in its name because Mao wished to use the campaign to teach the peasants how to recognize and root out corruption for themselves. He was deeply distressed over "degenerate elements" who had worked their way into the Communist party of the Soviet Union, and he wanted the people to know how to prevent a similar phenomenon from engulfing China. The 1964 party document "On Khrushchev's Phoney Communism" asserted: "The Soviet privileged stratum has gained control of the Party, the government, and other important organizations. The members of this privileged stratum have converted the function of serving the masses into the privilege of dominating them. They are abusing their powers over the means of production and of livelihood for the private benefit of their small clique." Although "revisionism" was not yet the problem in China that it was in Russia, "desperate forays by embezzlers, grafters, and degenerates" had corrupted the party. Mao believed it was necessary to "conduct extensive socialist education movements repeatedly in the cities and the countryside."[8]

In 1962 the goal of educating the peasants to learn how to recognize corruption was apparent when Mao supervised Peng Zhen, later the first prominent victim of the Cultural Revolution, and Chen Boda, for a time one of the most prominent promoters of the Cultural Revolution, in preparing what became known as "The Former Ten Points" document. The writers sought to organize a "revolutionary class army" that would "bring into full play the function of the poor and lower-middle peasant organizations in assisting and overseeing the work of the commune and brigade administrative committees."[9] Peasants were to learn to keep track of how cadres allocated work points, kept accounts, handed out supplies, and took care of warehouses and granaries, so they could make sure the transactions of the state were honest.

Mao warned that without renewed "class struggle, production struggle, and scientific experiment, the day would not be far off . . . when the resurgence of a counter-revolution becomes inevitable."[10] Although concerned, he was optimistic. He ruled out physical punishment for crimes and prescribed education to deal with cadres who had strayed from the virtuous socialist path. He personally told provincial leaders to be lenient with miscreants.

Other major leaders agreed on the need to eliminate corruption. But few shared Mao's enthusiasm for teaching the peasants how to control it. After violence erupted in a number of places in the countryside in spite of Mao's explicit cautions, a new party task force worked out a "Later Ten Points." Like the original "Ten Points," the "Later Ten Points" had a mild tone and talked about the need to involve peasant associations. It placed greater emphasis on the cadre role as well as on procedures for organizing the movement; but Mao approved the new formulation.

Liu Shaoqi, who in the early 1960s shared the official party leadership with Mao, enthusiastically backed this campaign. But Liu was dissatisfied with its slow pace and ineffectiveness, especially after Liu's wife reported seeing widespread corruption during an inspection visit to the countryside. In 1964 Liu issued a "Revised Later Ten Points" document. This pessimistic program showed little trust in China's local rural administrators. Liu emphasized the need for the "sending of a work team from the higher level."[11] He cast aside Mao's earlier instructions to deal leniently with rural officials and increased the role of the central leadership in the campaign. Liu wanted even the slightest complaints from

peasants to result in serious investigation by the central government, and he preferred that middle and rich peasants be treated
more harshly than before.

Liu caused hundreds of thousands of local cadres to be tar-
geted and expelled from the party, and for months purges and attacks disrupted the countryside. But the Socialist Education
campaign never received as much attention as the Cultural Revolution because it involved peasants, not intellectuals.

Mao stepped into the Socialist Education campaign to stop the
violence. Although he is often considered vicious for the way he
attacked his enemies, and though he was often ruthless, the fact is
that time and again it was Mao who tried to check the violence
that others encouraged.

In this case he supervised the drafting of a new "Twenty-three
Points" document, circumscribing the leadership mandate of the
outside work teams and affirming the soundness of the rural-level
structure. He abandoned the idea of overwhelming the local structure by sending in large-scale teams from outside. The document
noted: "In accordance with the '60 articles,' we should set a time
to carry out democratic elections. Terms of office for reelection, or
reappointment, should in general be limited to four years."[12]

By changing the focus of the movement from the peasants to
the leadership, Mao pinpointed the goal of the movement as the
need to "rectify those people in positions of authority within the
Party who take the capitalist road."[13] In effect Mao was saying that
the problem did not lie with local cadres who had engaged in
penny-ante embezzling but with the upper reaches of the party
bureaucracy.

Mao later told Edgar Snow that he determined to remove Liu
Shaoqi from the party leadership because Liu opposed Mao's in-
clusion of the phrase attacking "those people in positions of authority within the Party who take the capitalist road" at the January
1965 work conference where the "Twenty-three Points" were de-
bated. At this meeting Mao accused Liu and Deng Xiaoping of try-

ing to prevent him from combating revisionism in the party. "His performance was so effective," MacFarquhar writes, "that Bo Yibo recalled it with palpably bated breath almost twenty years later."[14] By early 1965 Mao's colleagues could have had little doubt that some kind of major divide had opened in the top ranks of the leadership.

Although Mao's differences with his colleagues probably had something to do with past resentments and slights, as others have argued, it is clear that he disagreed with them over how seriously to take the word "education" in the Socialist Education campaign. And his focus on educating the masses was not evidenced only in this one movement. Developing a program for mass education had been a topic of vital concern to Mao since his earliest days in Hunan. The former teacher and school principal continued throughout his life to see himself in one form or another as an educator. Few of his speeches and even his letters to colleagues do not display the tone of a teacher lecturing a pupil. He constantly berated party members on their need to improve their grammar and writing style. Throughout the 1950s and 1960s he continually promoted the education of the peasantry. He fretted that while reestablishing track schools that favored urban youths from privileged backgrounds, the party was cutting back and sometimes even eliminating rural schools.

Beginning in 1964, even as he wound down the Socialist Education campaign, Mao stepped up his calls for wider access to education. He wanted to make it easier for those with less advantaged backgrounds to compete in school. He ridiculed the rigid technical education given to students in the college preparatory classes, complaining, "Nowadays, first, there are too many classes; second, there are too many books. The pressure is too great." He advocated more equality between students and teachers. He even went so far as to praise cheating as an efficient approach to education: "At examinations, whispering into each other's ears and taking other people's places ought to be allowed. Your answer is good and I copy it, then mine should be counted as good." Even lazy students could draw encouragement from pronouncements like "Rather than keeping your eyes open and listening to boring lectures, it is better to get some refreshing sleep. You don't have to listen to nonsense, you can rest your brain instead."[15]

Many of Mao's statements sound like an irascible uncle who wants to provoke a little mischief among the offspring of his stuffy siblings. But though he may not have intended everything he said to be taken literally (a subtlety that many of his sycophantic followers missed), education was one area where Mao produced clear results during the Cultural Revolution. As one scholar has noted: "Education was the most contested terrain of the Cultural Revolution." The August 8, 1966, "Decision on the Cultural Revolution" proclaimed: "In the Cultural Revolution a most important task is to reform the old educational system and the old principles and methods of teaching."[16] Before the Cultural Revolution, relatively few middle schools or high schools existed in rural areas, where 85 percent of China's population lived. Even talented rural students generally received only a limited elementary school education. In order to continue their education, rural youths needed to secure permission to leave the countryside and move to an urban area. After leaving, few returned.

During the Cultural Revolution, teachers and students in rural areas heeded Mao's calls to address educational imbalances. While schools and universities in urban areas closed, rural Red Guards opened new ones in the countryside. Village production brigades established primary schools. In communes and districts throughout the countryside, the Red Guards promoted the formation of middle schools and high schools.[17]

Educated local youths who might have gone off to the cities for college or work now stayed in their home areas. Most became teachers. The local talent pool was supplemented by the "sent-down youths"—in the waning days of the Cultural Revolution, urban kids who were forced to go to rural areas after leaving city high schools. In his early days in Changsha as the founder of work-study societies, Mao had attempted to develop educational opportunities for poor workers and peasants, night classes for workers, and organizations to disseminate new books and essays. During the Cultural Revolution he put these long-cherished ideas into practice throughout China.

In the new locally promoted and financed rural schools, Mao urged a focus on increased literacy. The schools were rarely as good as the government-funded institutions in urban areas, but the curriculum they developed was better suited to local needs. Although many of these schools were closed after Mao died, in some parts of the country the rural schools established as a result of Maoist policies during the Cultural Revolution were still, as late as 2001, the only institutions that served peasant youths.

Dongping Han provides a moving personal testament to the changes brought to the Chinese countryside by the educational reforms of the Cultural Revolution. In the preface to his study *The Unknown Cultural Revolution: Educational Reforms and Their Impact on China's Rural Development*, Han notes that he grew up in a village in the Chinese countryside where children just a few years older than he "either never went to school or dropped out after one or two years of primary school."

> During the educational reforms of the Cultural Revolution, my village set up its own primary school, and hired its own teachers. Every child in the village could go to the village school free of charge. My village also set up a junior middle school with six other villages. Every child could go to this joint village middle school free of charge and without passing any examinations. The commune that included my village set up two high schools. About 70 percent of school-age children in the commune went to these high schools free of charge and without passing any screening texts. All my siblings except my elder sister, who was four years older than I, were able to finish high school.[18]

The era of the Cultural Revolution has often falsely been considered a period in which education came to a standstill. It is true that Mao tried to eliminate educational tracking, that universities closed for a time, and that many of the specialized agricultural schools and technical training schools for workers shut down or restricted enrollment. But overall during the "wasted decade," elementary school enrollment increased from 116.21 million in 1965 to 150.01 million in 1976. Middle-school enrollment grew from 9.34 million in 1965 to 67.8 million in 1977.[19] This was an increase of people attending middle school of more than 700 percent, or approximately thirty times the population growth during the period. This is an astonishing change, which obviously had a huge impact on Chinese life.

Not only lower-level education was altered by Mao's Cultural Revolution policies. Before the Cultural Revolution the high school curriculum had been overwhelmingly oriented toward the National College Exams. During the Cultural Revolution, Mao canceled the exams. The country developed a new curriculum that emphasized practical matters and relied less on memorization. As resources shifted to rural schools, some of China's high-end institutions suffered. As Suzanne Pepper has noted: "That declining quality accompanies the development of mass education is axiomatic, and the Chinese case was no exception." But while the children of the elite suffered under this new system, the children of peasants benefited.[20]

We can all sympathize with the plight of individual parents who want their bright, gifted children to receive a special education and instead find they must send them to schools geared to the masses. But the development of a massive number of new schools greatly helped China by boosting overall literacy, even though it meant that a few of the children of the privileged did not do as well as they might have.

In October 1967, when the government on a limited basis reopened the universities, closed a year earlier, admission to college was based on recommendation from one's work unit. This was not the most sophisticated system, but it was geared to the level of rural students. Abuses occurred when leaders recommended relatives and friends. Still, the new plan allowed peasant youths to gain a better education than would have been possible under the earlier policy.

The people as a whole not only benefited from Mao's improvement of education during the Cultural Revolution, but, as befits a movement with "culture" in its name, they also were exposed to stimulating cultural changes. In starting the Cultural Revolution, Mao was concerned about education but also about what a Red Guard document later called "all the ghosts and monsters who for many years have abounded in our press, radio, magazines, books, text-books, platforms, works of literature, cinema, drama, ballads and stories, the fine arts, music, the dance, etc."[21]

To chase out these old ghosts, Mao sponsored exciting artistic experiments throughout much of the 1960s. They produced stirring new syntheses in art, music, and literature and a new generation of Chinese artists who have only recently begun to receive recognition. Only lately has the artistic merit of many of the works developed during Mao's Cultural Revolution been recognized as scholars have finally begun to look seriously at the culture behind the Cultural Revolution.

After his death it became a matter of faith that Mao had sought to replace the rich culture of China with revolutionary slop, causing most of these works to be heaped into China's cultural attic to gather dust. The initial backlash against the art of the Cultural Revolution lingered for many years partly because its operas and ballets have been identified with Mao's wife Jiang Qing. Throughout the 1960s Mao had supported Jiang's efforts to commission new operas and ballets that emphasized revolutionary idealism and self-sacrifice for the national good. But in the chauvinistic climate of the post–Cultural Revolution era, Jiang Qing was dismissed as a "usurping concubine." Even the most sympathetic biography of Jiang is replete with opprobrium reflecting this representation—a power-crazed, dangerous woman, who "used her position to pay back old scores of a personal nature, not to realize political convictions."[22]

A more balanced judgment reveals that Jiang and Mao sponsored stirring syntheses of new and old forms. For instance, as one assessment explains, although "we often hear that the music of the Cultural Revolution was monolithic," in fact "the musical sounds were diverse, and their histories—before, during, and after the Cultural Revolution—complicated. The music encompassed a variety of styles, including those from Chinese traditional music (a term that usually refers to styles of music developed in China prior to the twentieth century). It also incorporated instruments and harmonies historically associated with 'Europe' and the 'West,'" even though the Cultural Revolution is usually considered a time when China sought to exclude foreign influences.[23]

It was not until the 1990s that the music of the Cultural Revolution began to be adopted by popular musicians. A work like the revolutionary ballet *White-haired Girl*, once championed by Jiang Qing, began to be appreciated for its celebration of the ability of common folk to triumph against the powerful forces of the government and society arrayed against them. As the curators of an exhibit in Heidelberg, "Rethinking Cultural Revolution Culture," noted in discussing the art of the Cultural Revolution:

> It presents a time of contradictions, when great leaders but also the most ordinary of people were exalted, when the Chinese Communist Party turned inward and yet was influenced by and sought to influence revolutionary struggles in other parts of the world. It also shows how, despite efforts by some to construct a monolithic culture and despite the reduplication through many media of certain key symbols and gestures and icons, artists working individually and as part of collective units continued to exercise considerable creativity within the limits imposed.[24]

It could, of course, be argued that however praiseworthy Jiang Qing's ballets were, there was something Stalinist about the way she allowed only Eight Model Ballets to be performed. "While this characterization is partly true, only a few years into the Cultural Revolution, eighteen works were officially designated as models; and these models constantly were revised and transplanted into different formats."[25]

Although the Cultural Revolution without question had its totalitarian aspects, one can find a range of individual and local initiative in what often appear to have been monolithic forms. This is seen most clearly in the most ubiquitous item distributed during the Cultural Revolution—the Mao badge. Most of these badges were not stamped out at a central factory but crafted by individual *danweis*—that is, workplace and neighborhood groups. A number of individuals made their own. There were an extraordinary number of varieties, not only in the pictures of Mao that were used but in the materials, the background and framing, and the size. Some are enormous, others more like dainty little pins. Some are exquisite, others ordinary. I was once given a Mao badge barely larger than the tip of my finger, its owner explaining that during the Cultural Revolution she was determined to wear the tiniest picture of Mao possible.

A similar variety exists in other Cultural Revolution objects, from posters to porcelain to the spontaneous songs of the Red Guards.[26] Despite broad cultural guidelines, the breakdown of central control, which was the main feature of the Cultural Revolution, gave the people an opportunity to put individual expression into the broad cultural forms sponsored by the government.

Since, as noted earlier, Mao never coherently discussed his purpose in promoting the Cultural Revolution, these cultural works are interesting vehicles for examining some of the movement's ideas. The first thing to note about them is, as already suggested, that although Mao's Cultural Revolution vision is often considered to be autarkic, the music his wife promoted (and he supported) in fact synthesized Western sounds and forms with traditional Chinese ideas. In spite of all the talk about Mao wishing to oppose foreign influences, works such as *White-haired Girl* popularized Western ballet. Although the culture of the Cultural Revolution is often considered to have been Stalinist, the story line of *White-haired Girl* emphasized not the role of officials or bureaucrats but the individual anti-authoritarian heroism of the father who fought against his oppressors before being beaten to death (unlike in the original opera where he committed suicide) and even more of the girl whom one writer has called "an embodiment of hatred, the spirit of revenge."[27]

The Cultural Revolution was also a period in which women had considerable power, and Jiang Qing used the model theater for challenging "the social sex-gender system in its portrayal of women. Major women characters act as agents in the public sphere as absolute equals with men. Moreover, they are free from their gender assignments as mothers, or sexual subordinates to men." One recent author, Di Bai, has gone so far as to suggest that some of Jiang Qing's characters "qualify culturally and socially as lesbians" in the sense that "they transcend gender by becoming *ci*, and their womanhood is a route to their liberation from a (hetero) sexist system."[28]

Although Di Bai is not here claiming that these characters were meant to be lesbians, it is interesting to note that Mao's doctor, Li Zhisui, asserted that Mao took an equal-opportunity approach to the subjects of his advances. He not only made passes at legions of attractive young women but often grabbed at the handsome young male attendants who stood by his bedside. Those who could not deal with this were reassigned.[29]

Mao's sexual proclivities may not have had much to do with the Cultural Revolution's attacks on the dominant patriarchal legacy of Chinese society, but in any event the efforts in this regard were disdained. The more complex works of the Cultural Revolution have been overshadowed by the destructive bullying of the teenaged Red Guards and silly propaganda such as Lin Biao's 1964 campaign to distill Maoist thought into the *Little Red Book*, a selection of quotations that later became the bible of the Red Guards. Cultural and political issues often became so interwoven that even today it is difficult to understand what was meant to be a genuine expression of sentiment, what was simply a random act of violence by a society in which all controls had been abandoned, and what was meant as a political attack.

Mao's cultural achievement during the Cultural Revolution offers a perspective on the incident said to have begun the movement. In 1965 he arranged for a member of Jiang Qing's group, the literary critic Yao Wenyuan, to write a detailed critique of the play *The Dismissal of Hai Rui* by Wu Han, a deputy mayor of Beijing. The play told the story of a distinguished sixteenth-century official, Hai Rui, who was dismissed from office after he tried to stand up to a powerful elder statesman whose callous actions harmed the peasantry.

In the early 1960s Mao himself had lauded this play, but in 1965 he approved Yao's article, which criticized the play for implying that high officials rather than the people themselves were needed to solve the peasants' problems. Yao raised the issue of whether peasant leaders or central bureaucrats should lead movements like the Socialist Education campaign. He complained that "In this play, Hai Rui is the hero. The peasants can only air their grievances to their lord and entrust their own destinies to the Honorable Hai." Hai Rui's fault lay in trying to get the government to act on behalf of the peasantry, rather than teaching the peasants how to act for themselves. Yao reminded his readers: "It is necessary to oppose bureaucratism."[30]

Yao's attack on the play seems bizarre and has often been dismissed as a personal vendetta, perhaps resulting from a conviction that the play was a thinly disguised attack on Mao's dismissal of Peng Dehuai during the Great Leap Forward. But in fact Yao's article did not personally attack the playwright. It concentrated on issues, as Mao himself had occasionally done when he commented on the political messages in various movies, novels, and articles. The very fact that Mao chose to begin a major revolutionary campaign with the criticism of a play demonstrates the attention Mao paid to cultural matters and how serious were his intentions to establish a new kind of art and literature in China, one which emphasized the importance of action from below rather than in Stalinist style from above.

Yao's article set in motion a complicated political endgame. Wu Han, the author of the play, worked for Peng Zhen, the mayor of Beijing. Peng was the head of the party's culture group and was known for his eagerness to persecute intellectuals whose writings showed even a hint of unorthodox ideas. Peng nonetheless insisted that any mistakes his assistant had made in writing the play were academic rather than political. He tried to block Mao's attempts to have the article reprinted in a prominent Beijing publication, apparently not realizing at first that it had the chairman's sanction.[31]

Few other party leaders showed Peng's backbone.[32] Both Zhou Enlai and Deng Xiaoping echoed Mao's charge that Peng Zhen had turned Beijing into an independent kingdom. In May 1966 Liu Shaoqi chaired a Politburo meeting that officially dismissed Peng as well as three other officials whom Mao had demoted a few months earlier. One was the army chief of staff, Luo Ruiqing. Mao's loyal defense chief Lin Biao saw him as a rival and wanted him out of the way. The other two were Lu Dingyi, director of the Central Propaganda Department, and Yang Shangkun, director of the Central Committee general office. Yang controlled the flow of information into and out of the Central Committee; Lu controlled the media. Mao held a personal grudge against Yang, who a few years earlier had authorized security officials to bug Mao's private quarters and train compartment, an incident that became known after some of those doing the bugging proved indiscreet in discussing details of Mao's liaisons with a string of younger women. But Mao now concentrated his wrath on Yang and the others not just for personal reasons but because he wanted direct control of the Beijing party apparatus and the critical propaganda ministries.

Lin Biao electrified the atmosphere by accusing the four purged men of plotting a coup d'état against Mao and by announcing that in order to prevent this action, Mao had "dispatched personnel and had them stationed in the radio broadcasting system, the armed forces, and the public security systems." The polemicist Yao Wenyuan turned up the heat by claiming that Wu Han and two collaborators, Deng Tuo, a former editor of *People's Daily*, and Liao Mosha, a novelist, had plotted together to use veiled language to satirize Mao.[33] Yao Wenyuan implied that Wu and Deng were part of a conspiracy to undermine the chairman's power and authority.

With tensions escalating, the Politburo created a Central Cultural Revolution Group, chaired by Zhou Enlai, to take charge of the movement. Zhou was placed in charge of the Central Case Examination Group, a body set up to manage the purge of all senior "counter-revolutionary revisionists." The ease with which Mao lined up the senior members of his government in support of his campaign belies the notion that the Cultural Revolution was simply a power struggle by an aging chairman pushed to the back burner of Chinese politics.[34] Mao had political power before the Cultural Revolution. He was now using this power to change the direction of the political process and to push his cultural and educational agenda.

Mao's direction became clearer on May 25, 1966, when a woman philosophy lecturer named Nie Yuanzi gathered together six of her friends and mounted a wall poster on the campus of Beijing University. The poster denounced school officials for curtailing the discussion of Wu Han's play, *The Dismissal of Hai Rui*. Nie detailed the relationship between Peng and Beijing University president Lu Ping. She revealed factional ties between the three top men in Beijing's political and academic power structure—

Peng Zhen, Wu Han, and Lu Ping—implying that the party organization these men dominated was corrupt. She urged "revolutionary intellectuals" to "go into battle."

A few days later Mao publicly praised the poster. The media took the hint and editorialized in favor of the dissidents. Party business in China, especially a purge, was supposed to take place behind closed doors. Nie, a local party secretary, had written of behind-the-scenes relations and had made a public case against a high party official. Politics had been brought into the open. When the chairman of the Chinese Communist party supported her, similar wall posters appeared on campuses throughout the country. Some were placed on public buildings, including one on the Beijing Municipal Office that attacked the head of the citywide party organization. Throughout China student rebel groups formed to fight school authorities.

In early June 1966 high-level party officials organized work teams that moved into the schools, adopting the same tactic that Liu had used during the Socialist Education movement. The teams assured the students that their struggle was well motivated but suggested that the authorities could handle their grievances. The students were told that "a distinction should be made between inside and outside the party": "wall posters should not be put up in the streets," and "meetings should be held only on campus."[35]

Needing people they could trust, Deng and Liu called on relatives. Liu Shaoqi's wife and daughter joined the work team at Beijing University. The teenaged children of other high-level party officials, spurred on by Maoist calls for student activism, organized the first Red Guard groups.

Mao remained mostly above the fray. In late July 1966 he was photographed battling the waves of the Yangzi River for two hours. The Chinese media swarmed all over the story. At seventy-two Mao had shown he was still strong and hardy.

Returning to Beijing, where he had been long absent, Mao ordered the withdrawal of the work teams from the campuses, condemning their "crackdown on the masses." He made it clear that "The campaign was not aimed at the common people, nor was it to try to single out rightists among the masses." He also demanded the destruction of the dossiers compiled against so-called rightists by the supporters of Deng and Liu, so that the slanders compiled by party authorities against innocent people could not be used in the future. Although Mao's actions have usually been interpreted as a cynical political ploy to undermine the authority of Liu and Deng, the fact is that they removed government pressure from the backs of the student rebels—a tactic to which Mao returned again and again, allowing them to continue the undermining of the party. As he told one Cultural Revolutionary group, "There should be a wholesale cut in secretaries." He also emphasized that "we mustn't arrest people indiscriminately." Only for "murder, arson, and spreading poison."[36]

In August 1966 the government officially labeled Liu Shaoqi "the leading person in authority taking the capitalist road" and Deng Xiaoping the "second leading person in authority taking the capitalist road." In late fall the two disappeared from public view. Liu died in 1969 after being transferred out of Beijing. Deng spent seven years in the countryside.

If the Cultural Revolution was simply a Stalinist-type movement by Mao to purge the government of his deputies and strengthen the power of the state, his actions following the disgrace of Liu and Deng certainly do not support that interpretation. Mao did not move to take stronger control of the government for himself; he cleared the way to allow the masses, or at least the Red Guards, to do most of the purging on their own. On August 5, 1966, Mao mounted his own wall poster urging students to "bombard the headquarters." This was a call to attack the Chinese Communist party, which Mao referred to as a "bourgeois dictatorship."[37]

Mao's actions sparked the formation of the Revolutionary Red

Guards. They organized to oppose the established Red Guard groups, which now became known as the Royalist Red Guards. The members of these new Revolutionary Red Guard groups included students who had been sneered at, some from landlord and merchant backgrounds who, in the complicated politics of post-1949 China, had become the most disparaged elements in the society. Encouraged by Mao, they formed throughout the country. To this point Red Guard groups had been largely confined to the capital. Now they marched on party headquarters in towns throughout China, raiding secret files and forcing party leaders from their offices. They posted secret speeches and documents on the walls of buildings. Security forces complained to Mao that the students were publishing state secrets. He appeared unconcerned. As restraints on the Revolutionary Red Guards were thrown off, their actions became more frenetic and disorganized.[38]

The Royalist Red Guards countered by preventing the Revolutionary Red Guards from entering party buildings, where they arrested and condemned party bureaucrats. The two sides sometimes fought each other in pitched battles. By late August the violence began to reach terrible proportions.[39]

The most strident and activist of these Red Guard groups formed not in the universities but in the middle schools. University students were generally content to beat and humiliate their professors, forcing these distinguished elderly men and women to empty out latrines and to stand for hours enduring insults. The real zealots were impressionable teenagers. They vandalized street nameplates and store signs, closed barbershops, sealed off the offices of the democratic parties, and destroyed religious temples and historical relics. Their wanton destruction of property and vicious assaults on intellectuals helped reinforce the idea that this was an anti-cultural movement. Occasionally Mao or Zhou Enlai stepped in to save an individual or an artifact they learned was under attack. Some brave persons took similar initiatives, but for the most part there were no restraints on the youthful ruffians.

Eventually the Red Guards singled out large numbers of teachers, branding them "monsters and demons." The students locked many of these teachers in small rooms or cowsheds, beating and torturing them for days, sometimes months. When the Red Guards searched neighborhood houses for counterrevolutionary material, they often stole valuable jewels and other art objects.

Some of China's most talented artists were driven to suicide. In factories and offices throughout China, party secretaries, anxious to show that they too were part of the campaign, reported so-called rightists in their own units. People with personal grudges denounced one another, frequently with little or no evidence. Countless others were beaten, abused, and driven to early deaths. In the fall of 1966 street fights erupted among the different groups as the power struggle began to involve more senior officials of the party. Among the victims was one of Deng Xiaoping's sons. Captured and tortured, his comrades either pushed him or forced him to jump from an upper-story window. He survived, crippled from the waist down.

Everywhere in urban areas the cultural atmosphere was chaotic. Loudspeakers on street corners blared Mao's quotations. No one dared leave home without a Mao button pinned on his jacket and often a Mao book in hand. Blue jeans, makeup, and other signs of Western deviance were strictly prohibited. Families who lived in large apartments and houses found their dwellings subdivided, and new families moved in.

The Central Case Examination Group, chaired by Zhou Enlai, investigated more than a thousand officials accused of rightist crimes, torturing them until they confessed. Similar provincial-level groups investigated millions more. Massive Red Guard rallies borrowed high-level rightists from prisons for struggle sessions. These kinds of traumas were too much for someone like the aging Liu Shaoqi. Cut off from adequate medical care, he fell ill and died.[40]

Mao had encouraged the Red Guards to seize power, and in

August 1966 he had relaxed police controls. The actions of Deng and Liu at the start of the Cultural Revolution sparked some of the initial confrontations. None of the leaders orchestrated the violence. Mao was rarely inclined to help former colleagues who were now in trouble. But no evidence has emerged that Mao knew specifically what was happening to people like Liu. Even when Mao castigated the Red Guards for fighting and insisted on an end to the violence and destruction, these directives were not obeyed well. As the political scientist Lynn White has argued, long-standing structural and administrative policies had developed a culture in which violence easily erupted when controls loosened. Tony Saich has noted that brutal totalitarian methods had long been a feature of the party's culture: "Certainly, Mao would not have been able to destroy so many of his closest followers without that acceptance, and without the seeds of the Mao cult that were developed in Yan'an and which attained preposterous heights during the Cultural Revolution."[41]

Huang Zhang, the official party biographer of Liu Shaoqi, has pointed out how throughout 1966 and well into the spring of 1967, Mao went out of his way on several occasions to associate himself with Liu, even when he was under attack. In October 1966 Mao told a party group, "We should allow Liu and Deng to make revolution and to reform themselves." According to Huang, Mao's views changed as a result of the efforts of Lin Biao, Kang Sheng, and Jiang Qing to fabricate evidence against Liu. But even Huang produces no evidence to show that Mao knew precisely what was happening to Liu. What he shows is that not only the so-called Gang of Four (Mao's wife Jiang Qing; the onetime Shanghai propaganda department official Zhang Chunqiao; the polemicist Yao Wenyuan; and the erstwhile Shanghai labor leader Wang Hongwen) but also Zhou Enlai were part of the body that investigated and ultimately ruled against Liu. But after all their investigation and evidence, Mao still refused to allow them to hand Liu over to the state for punishment.[42]

Mao was willing to allow the masses to carry out much of the campaign more or less spontaneously. Stalin had set out to liquidate officials who disagreed with him, as well as their supporters; Mao did not. This does not excuse the killings of many people during the Cultural Revolution and the subjection of countless numbers to several years of torture and unpleasantness. Yet to a great extent these events occurred not as a result of Mao's conscious policies.

Because of Mao's efforts, the official avenues of communication between top and bottom briefly almost disappeared. Even when Maoist leaders attempted to contact the various Red Guard groups, hoping to give them personal instruction, they found it difficult. The central government could no longer control day-to-day affairs. New rebel factions formed daily. The situation grew more chaotic when Revolutionary Red Guards attempted to seize power in factories, sometimes struggling with workers.

Workers too were rising to take over their own governance. A former Red Guard member has suggested that in December 1966, "For the first time the broad ranks of workers were able to give their superiors a piece of their mind without fear of being beaten down as anti-party, anti-socialist elements." The "rank and file took the cadres to task." They reprimanded them over "the unreasonable treatment they had been subject to over the years. Petitioners began to pour into Beijing, making clear their complaints about items ranging from the 'insufficiency of labor insurance' to the lack of employment for high school graduates." In some places, to restrain the leftists, "factories disbursed long-overdue overtime pay, raised the limits of compensation on certain items of medical insurance, and expanded the coverage."[43]

Elsewhere workers joined with students to push for a new, more representative form of government. As Elizabeth Perry has shown, these rebel worker groups represented "countercultural undercurrents," while those who formed Red Guard groups to oppose the workers' changes represented the party mainstream. Although the various worker groups often struggled at cross-purposes, Mao supported those groups that represented new cultural and political trends. In January 1967 in Shanghai, a mass movement supported by Mao overthrew the municipal authorities.[44]

When chaos loomed, however, Mao began to rein in the movement. He reminded supporters, "There will always be 'heads.'"[45] In February a three-way alliance of rebels, army representatives, and veteran cadres reestablished the government in Shanghai. Similar alliances tried to bring order to other parts of the country. At first the army seemed to help the Revolutionary Red Guards in their struggle against the party. But often army leaders supported the old conservative party organization or, on more than a few occasions, the Red Guard factions composed exclusively of the children of military commanders. In some places, by late spring, leftist Maoist groups who had welcomed the army as an ally were struggling against it.

During the summer of 1967 fighting between different Red Guard units increased. At the end of July Mao's wife, Jiang Qing, told the Revolutionary Red Guards to "defend yourselves with weapons."[46] The struggle against the old party organization intensified. Pitched battles raged in many cities. In September Mao called for an end to the turmoil. He ordered the army to intervene and forbade people to interfere with its functions. Slowly and sporadically the government restored order, though so thoroughly had party ranks been devastated that it was to be almost two years before calm again prevailed.

A common assertion is that the Cultural Revolution reconfirmed the old power structure, but this does not seem to have been the case—at least not until after Mao died. In Shanghai, for instance, Elizabeth Perry and Li Xun found that the "new core leadership at all levels" after 1967 "included a substantial number of worker rebels."

During the previous seventeen years of Communist rule, worker representatives had been selected for their diligence at work or their obedience to party directives and had served as little more than tokens at people's congresses. By contrast, the "new cadre" corps of worker rebels evidenced a keener understanding of political operations and a greater willingness to speak their minds.[47]

This change occurred not only in urban areas. In his examination of a poor rural area in Shandong during the Cultural Revolution, Dongping Han has noted that Jimo County experienced a radical change in the power structure of the local villages during this period. As he puts it:

> In sum, the empowerment of ordinary villagers during the Cultural Revolution promoted a change of political culture in rural areas. Before the Cultural Revolution, production team leaders were appointed by village leaders and village leaders were in turn chosen by commune leaders. Ordinary villagers had little to say in the process. In the villages I have studied, this practice changed during the Cultural Revolution. Production team leaders were elected by production team members. If the production team leaders did not do a good job, they would lose their position at the end of the year. In some cases, the production team leaders had to be replaced every year.[48]

Limited research by Han and others indicates that what he found in Jimo County was true in many other rural areas as well. While Mao failed to create anything like a democracy, during the Cultural Revolution he did manage to infuse the government with a group of women and workers who, unlike their predecessors, looked, talked, and thought like the people they represented. Unfortunately, most of those who came to office during the Cultural Revolution were removed after Mao's death in 1976, though in rural areas some of the changes may have had a more lasting effect. The election of village leaders, which first occurred in many areas during the Cultural Revolution, became universal throughout China in the 1990s. Unfortunately these election practices have never been extended up to the ranks of the central government.

Not only was Mao's Cultural Revolution empowering in many ways—educationally, culturally, and even politically—but it was far from the economic disaster it is often thought to have been. Along with the growth of rural education and the change in educational direction, Mao began to reduce central control over agricultural policy, promote local self-sufficiency, and encourage cooperative, labor-intensive initiatives. In 1968, as the Cultural Revolution began to ebb in the cities, Mao again turned his attention to the countryside. For the next ten years the Chinese countryside was subjected to almost continuous local and central campaigns. In their slack times groups of peasants were encouraged to form work brigades to dig irrigation ditches, terrace and level fields, and improve the land. David Zweig has noted: "These capital construction campaigns became a regular part of the rhythm of peasant lives." Pooling resources, peasants began to use "new technologies, such as tractors and diesel pumps. Land leveling facilitated the introduction of this technology, and high rates of capital formation supplied funds for localities to buy equipment."[49]

Although the Cultural Revolution provoked harmful and horrific struggles in many rural areas, agricultural production increased during the period. Lower production of chemical fertilizers hurt farm productivity, and the Maoist suppression of rural markets reduced income and created a lack of incentive for certain crops. But distribution problems were eased as the result of the emphasis on lower consumption, especially in urban areas, as well as the dispersal of at least 12 million people to the countryside. Most important, because of the recognized errors of the Great Leap Forward, the kind of radical extractive policies that had characterized the earlier period were largely absent during the Cultural Revolution. Nor were there further attempts at collectivization.[50]

As Dali Yang has noted, "Even though Mao launched the Socialist Education movement in 1962, championed Dazhai as a model of self-reliance beginning in 1964, and unleashed the Cultural Revolution in 1966, he would never again push for the transition to brigade or commune ownership. Instead of social mobilization, Mao turned to agricultural mechanization and other technical steps for improving agricultural output."[51]

The biggest change in rural areas resulted from the diminution of government control and authority during the Cultural Revolution. As Dali Yang has shown, in the aftermath of the Great Leap Forward efforts by the state to remake the rural economy slowed dramatically. During the Cultural Revolution a weakened and distracted state gave an increasingly better-educated peasantry the opportunity to make decisions on their own. Some decided to decollectivize and to grow crops suited to their areas instead of only grain. This was in spite of slogans emphasizing learning from the model collective, Dazhai.[52]

Not all of Mao's efforts were beneficial, especially his insistence on developing land in areas not suited for farming. Mao's encouragement of mono cropping drained the soil, creating erosion problems and forcing China to turn to imports for a number of key products. Although agricultural production rose throughout the period, in 1977 the per capita production of grain was still slightly lower than it had been in 1957. According to official statistics, agricultural growth during the Cultural Revolution was positive but meager.[53]

Statistics from the period of the Cultural Revolution, it should be noted, are notoriously unreliable. One researcher who looked at local records and did interviews in Jimo County in Shandong province found that agricultural production in this area more than doubled during the period. As Dongping Han writes, "Before the Cultural Revolution, farmers could afford to eat wheat flour only on special occasions, when entertaining guests or celebrating at festivals. With the increases in wheat and corn production, their diet improved greatly."[54]

Han's findings in this North China county correspond with Philip Huang's documentation of substantial increases in crop yields in the Yangzi Delta area during the decade. Given the problems with central government statistics during the period, it is not at all unlikely that Han's finding may be true for other areas of the country. Dwight Perkins, probably the most distinguished economist studying modern China, has written in the authoritative *Cambridge History of China* that the Cultural Revolution did not adversely affect agricultural growth.[55]

One reason why there probably was an improvement in agriculture during what are called the "Cultural Revolution Years" is because Mao's emphasis on mechanization during this period produced positive changes for agriculture. Lynn White has noted, "On the Yangzi delta, by the early 1970s, two new conditions appeared: First the productivity of rural labor rose, because field work had mechanized quickly at that time. Second, the state could not take its previous high rake-off from the profits of rural processing, because it had lost much of its monitoring ability through maltreatment of its own bureaucrats during the late 1960s, as well as much of its legitimacy among peasants because of the early 1960s famine."[56]

Beyond question, Mao liked collectivization and saw a return to markets as capitalist revisionism. But he also wanted less bureaucratic control, which paradoxically led to the unintended result of dismantling the collectives.

The common impression that Mao's Cultural Revolution policies created widespread rural poverty is not true. By weakening the central government and bureaucracy, Mao gave rural areas an opportunity to take advantage of the government's weakness and abolish the collective production system, something that led to a great increase in agricultural production in many areas in the early to mid-1970s. The dismantling of central planning in agriculture left the state incapable of extracting the kind of wealth from the countryside that it had in the early Communist period.[57]

As Mao had hoped and planned, a better-educated and more

mechanized peasantry was better able to chart its own course, though ultimately they took a different path from what Mao might have planned for them. According to Lynn White, "Shanghai suburbs in 1965 . . . were only 17 percent machine-tilled. By 1972, this portion was already 76 percent." By the mid-1970s this rapid mechanization of agriculture and the use of new seed, better adapted to local areas, had spread throughout much of China, creating a new green revolution.[58]

Mao took the Chinese government out of the business of controlling the day-to-day lives of the Chinese peasantry. After the Cultural Revolution, when the central bureaucrats returned to power, the peasantry refused to accept the old extractive policies. The better-educated peasantry who emerged from the Cultural Revolution broke up the collectives and took advantage of the mechanization and communal projects accomplished during the Cultural Revolution to create the rural explosion of the 1980s and 1990s and produce a positive legacy for the movement.

Whatever the growth rate of agriculture during the decade of the Cultural Revolution, there is no question that industry grew even more rapidly during the period. Between 1966 and 1976, industrial production in China grew annually at a rate of at least 8 percent, high by any standards, and by many accounts it was substantially greater. Living standards and consumption remained depressed, because this growth rate was financed by huge public investment. But the rate of growth that Mao achieved during what has been called the Ten Wasted Years was high even in comparison with the post-Mao years.[59]

One of the problems in assessing the Cultural Revolution is that of periodization. Although the movement is usually thought to have lasted a decade, in fact the heart of the Cultural Revolution lasted only a few years. During its high tide, industrial production fell. But by 1969 it had resumed its growth. After 1971, when Maoist policies were in place but the chaos of the movement had subsided, "overall growth was exponential." After Mao's death, although it continued to be high, it was merely linear.[60]

One of the main reasons for this growth was that after he had carried out the Cultural Revolution, Mao returned to emphasizing rural industrialization. He gave local governments the right to their own independent finances. They hired their own workers, creating a vast rural industrial base outside the central plan. The government also made state capital available for rural industry. Some programs were wasteful and redundant, to be expected in a time of economic transition, but local industries became a source of economic dynamism. As Christine Wong writes,

> By 1979, at the end of the Cultural Revolution, there were nearly 800,000 rural industrial enterprises, plus almost 90,000 small hydroelectric stations, scattered in villages and small towns, employing some 24 million workers and producing an estimated 15 percent of the gross value of industrial output. They dominated in the agriculture-related industries, producing all the farm tools and nearly all the small and medium-sized farm machinery, more than half of the chemical fertilizers, two-thirds of the cement, and 45 percent of the coal output.[61]

Mao not only pushed the establishment of small industries but also sought to change the structure of the large traditional industries. As early as 1964 he began forcing the Central Economic Planning Commission to place formerly state-controlled industries under the direction of local governments. Barry Naughton notes:

> In 1965, 10,533 enterprises, accounting for 47 percent of state-run industrial output, had been under central ministerial control. By 1971 only 142 factories, accounting for 8 percent of state industrial output, remained under central control. Moreover, in 1970, the entire planning apparatus—including the former Planning and Economic commissions, Material Supply Bureau and Statistical Bureau—was amalgamated into a single "revolutionary committee" with only 610 employees, 12 percent of the former personnel.[62]

Mao wanted more financial and investment decisions to be made by local government, not the central authorities. He made factories increasingly self-reliant, subject only to the demands of the party and the administrative organs of their locality or region. Central control was not completely dissolved; broad decisions still followed party policies dictated from above. But the changes that Mao brought to the Chinese economy were momentous, even though some of their benefits did not appear until the 1980s and 1990s. According to Lynn White:

> Because the Cultural Revolution incapacitated most central ministries, much localization of control over property during the early 1970s occurred by default. The State Planning Commission had expired by 1969, and Zhou Enlai set up a temporary group to fill the void—but expert administrators were still demoralized, so that few plans would have been enforceable in any case. All the industrial ministries, the People's Bank, and the Ministry of Finance were similarly decimated. Socialism is a difficult proposition for a state without planners.[63]

Mao's attacks on the bureaucracy, his efforts to level distinctions between mental and manual laborers, and his empowerment of workers and education of peasants made the distribution of income in China among the most balanced in the world, exceeding that of almost every other Asian country.[64] Ironically, Mao seemed unable to level the disparity between urban and rural income, something he cared about greatly. To be sure, the emphasis was on austerity. The fact that everyone was suffering equally did not necessarily make people feel better. Still, the relative equality that Mao created during the Cultural Revolution gave the leaders who came to power after his death some breathing space.

At least one of Mao's economic policies carried out through much of the Cultural Revolution did prove to be enormously wasteful. In 1964 he relocated large portions of China's industrial complex into the inland mountainous regions, where he felt it would be safe from the reach of American bombers, which China perceived as a growing threat after the American escalation of the Vietnam War. He extended railroad lines into western China and built steel plants, automobile factories, and other heavy industry in previously undeveloped areas.

This so-called Third Front policy, which was independent of the Cultural Revolution, wasted resources. Between 1965 and 1971 the central government put about half of China's basic construction expenditures into the Third Front. The steel and automobile industries established in the interior could not compete with the older coastal industries, and their factories turned into white elephants. In 1971, when the United States and China began to reconcile and China realized that the chances of an American invasion were slim, Mao ended the Third Front investments. Although it may be argued that some of Mao's decisions during this period were a reasonable response to the threat of war, and that some of this construction at least helped integrate inland regions into the national industrial economy, the waste of so much of the country's resources in order to build factories in caves and other remote places was absurd.

Yet Mao's Third Front was essentially a sideshow. Mostly he wished to remove the central government from the management of the economy, a policy Deng Xiaoping sought to reverse when he returned to office in 1974. Deng failed only because the Gang of Four, Mao's sometime allies during the Cultural Revolution, strenuously opposed Deng. In 1975 they succeeded once more in pushing Deng from office and putting an end to his recentralization attempts.[65] By the time Deng returned to power after Mao's death in 1976, Mao's decentralization policies could not be easily reversed.

Mao's Cultural Revolution not only had a positive, long-lasting impact on the Chinese economy, it also helped created the basis for an anti-authoritarian culture. As already noted, village elections first occurred in many places during the Cultural Revolution. At the same time some workers and peasants were taking onto themselves the rights of local self-government, some Red Guard groups were attempting to develop a democratic theory. In the autumn of 1966 two high school students in Beijing, writing under the pseudonym of Yilin-Dixi, were influenced by Maoist attacks on the government to point out that the problems besetting China were not just the fault of individual bureaucrats. They wrote that "the proletarian dictatorship needs to be ameliorated, the socialist system needs to be reformed," and that "the people's democratic dictatorship has become obsolete."[66] They called for the country to emulate the Paris Commune.

In the summer of 1967 a Revolutionary Red Guard organization known as Sheng Wu Lian, or the Hunan Provincial Proletarian Revolutionaries' Great Alliance Committee, responding to Mao's criticism of Chinese officialdom, suggested that the relationship between leaders and followers in China had become that of "exploiters and exploited." As a middle-school student named Yang Xiguang wrote, "At present over 90 percent of our high-ranking officials have actually formed into a unique class—the 'red' capitalist class."[67] The Cultural Revolution had concentrated on personalities, the student argued, and had never confronted the power basis of this group—the undemocratic bureaucratic system that created it. Nor had the Cultural Revolution touched the chief group that kept the bureaucracy in power—the military.

Other students formed similar conclusions. The Cultural Revolution's attacks on the party organization and the vicious response of the party to these criticisms destroyed its legitimacy for many people. By breaking down organizational control and forcing people to criticize almost everything they had been told to take for granted, especially the organization of the Chinese Communist party, Mao helped foster a spirit of independent judgment and self-reliance. Some learned to organize the kinds of action groups—with others of similar interests and backgrounds—that

Mao had endorsed in one of his first writings on Chinese society.[68] Many began to doubt authority.

In 1989 many of the Chinese students who camped out in Tiananmen Square believed that the far-reaching economic and political reforms of the 1980s would have been impossible without a Cultural Revolution. As one of its consequences, Chinese authorities in the 1980s had a weakened institutional base and were forced to respond to the needs and wants of the people to an unprecedented degree in order to revive the economy. The demonstrators in Tiananmen drew inspiration from the Sheng Wu Lian and other neodemocratic groups. They had been inspired by Mao's idea that the Chinese Communist party had been usurped by a new bureaucratic class, one as corrupt and autocratic as those opposed by the students of the May Fourth generation and earlier. It is not surprising, therefore, that in post-1989 China the country's authoritarian rulers have tried to repress any discussion of the Cultural Revolution.[69]

Mao did not simply bring some young Chinese a democratic political awareness. He also touched the souls of many young people, giving them a new sense of personal identity and accomplishment. This has been particularly so for Chinese women, in spite of what has been referred to as the "problematic" manner in which they have been depicted in movies such as *Xiu Xiu: A Senddown Girl* (1999) and in the popular victim-genre memoirs written disproportionately by women.[70] Mao had been an advocate of women's rights from his earliest days in Hunan. Although women's issues were mostly shunted aside during the Stalinist phase of the party in the 1940s and 1950s, during the Cultural Revolution Mao succeeded in helping imbue women with a positive sense of self-worth that exceeded even his own expectations.

In a recent work reflecting on their Cultural Revolution experiences, a group of Chinese academic women declared that Maoist thought and their lives as Red Guards had helped them develop into strong independent thinkers and had fostered their feminist identity. As one of the writers exulted: "I am delighted to have found in feminism a cause of my own, for the demise of the Maoist revolution did not extinguish my youthful dream of a society of equality and justice, a dream shared by numerous feminists worldwide. I am stuck with the identity of 'agents of social change' endowed by the Maoist state."[71]

This is exactly the "sense of emancipation among Red Guards" that Bill Brugger witnessed in 1966.[72] Not only women benefited from the experience. Many of those whom Mao encouraged to explore China and think on their own in the 1960s became the country's entrepreneurs in the 1980s.

Until very recently this sense of self-realization that Mao afforded many young Red Guards is something they have been prevented from admitting. The same group of women writers mentioned above has noted that former Red Guards who acknowledged remembering positive feelings from this period were told that, like the survivors of Nazi concentration camps, they had been so traumatized by their experiences that they could no longer remember what had really happened to them.[73]

The Cultural Revolution began to wane in 1969. Earlier Mao had designated army commander Lin Biao as his heir apparent, because Lin's support ensured Mao's victory over the party organization of Liu Shaoqi and Deng Xiaoping. But Mao believed that civilians needed to control the military, not the other way around. Gradually the relationship between Lin and Mao weakened. In 1971 Lin Biao died in a plane crash as he attempted to flee the country. (Fearful that the chairman would soon turn on him, Lin had been considering a coup d'état against Mao.) By 1973 Mao had rehabilitated Deng Xiaoping, and the two worked together to restrict the independent power of the military.

Mao had never wished to isolate China from the West. When the newly elected President Richard Nixon offered the possibility of relations with the United States, Mao took the opportunity. He ordered the Chinese foreign ministry to invite his American friend Edgar Snow to China, and then summoned Snow to be photographed with him on the walls overlooking Tiananmen on October 1, 1969, China's National Day, an unprecedented honor for a foreigner.

Mao's gesture escaped notice in the West. As Henry Kissinger, who was Nixon's national security adviser at the time, put it: "What they conveyed was so oblique that our crude Occidental minds completely missed the point."[74] The United States had become so alienated from China that no one in the American government was still capable of reading its signals, even when Mao repeated the message more overtly the next year.

In 1971, after Washington began its own initiative, Mao invited Kissinger to visit China. The following year Nixon came to the country. This initial diplomatic accord between China and the United States ended the country's twenty years of estrangement from the West.

In the brief period from 1972 to 1974—a time considered part of the "wasted decade" of the Cultural Revolution during which Mao had supposedly become a crazed ideologue—foreign trade jumped from approximately $4.5 billion (in constant 1963 prices) in 1972 to $6.1 billion in 1974, an increase of 30 percent.[75] The accord with the United States not only increased China's trade but allowed it to extricate itself from the Vietnam War and leave the Russians and the Vietnamese to fight the Americans. Under Mao's watch, China improved its relations with other Western nations and with Japan as well. In 1972 it again began sending young people abroad for study. Although Mao has often been painted as a xenophobic isolationist, in the early 1950s it was he who had pushed China's integration into the Soviet bloc. It was not the right decision, but it was also not the act of a xenophobe. In the early 1970s he started China's integration into the world capitalist economy. Because of Mao's relative silence late in life, one can

argue that he wished to recreate a Stalinist state in China, eliminating markets and placing the economy more firmly under the
control of the central government; but even if these were his
wishes, he succeeded in fostering a market economy by breaking
down central controls and beginning China's assimilation into the
world economy.

The nearest that Mao came to explaining why he started the
Cultural Revolution occurred in a speech in October 1966. The
purpose of the movement, he said, was to unite the "two lines." He
referred to the first and second lines of command set up by the
party, so that the CCP would not suffer the same problems of transition after Mao's death that occurred in the Soviet Union after
the death of Stalin. Mao suggested that the two lines of command
did not work. He wanted to reinvigorate the party.[76] Without a
change, China ran the risk of developing the same kind of revi-
sionist ideology that the Soviet Union had established.

Because of the Cultural Revolution, China did not go the way
of the old Soviet Union. The movement called into question the
very legitimacy of the Communist party. It so weakened the Chinese bureaucracy that it lost its stranglehold over people's lives. It
led to a questioning of norms that resulted in the permanent re-
moval of China from the path traveled by the old Soviet Union. As
Elizabeth Perry and Li Xun have put it: "The irreverent style of
the rebels was fertile soil for the growth of a general disrespect for
party authority, with serious implications for the future of Chinese
politics."[77]

It was this disregard for party rules that so infuriated Mao's victims. Party members had long acknowledged the right of Mao to
rectify and criticize other members. But such action was supposed
to take place within the confines of the party. Time and again in
the 1930s and 1940s, party members such as Zhang Guotao, Wang
Ming, and even Mao himself had relinquished opportunities for
personal advancement because of their willingness to observe the
team rules. With the Cultural Revolution Mao finally recognized

that although the team rules gave him supreme authority, they were fundamentally flawed and needed to be broken. To accomplish this he had to act in a very un-Stalinist manner by allowing the masses, or at least the Red Guards, more or less free rein to take matters into their own hands for a while. This does not mean that everything Mao did during the Cultural Revolution was good for China; far from it. As Bill Brugger, an eyewitness to the movement, has noted in his relatively sympathetic assessment of what happened, there were "elements of Stalinism" but also "elements of democracy" to be found in the Red Guards.[78]

Shortly before his death Mao tried to assess his life for a group of his followers. He noted that he had achieved two major victories: the first was to defeat Jiang Kaishek and the Japanese, the second was the Cultural Revolution. "Here I don't have many supporters, and I have quite a few opponents. The Great Cultural Revolution is something that has not yet been concluded. Thus I am passing the task on to the next generation. I may not be able to pass it on peacefully, in which case I may have to pass it on in turmoil. What will happen to the next generation if it all fails? How will you cope? Heaven only knows!"[79]

In saying this Mao was aware that though he may not have clarified his intentions for the Cultural Revolution, even on his deathbed, he felt that it would take China in a completely new direction. The Cultural Revolution marks one of the few moments in world history when a leader looked out over the changes he wrought, realized they were wrong, and set out to reverse them. It was not only a remarkable effort but, coming after the setbacks of the Great Leap Forward, a truly monumental one. With the Cultural Revolution, Mao reinvigorated China. The lesson he took from the Great Leap was that for China to continue to make progress, the party structure had to be limited and decentralized. Unfortunately Mao was not as successful as he might have hoped. The party bureaucrats returned, though not as powerful as before, and many of them were understandably upset about the Cultural

Revolution's attacks upon their lives and reputations. What is truly surprising is that so many American critics have accepted their estimates of the movement and of Mao as tyrant.

In many respects Mao was like a father who tells his children to "do their own thing." He may not like the results of what they have done, but he gave them the opportunity to do it. Mao set the stage for the country's future growth and prosperity. He created an exciting new culture that has only recently begun to be appreciated. His final campaign improved education, speeded up industrialization, and opened China to the outside world—not bad for a movement that is usually vilified in both China and in the West.

NINE

An Assessment

❧ MAO DIED on September 9, 1976. After his death, as his reputation plummeted among opinion-makers East and West, a counterphenomenon occurred. Chinese taxi drivers began to hang his picture on the dashboards of their cabs. Peasants placed his image on their household shrines. Striking workers carried Mao's portrait with them on demonstrations and spoke out longingly of the job security they had enjoyed under his rule. What I have tried to show in the pages of this book is that the masses were correct. Mao enriched the lives of the Chinese people.

Despite Mao's continued high standing in the eyes of the Chinese masses, most Chinese urbanites today feel disillusioned with the government and the movement he helped shape. Trying to describe the antipathy many in China now have for their country's current socialist state, Paul Pickowicz has characterized China since the death of the Great Helmsman as "postsocialist." According to Pickowicz, "Postsocialism, the ideological counterpart of postmodernism, refers to a cultural crisis that is unique to societies that have undergone decades of Leninist-Stalinist (i.e. what I call traditional socialist) development." In elaborating Pickowicz's ideas, Ben Xu has suggested, "Just as post-modernism underscores the crises of history, reason, and subjectivity inherent in modernism, so does postsocialism reveal the anomies rooted deeply in the Leninist-Stalinist system and the single-party dictatorship of socialism."[1]

Although the Chinese masses feel this disillusionment with socialism, it does not taint their image of Mao. What the Chinese masses understand far better than most Western and Chinese opinion-makers is that Mao struggled *against* the totalitarian bureaucratic state that has today created this "postsocialist" crisis in China. They know that China's current rulers have much less faith in the Chinese people than Mao did—and that this lack of faith contributes to the negative view of the Cultural Revolution espoused by China's current intellectual and political establishment. As Xudong Zhang notes in a recently published essay, there is a convergence in today's China between the ideas of "official" state intellectuals and "critics of the Chinese totalitarian state" who want market-oriented change and greater private ownership. The two sides find common ground in their adamant distrust of mass democracy and their dislike of equality and social justice, associating these "dangerous" ideas with the Cultural Revolution. Both factions in effect desire to protect a wealthy "middle class" they believe should have "freedom against democracy."[2]

Not only does China's political and intellectual establishment identify Mao with the mass democracy they despise, they refuse to acknowledge that it was Mao's weakening of the planned central state that allowed his successors to take credit for many of the positive features associated with the present government and society. In an irony of history, Mao's heirs have received accolades for changes forced upon them as a result of the same Cultural Revolution they have disavowed.

Even in the area most closely identified with the achievements of the post-Maoist regime—improving the material well-being of the Chinese people—Mao's record, as I have noted, was good. From 1953 until 1977, Chinese industry grew at an average rate of 13.134 percent (even including the disastrous Great Leap Forward years) while from 1978 to 1995 Chinese industry grew at a rate of only 12.4 percent. If the period is extended to include the steep rise in Chinese industrial production that occurred from 1949 to 1953, years that were certainly under Mao's watch, the comparative rate of increase of Chinese industry realized under Mao becomes truly spectacular.[3] Industrial growth is the area in which Mao's comparative economic record shines the most, but in most other areas the overall economic growth under Mao was also impressive.

Mao, however, did more than improve the material life of the Chinese people. By taking ideas seriously, he radically changed the culture of China, helping for the first time to expose hundreds of millions of Chinese to new thoughts and possibilities. Mao's views on learning appeared in a published conversation he once had with a niece, who complained to him about a fellow student who wasted time reading the supposedly reactionary old novel *Hong Lou Meng* (translated either as *Dream of the Red Chamber* or *Story of the Stone*). Mao assured her that such works should be read. He suggested that she look at a poem by the famous Tang dynasty writer Du Fu. The confused niece asked, "What precaution should I take against its influence?" He answered: "You are always metaphysical. Why should you take precaution? No. You should receive some influence. You should go deep in it and then emerge from it." He even added the Bible and Buddhist sutras to her reading list.[4]

The hard statistics on education make it clear that Mao's exhortations to his niece to broaden her understanding of the world were not just posturing. Mao worked hard to create a literate and aware populace. Primary school enrollment and per capita education grew dramatically during Mao's rule, especially during the Cultural Revolution years. Although China today is often considered a more open and enlightened place than it was during the Mao years, the figures indicate that in recent decades this enlightenment has not extended to the broad masses. Since Mao's death, basic educational opportunities have dwindled for tens of millions of Chinese children, a fact that bodes poorly for everyday life in China in the coming years.

Beyond what the records of education and industrial growth during the Mao era illustrate, Mao must be given much of the credit for reducing the stultifying bureaucratic controls that threatened to engulf the country in the 1950s and early 1960s. He did what most people today claim they want a leader to do—he broke with the bureaucrats who surrounded him. His achievement is especially significant because of the Stalinist leanings of those bureaucrats. Few people today on either the left or the right defend Stalinism, and Mao deserves praise for breaking with the consensus politics of the Stalinists in order to weaken the party through which they ruled, even though this was the same party Mao himself had once helped create. Furthermore Mao's break with the Stalinist bureaucrats was fundamental, occurring at the very root of its culture. Since it was the culture of the society that allowed this kind of organization to flourish and that led to the violence of the Cultural Revolution and the Great Leap, Mao should be applauded for working to develop a new ethos devoted to greater sexual, educational, and economic equality.

As I have made clear, Mao must be held responsible not only for the disaster of the Great Leap but also for many of the innocent, cruelly tortured victims of the Cultural Revolution. It is not much consolation to the victims of his campaigns that Mao, unlike Stalin, never went over the lists of people to be imprisoned or executed and was probably largely unaware of most of the egregious assaults of the Cultural Revolution. Mao also fell short in his personal life. He was, as Frederick Teiwes has put it, a "randy old bastard who abused his authority" to have sex with a great many women.[5] It does not let him off the hook that those who refused him suffered no ill consequences, or that the personal picture of Mao that emerges from Li Zhisui and the various bodyguards and secretaries who have written memoirs of life with Mao is of someone who most often worked to reconcile the varying demands of those around him in his private court, not of a person who constantly ranted, raved, and plotted against others. This does not make Mao a nice guy, but nice guys do not transform nations, and no country has ever emerged painlessly from a Stalinist system.

Mao may not have been the "sun in the sky" that China's old sycophantic culture designated him in the 1960s. The deconstruction of worshipful attitudes toward officialdom that Mao engineered during the Cultural Revolution has rightly diminished the awe he once inspired, even if the old man might not have appreciated the slew of Chinese artists who have now reduced his image to postmodern kitsch. But no one can deny that Mao was a great leader who transformed China. In a postsocialist age, Mao still ranks as a socialist hero. In an anti-totalitarian time, Mao can still inspire awe for his struggles against bureaucracy and his efforts to educate and empower the common people. The rural boy from Hunan may not have even heard the name Marx until he was in his mid-twenties, but his own name will inspire discussion for years to come, and his influence—largely positive—will be felt in China for generations.

Acknowledgments and
A Note on Sources

I AM GRATEFUL to Leanne Star, who helped edit and sharpen this manuscript. The good prose that was there before Ivan Dee began to apply his miraculous hand is due to her work. The mistakes that remain are my own.

I also wish to thank the Center for East Asian Studies at the University of Chicago, which for the last several years has provided me the research facilities that made this book possible. Dali Yang not only facilitated my use of this great library but made it possible for me to listen to the comments and ideas he has made over the years at various symposiums and talks. Katie Lynch and Alex Day graciously read the manuscript for me on short notice and offered valuable suggestions. Ed Friedman helped sharpen my thoughts by sending me so many e-mails disagreeing with my ideas about the Cultural Revolution that I finally—and to little avail—begged him to cease and desist.

Mao's works have been assembled in numerous collections, many of which do not completely agree. Different people recorded some of Mao's talks, and their note-taking abilities varied. More critically, many of Mao's important works were later edited: he had the right to revise and change his rough texts and speeches be-

fore they were officially published. In some cases these polished
works might represent his real thoughts better than his impromptu
remarks. But since many of Mao's writings were altered for political purposes, the edited texts sometimes convey meanings and
ideas different from those he meant when he first spoke. In recent
years it has become increasingly clear that much of what has long
passed for Mao's edited works, and a number of his unedited ones
as well, were written by or in collaboration with others, Mao
merely assenting to have the works published under his name.
Hence the official version of Mao's post-CCP writings, *Mao Zedong xuanji* (*The Selected Works of Mao Zedong*), must be treated
with some suspicion. Obviously this is also the case with the official translation of Mao's works, *The Selected Works of Mao Zedong*.[1]

Fortunately, since Mao's death a number of both official and
unofficial compilations of Mao's writings have been published.
The most comprehensive version of Mao's pre-1949 works has
been assembled by Takeuchi Minoru and his associates in *Mo
Takuto shu* (*Collected Writings of Mao Zedong*) and *Mo Takuto
shu hokan* (*Supplements to Collected Writings of Mao Zedong*).[2]
Professor Takeuchi's efforts have been fleshed out and verified by
several collections that have appeared in China in recent years.

Red Guards assembled the first unedited compilation of Mao's
post-1928 writings in the 1960s under the title of *Mao Zedong sixiang wansui* (*Long Live the Thought of Mao Zedong*).[3] Since one
of the most important points I make in this book is that the Cultural Revolution laid bare the pretensions of China's Stalinist political structure, it is interesting to note that it was under the
auspices of the Cultural Revolution that these original manuscripts of many of Mao's most important CCP writings and talks
were compiled and published—in order to reveal what Mao actually said before the bureaucrats around him began editing his
ideas.

Some of this material can now be found in *Jianguo yilai Mao*

Zedong wengao (*Manuscripts of Mao Zedong from the Period After the Nation's Founding*). The thirteen volumes published cover the period from 1949 to 1976. This is a generally reliable compilation of original and unedited notes, letters, and cables written by Mao to others—both Chinese and foreign (e.g., Stalin). Other collections of Mao's writings, such as *Mao Zedong junshi wenxuan* (*Selected Military Writings of Mao Zedong*), supplement this work. There is now also a detailed chronological biography of Mao edited by Fang Xianzhi, *Mao Zedong nianpu* (*Chronology of Mao Zedong*) 1893–1949, 3 volumes.[4]

There are several excellent English-language compilations of Mao's writings, which have extensive annotations and explanations. The most important and authoritative is the multi-volume work edited by Stuart Schram and his associates at the John King Fairbank Center for East Asian Research of Harvard University, under the title *Mao's Road to Power*. Upon my completion of *Mao*, Schram had published the first five volumes of this project, making available a more or less complete text of Mao's writings up to July 1937. For the years to 1937 I have therefore in almost every case cited Schram. He earlier published another important compilation of Mao's unedited writings, which I have also used to some extent: *Chairman Mao Talks to the People: Talks and Letters, 1956–1971.*[5]

Besides Schram's translations, there are two other important English-language compilations of Mao's writings for the period 1949–1958. The first is the two-volume work edited by John K. Leung and Michael Y. M. Kau, *The Writings of Mao Zedong*. This work translates almost all of Mao's writings from 1949 to December 1957. It is important not only for its annotations and references but also because it provides both the official edited version and the unofficial *wansui* unedited form of Mao's most important texts. Another extremely valuable, smoothly written translation of Mao's unedited writings has been published by Roderick MacFarquhar, Timothy Cheek, and Eugene Wu, *The Secret Speeches of Chair-*

man Mao: From the Hundred Flowers to the Great Leap Forward.
This includes Mao's 1958 speeches that are not to be found in the
Leung and Kao books.[6]

The foregoing titles comprise just a partial notation of the hundreds of volumes of Mao's works translated in many different
English-language editions, not to mention the innumerable
Chinese-language collections of his works, many of which I cite
throughout this book.

Notes

Chapter One: The Image

1. *Mao: The Real Man* (First Run/Icarus Films, 1995), a video by Szilveszter Siklosi.

2. Jiang Zemin, "Mao Zedong's Historic Contributions" (December 26, 1993, speech given to commemorate the 100th birthday of Mao Zedong), translation from *Beijing Review*, January 10–16, 1994, Vol. 37, p. 9. Jiang here was merely repeating an earlier assessment by Deng Xiaoping.

3. Edgar Snow, *Red Star over China* (New York, 1961), 71. Stewart Alsop, *New York Herald Tribune*, March 18, 1951. This and most of the other media quotes that follow have been collected in Alain Bouc, *Mao Tse-tung: A Guide to His Thought*, trans. Paul Auster and Lydia Davis (New York, 1977). *Time*, April 12, 1954. Tilman Durdin, *New York Times*, May 27, 1962. Harold Schechter, *Time*, September 26, 1969.

4. Simon Leys, "Mythmaker," a review of *André Malraux: A Biography by Curtis Cate*, *New York Review of Books*, May 29, 1997, 25–27.

5. Henry Kissinger, "The Philosopher and the Pragmatist," *Newsweek*, March 3, 1997, 45–46. Kissinger here is repeating what he says in his memoirs. Interesting is his comparison of meetings with Deng and Mao, and his description of Deng as "more nationalistic." To look at the newly released interviews, see William Burr, "The Beijing-Washington Back Channel and Henry Kissinger's Secret Trip to China (September 1970–July 1971)," National Security Archive Electronic Briefing Book No. 66 (February 27, 2002). This can be accessed at: http://www.gwu.edu/~nsarchiv/NSAEBB/NSAEBB66/.

6. Philip Short, *Mao: A Life* (New York, 1999). Jonathan Spence, *Mao Zedong* (New York, 1999). Ian Buruma, "Divine Killer," *New York Review of Books*, February 24, 2000, 18–25.

Chapter Two: Growing Up Normal

1. See, for instance, the book by Siao Yu, *Mao Tse-tung and I Were Beggars* (London, 1961). Siao Yu, who became an opponent of Communist rule, had been a classmate and friend of Mao's. When he describes incidents from Mao's early life before he met Mao, and by his own admission relies on secondhand stories, he makes Mao out to be churlish and temperamental. But when he describes his own face-to-face encounters with Mao, he sees Mao as a polite and considerate friend who was held in high regard by his teachers.

2. Snow, *Red Star*, 123. Whether the father should be considered a "rich peasant" or a "middle peasant" may seem like a pedantic distinction, but it matters greatly in how the Chinese Communists distinguished a family's political and social ranking. Communists generally thought of middle peasants as a basically progressive group; but they often labeled rich peasants as a reactionary group whose land should be expropriated. At the time Mao was talking to Snow, the Communists were trying to persuade rich peasants to participate in the anti-Japanese struggle. In identifying himself as someone of rich peasant origin, Mao may have been trying to show this group that he had some affinity with them. Mao's distinguished American biographer, Stuart Schram, has argued that Mao overstated the father's wealth and status for reasons of familial pride or perhaps politics. Even in the rich soil of the Hunan countryside, the family's three and a half or four acres, though marking them as well off, would not really make them rich peasants. Nonetheless the father made a decent living and over the years gradually improved his status.

3. "Yang Changji's Record of a Conversation with Mao Zedong" (April 5, 1915), in Stuart Schram, ed., *Mao's Road to Power: Revolutionary Writings, 1912–1949*, Vol. I, *The Pre-Marxist Period, 1912–1920* (New York, 1992), 60. As Schram notes, every article in Vol. I is taken from *Mao Zedong zaoqi wengao, 1912.6–1920.11* (*Draft Writings by Mao Zedong for the Early Period, June 1912–November 1920*), (Changsha, 1991); Takeuchi Minoru, ed., *Mo Takuto shu* (*Collected Writings of Mao Zedong*), (Tokyo, 1983); or *Mo Takuto shu hokan* (*Supplements to Collected Writings of Mao Zedong*), (Tokyo, 1983–1986).

4. Siao Yu, *Mao Tse-tung and I*, 6.

5. Philip Short speculates on this. *Mao*, 30.

6. Snow, *Red Star*, 121–134, 127, 125.

7. Ibid., 126–127.

8. Siao Yu, *Mao Tse-tung and I*, 6–11.

9. For example, Chen Duxiu, the aging founder of the Chinese Communist party, who throughout his life kept keenly abreast of trends among Chinese youth, wrote a prison autobiography at about the same time that Mao told Snow his story, in which he claimed to have had a miserable childhood. Chen told his readers that his father died before Chen could even know him, and that a tyrannical grandfather then raised him. What Chen failed to mention, however, is that

after his grandfather's death he was adopted by a wealthy and powerful uncle and grew up in a comfortable and privileged household. See Lee Feigon, *Chen Duxiu: Founder of the Chinese Communist Party* (Princeton, 1983).

10. As both Spence, *Mao Zedong* (34–35), and Short, *Mao* (89), point out, he dawdled in getting home, stopping first in Shanghai, perhaps not fully cognizant of how ill his mother was. But he did arrive well before her death, from what today would be an easily treatable problem. Mao Zedong, "Letter to Seventh and Eighth Maternal Uncles and Aunts" (April 28, 1919), in Schram, *Mao's Road to Power*, Vol. I, p. 317. Mao Zedong, "Mao Zedong's Funeral Oration in Honor of His Mother" (October 8, 1919), in Schram, *Mao's Road to Power*, Vol. I, p. 419.

11. Snow, *Red Star*, 136.

12. Ibid., 137–138.

13. Actually he entered the Fourth Hunan Normal School, but the next year this school merged with the First Provincial Normal School, and it was the latter school from which Mao ultimately graduated. *Snow, Red Star*, 149.

14. "Yang Changji's Record of a Conversation with Mao Zedong" (April 5, 1915), in Schram, *Mao's Road to Power*, Vol. I, p. 60.

15. Li Jui, *The Early Revolutionary Activities of Comrade Mao Tse-tung*, trans. Anthony W. Sariti (White Plains, N.Y., 1977), 41. Siao Yu, *Mao Tse-tung and I*, 31.

16. Mao Zedong, "Marginal Notes to: Friedrich Paulsen, A System of Ethics" (1917–1918), in Schram, *Mao's Road to Power*, Vol. I, p. 205.

17. Mao Zedong, "Evening School Journal, Volume One" (November 1917), in Schram, *Mao's Road to Power*, Vol. I, p. 145.

18. Mao Zedong, "A Study of Physical Education" (April 1, 1917), in Schram, *Mao's Road to Power*, Vol. I, pp. 115, 116, 118.

19. Snow, *Red Star*, 146.

20. Ibid., 149. Mao Zedong, "Letter to Tao Yi" (February 1920), in Schram, *Mao's Road to Power*, Vol. I, p. 493.

21. Mao Zedong, "Manifesto on the Founding of the Xiang River Review" (July 14, 1919), in Schram, *Mao's Road to Power*, Vol. I, pp. 318–320.

22. Snow, *Red Star*, 154. Mao Zedong, "The Arrest and Rescue of Chen Duxiu" (July 14, 1919), in Schram, *Mao's Road to Power*, Vol. I, pp. 329–330.

23. Mao Zedong, "For the Germans, the Painful Signing of the Treaty" (July 21, 1919), in Schram, *Mao's Road to Power*, Vol. I, pp. 357–366, especially 365.

24. Mao Zedong, "The Great Union of the Popular Masses" (July 24, July 28, August 4, 1919), in Schram, *Mao's Road to Power*, Vol. I, pp. 378–389. "Introduction" in Schram, *Mao's Road to Power*, Vol. I, p. xxxiii.

25. Mao Zedong, "The Great Union of the Popular Masses," 389.

26. "Introduction" in Schram, *Mao's Road to Power*, Vol. I, p. xxxvi. Indeed, several times during this period Mao consulted with and wrote to Hu Shi, seeking his advice on Hunan. See Mao Zedong, "Letter to Hu Shi" (July 9, 1920), in Schram, *Mao's Road to Power*, Vol. I, p. 531.

27. To get an idea of the kinds of ideas that Mao and Tao Yi shared, especially their common views of the women's movement, see Mao Zedong, "Letter to Tao Yi" (February 19, 1920), in Schram, *Mao's Road to Power*, Vol. I, pp. 491–495. Schram discusses their relationship on 491, n. 1.

28. Mao Zedong, "The Women's Revolutionary Army" (July 14, 1919), in Schram, *Mao's Road to Power*, Vol. I, p. 353.

29. Snow, *Red Star*, 145. Spence, *Mao Zedong*, 5.

30. Mao Zedong, "The Work of the Students" (December 1, 1919), in Schram, *Mao's Road to Power*, Vol. I, p. 451.

31. Spence, *Mao Zedong*, 43.

32. Snow, *Red Star*, 75. Mao Zedong, "Reply to Zeng Yi from the Association for Promoting Reform in Hunan" (June 23, 1920), in Schram, *Mao's Road to Power*, Vol. I, p. 527.

33. Mao Zedong, "Oppose Unification" (October 10, 1920), in Schram, *Mao's Road to Power*, Vol. I, pp. 582–583.

34. Li Jui, *Early Revolutionary Activities*, 154.

35. Spence, *Mao Zedong*, 44.

Chapter Three: Party Man

1. Siao Yu, *Mao Tse-tung and I*, 68–69.

2. Ibid., 41.

3. Snow, *Red Star*, 157.

4. Angus McDonald, "Mao Tse-tung and the Hunan Self-Government Movement, 1920," *China Quarterly* 68 (February 1976), 751–777. Mao's advocacy of self-government placed him in the gradualist camp of the American-educated scholar Hu Shi, who opposed Marxist ideas. See Hu Shi's and Li Dazhao's famous "problems" versus "isms" debate in the summer of 1919, in which Hu published his criticism of isms like Marxism: "Duo yanjiu xie wenti, xiao tan xie zhuyi" (More study of problems, less talk about isms), *Meizhou pinglun* (*Weekly Critic*), Vol. 31 (July 20, 1919). The debate continued in a series of articles and exchanges between Li and Hu. For a discussion of this, see Maurice Meisner, *Li Ta-chao and the Origins of Chinese Marxism* (Cambridge, Mass., 1967), 105–114. Although Hu Shi also supported the federalist movement, he did not write on it until 1922. See Jerome B. Grieder, *Hu Shih and the Chinese Renaissance: Liberalism in the Chinese Revolution, 1917–1937* (Cambridge, Mass., 1970), 195.

5. Mao Zedong, "Letter to Xiao Xudong, Cai Linbin, and the Other Members in France" (December 1, 1920), in Schram, *Mao's Road to Power*, Vol. II, pp. 8–11, 7.

6. Alexander Pantsov, *The Bolsheviks and the Chinese Revolution, 1919–1927* (Honolulu, 2000), 31.

7. See J. Van De Ven, *From Friend to Comrade: The Founding of the Chinese*

Communist Party, 1920–1927 (Berkeley, 1991), especially 55–99. Schram, *Mao's Road to Power*, Vol. II, "Introduction," p. xxii.

8. See Mao Zedong, "Letter to Zhou Shizhao" (March 14, 1920), in Schram, *Mao's Road to Power*, Vol. I, p. 504. For more on Hu's influence on Mao, see Chapter 2 of this book. See also Schram, *Mao's Road to Power*, Vol. II, "Introduction," p. xxiii.

9. The Trotskyist Peng Shuzhi, a revolutionary rival of Mao's, later published the account to prove Mao's disregard for his colleagues, though what it really seemed to show was Mao's eccentricity. See Peng Shuzhi, *L'Envol du Communisme en Chine: Memoires de Peng Shuzhi* (*The Take-off of Communism in China: Memoirs of Peng Shuzhi*), ed. Claude Cadart and Cheng Yingxiang (Paris, 1983), 159–160.

10. Cheng Ch'ao-lin, *An Oppositionist for Life: Memoirs of the Chinese Revolutionary Zheng Chaolin*, ed. and trans. by Gregor Benton (Atlantic Highlands, N.J., 1997), 47.

11. Mao Zedong, "The Greatest Defects of the Draft Provincial Constitution" (April 25–26, 1921), in Schram, *Mao's Road to Power*, Vol. II, p. 41.

12. Mao Zedong, "Report on the Affairs of the New People's Study Society" (Summer 1921), in Schram, *Mao's Road to Power*, Vol. II, pp. 73–74, 78.

13. Mao Zedong, "Some Issues That Deserve More Attention" (May 1, 1922), in Schram, *Mao's Road to Power*, Vol. II, p. 107.

14. For an insider's discussion of this, see Chen Duxiu, "Gao chuandang tongzhi shu ("A letter to all party comrades"), Shanghai, December 10, 1929. See also Pantsov, *Bolsheviks*, 56. For an even more complete discussion that includes many relevant documents, see Tony Saich, *The Origins of the First United Front in China: The Role of Sneevliet (Alias Maring)* (Armonk, N.Y., 1995).

15. See Saich, *Origins*, 580. Mao had written the same thing in an article published a few months earlier. "The Foreign Powers, the Warlords, and the Revolution" (April 10, 1923), in Schram, *Mao's Road to Power*, Vol. II, pp. 157–161. See also the discussion of this issue in ibid., xxix–xxx.

16. Chang Kuo-t'ao, *The Rise of the Chinese Communist Party*, 1921–1927 (Lawrence, Kans., 1971), 311. Zhang claimed that Mao was originally on his side but switched when it became clear that the vote would go against him, though this does not seem to have been the case (see Maring's notes referred to above).

17. Mao was even chosen to draft the resolution on the peasant movement for the convention. See "Resolution on the Peasant Question" (June 1923), in Schram, *Mao's Road to Power*, Vol. II, pp. 164. Mao Zedong, "The Beijing Coup d'Etat and the Merchants" (July 11, 1923), in Schram, *Mao's Road to Power*, Vol. II, pp. 178–182.

18. For a biography of Tan Yankai, see *Biographic Dictionary of Republican China* (New York, 1967–1979), Vol. III, pp. 220–225. For a biography of Zhao Hengti, see ibid., Vol. I, pp. 143–144. Mao Zedong, "The Cigarette Tax" (August

29, 1923), in Schram, *Mao's Road to Power*, Vol. II, p. 190. Cheng Ch'ao-lin, *Oppositionist for Life*, 69.

19. Mao Zedong, "The Struggle Against the Right Wing of the Guomindang" (July 21, 1924), in Schram, *Mao's Road to Power*, Vol. II, p. 217.

20. See David Bachman, *Chen Yun and the Chinese Political System* (Berkeley, 1985), 69. See also Frederick Teiwes, "Mao and His Lieutenants," *Australian Journal of Chinese Affairs* 19/20 (January–July 1988), 47–48.

21. Mao Zedong, "Analysis of All the Classes in Chinese Society" (December 1, 1925), in Schram, *Mao's Road to Power*, Vol. II, pp. 249–267. Schram notes that the article was first thought to have been issued on March 1, 1926, but actually appeared on December 1, 1925. Schram, *Mao's Road to Power*, Vol. II, "Introduction," pp. xli, xliv.

22. Feigon, *Chen Duxiu*, 188. See Van De Ven, *From Friend to Comrade*, especially 147–199.

23. Snow, *Red Star*, 161. Schram, *Mao's Road to Power*, Vol. II, "Introduction," p. xli.

24. "Resolution Concerning the Peasant Movement: Resolution of the Second National Congress of the Chinese Guomindang" (January 19, 1926), in Schram, *Mao's Road to Power*, Vol. II, pp. 359–360.

25. Mao Zedong, "An Analysis of the Various Classes Among the Chinese Peasantry and Their Attitudes Toward the Revolution," (January 1926), in Schram, *Mao's Road to Power*, Vol. II, pp. 304, 303–309. Mao Zedong, "Analysis of All Classes in Chinese Society" (December 1, 1925); "Reasons for the Breakaway of the Guomindang Right and Its Implications for the Future of the Revolution" (January 10, 1926); "Resolution Concerning the Peasant Movement" (January 19, 1926); "The National Revolution and the Peasant Movement" (September 1, 1926) (this one less so than the others); "Report on the Peasant Movement in Hunan" (February 1927). Mao Zedong, "Reasons for the Breakaway of the Guomindang Right and Its Implications for the Future of the Revolution" in Schram, *Mao's Road to Power*, Vol. II, pp. 320–327.

26. Mao Zedong, "Report on the Peasant Movement in Hunan," in Schram, *Mao's Road to Power*, Vol. II, p. 432–433.

27. Ibid., 436.

28. Ibid., 434, 435.

29. Mao Zedong, "Report to the Central Committee on Observations Regarding the Peasant Movement in Hunan" (February 16, 1927), in Schram, *Mao's Road to Power*, Vol. II, p. 426. Benjamin I. Schwartz, *Chinese Communism and the Rise of Mao* (New York, 1951), 74.

30. Snow, *Red Star*, 162.

31. Mao Zedong, "Remarks on the Report of the Representative of the International at the August 7 Emergency Conference" (August 7, 1927), in Schram, *Mao's Road to Power*, Vol. III, p. 31.

Chapter Four: Rethinking Mao—The Long March

1. For a helpful discussion of this issue, which raises many of the same themes discussed in this chapter, see Tony Saich, "The Chinese Communist Party During the Era of the Comintern (1919–1943)," article prepared for Juergen Rojahn, "Comintern and National Communist Parties Project," International Institute of Social History, Amsterdam. The paper is available at: http://ksghome. harvard.edu/~.asaich.Academic.KSG/COMIN-F.html.

2. Mao Zedong, "The Greatest Friendship" (March 9, 1953), in Michael Y. M. Kau and John K. Leung, ed., *The Writings of Mao Zedong, 1949–1976*, Vol. I, *September 1949–December 1955* (Armonk, N.Y., 1986), 331. This was not just empty funeral talk. As early as August 1927, after listening to the new Comintern representative, Besso Lomindaze, Mao began his comments to the CCP conference with the words, "The whole of the Comintern representative's report is very important." See Mao Zedong, "Remarks on the Report of the Representative of the International at the August 7 Emergency Conference" (August 7, 1927), in Schram, *Mao's Road to Power*, Vol. III, p. 29.

3. See the discussion in Schram, "Introduction" to *Mao's Road to Power*, Vol. III, p. xxv.

4. Benjamin Yang has pointed out that these groups were really peasant self-defense forces. See his *From Revolution to Politics: Chinese Communists on the Long March* (Boulder, Colo., 1990), 27.

5. This is nicely covered in Schram, "Introduction" to *Mao's Road to Power*, Vol. III, p. xv–lxv. See the discussion in ibid., xxxiii.

6. Mao Zedong, "A Letter from the Front Committee to the Central Committee" (April 5, 1929), in Schram, *Mao's Road to Power*, Vol. III, p. 155. Snow, *Red Star*, 170.

7. Ibid., 171.

8. Schram, "Introduction" to *Mao's Road to Power*, Vol. III, p. xlii. A translation of "Political Resolution of the Sixth National Congress" (July 9, 1928) is available in Tony Saich, ed., *The Rise of the Chinese Communist Party: Documents and Analysis* (Armonk, N.Y., 1996), 341–369. See also "Resolution on the Peasant Question" (July 9, 1929), ibid., 369–376.

9. Mao Zedong, "Xunwu Investigation" (May 1930) in Schram, *Mao's Road to Power*, Vol. III, pp. 296–418.

10. Mao Zedong, "Draft Resolution of the Ninth Congress of the Communist Party in the Fourth Red Army" (December 1929), in Schram, *Mao's Road to Power*, Vol. III, pp. 195–230.

11. For further discussion, see Feigon, *Chen Duxiu*, 200–204. See Mao Zedong, "Letter from the Fourth Army of the Chinese Red Army (The Red Army of Zhu and Mao) to the Soldiers of the Guomindang Army" (January 1930), in Schram, *Mao's Road to Power*, Vol. III, pp. 247–255.

12. Mao Zedong, "Letter to Comrade Lin Biao" (January 5, 1930), in Schram, *Mao's Road to Power*, Vol. III, pp. 234–246.

13. According to most reports, the youngest son died, though Salisbury claims that he was told that the boy was found many years later working as an accountant in a commune. See Harrison E. Salisbury, *The Long March: The Untold Story* (New York, 1985), 361. For He Zizhen's story, see Wang Xingjuan, *Jinggang du juan hong: He Zizhen fengyu rensheng (Jinggang's red azalea: the trials and hardships of He Zizhen's life)* (Liaoning, 2000). Also Wang Xingjuan, *Li Min, He Zizhen yu Mao Zedong (Li Min, He Zizhen and Mao Zedong)* (Beijing, 1993). See also Lee Xiao Hong Lee and Sue Wiles, *The Women of the Long March* (Sydney, 1999). Until recently He Zizhen's life has received much less attention than that of the wives who went before and after her — at least in part because she later suffered from mental problems. But after Mao's death she did get to tell her story, as reported in the above Wang Xingjuan books, especially the first one.

14. Much of this discussion is derived from Stephen C. Averill, "The Origins of the Futian Incident," in Tony Saich and Hans Van De Ven, ed., *New Perspectives* (Armonk, N.Y., 1995), 79–116. See also the discussion of this incident in Yung-fa Chen, "The Futian Incident and the Anti-Bolshevik League: The 'Terror' in the CCP Revolution," in *Republican China*, Vol. 19, no. 2 (April 1994), 1–51.

15. Averill, "Origins of the Futian Incident," 107.

16. Stephen Averill and Stuart Schram, "Introduction" to *Mao's Road to Power*, Vol. IV, pp. xliv–xlv.

17. Ibid., xlvi.

18. Ibid., lii–lx.

19. Yang, *From Revolution to Politics*, 67.

20. Mao Zedong, "This Year's Elections" (September 6, 1933), in Averill and Schram, *Mao's Road to Power*, Vol. IV, pp. 533–534.

21. Mao Zedong, "Report of the Central Executive Committee and the Council of People's Commissars of the Chinese Soviet Republic to the Second National Soviet Congress" (January 24–25, 1934), in Averill and Schram, *Mao's Road to Power*, Vol. IV, p. 699. This was something he had emphasized as early as 1929, when he and Zhu De issued the following notice: "Unifying the whole of China is reason for the nation to rejoice. As for Manchus, Mongols, Hui, and Tibetans, they will determine their own statutes." See Mao Zedong and Zhu De, "Notice Issued by the Fourth Army Headquarters of the Red Army," in Schram, *Mao's Road to Power*, Vol. III, p. 138. This early statement was astonishing in that it acknowledged that the old Qing empire, which had united Chinese and minorities areas under a Manchu-dominated government, was not the same place as the Chinese nation, something later Chinese nationalists and Communists were unwilling to admit. "Interview with Edgar Snow on Foreign Affairs" (July 15, 1936). This is the original interview manuscript that became the basis for *Red*

Star over China. As printed in Schram, *Mao's Road to Power,* Vol. V, p. 254. Mao Zedong, "Proclamation of the Central Soviet Government to the People of Inner Mongolia" (December 10, 1935), in Schram, *Mao's Road to Power,* Vol. V, pp. 71–72. Mao Zedong, "Declaration of the People of Muslim Nationalities by the Central Government" (May 25, 1936), in Schram, *Mao's Road to Power,* Vol. V, p. 202.

22. Otto Braun, *A Comintern Agent in China, 1932–1939,* trans. Jeanne Moore (Stanford, 1982), 55–56.

23. Gregor Benton, *Mountain Fires: The Red Army's Three-Year War in South China, 1934–1938* (Berkeley, 1992), 5.

24. Schram, "Introduction" to *Mao's Road to Power,* Vol. V, p. xl. Yang, *From Revolution to Politics,* 123–124. See also Thomas Kampen, *Mao Zedong, Zhou Enlai and the Evolution of the Chinese Communist Leadership* (Copenhagen, 2000), 66–67.

25. Michael Sheng, *Battling Western Imperialism* (Princeton, 1997), 20–21. See also Michael Sheng, "Mao, Stalin, and the Formation of the Anti-Japanese United Front, 1935–1937," *China Quarterly,* no. 129 (1992), 149–170.

26. See Kampen, *Mao Zedong . . . ,* 76–77.

27. Wang, *Jinggang du juan hong,* 184–190. Salisbury, *Long March,* 173. See also Lee, *Women,* 34–36. Salisbury, *Long March,* 174. Wang, *Jinggang du juan hong,* 218–219.

28. Snow, *Red Star,* 201–209.

29. Schram, "Introduction" to *Mao's Road to Power,* Vol. V, p. xlii.

30. He later claimed he was more or less kidnapped. See, for instance, Salisbury's account which calls him a "captive general." Salisbury, *Long March,* 245–246.

31. Robert Farnsworth, *From Vagabond to Journalist: Edgar Snow in Asia, 1928–1941* (Columbia, Mo., 1996), 222.

32. Snow, *Red Star,* 217. A useful discussion of the changes in Mao's position can be found in Schram, "Introduction" to *Mao's Road to Power,* Vol. V, pp. li–liii. See also Sheng, *Western Imperialism,* 31–40.

33. Snow, *Red Star,* 217.

34. Yang, *From Revolution to Politics,* 182–186. The date is in fact in doubt. Yang says that Mao was shown the document in November, as does Schram. See Schram, "Introduction" to *Mao's Road to Power,* Vol. V, pp. lii, n. 62. Tony Saich implies they may have seen the document as early as October. See Saich, "The Chinese Communist Party During the Era of the Comintern (1919–1943)." Mao Zedong and Zhu De, "Manifesto of the Central Government of the Chinese Soviet Republic and of the Revolutionary Military Commission of the Workers' and Peasants' Red Army on Resisting Japan and Saving China" (November 28, 1935), in Schram, *Mao's Road to Power,* Vol. V, pp. 54–56. Garver, who argues that Mao won the CCP leadership without Comintern support, points to the length of time it took Mao to "finally accept the Comintern's new United Front line." See John

W. Garver, *Chinese-Soviet Relations, 1937–1945* (New York, 1988), 13. Mao Ze-dong, "The Zhiluozhen Campaign, and the Present Situation and Task" (November 30, 1935), in Schram, *Mao's Road to Power*, Vol. V, p. 62. See also Sheng, *Western Imperialism*, 24–29.

35. Schram, "Introduction" to *Mao's Road to Power*, Vol. V, p. lii. See also in the same volume, Mao Zedong, "Letter to Zhang Wentian on Changing the Policy Toward Rich Peasants and Other Questions" (December 1, 1935), 66–67. Also "Order of the Central Executive Committee of the Chinese Soviet Republic on Changing the Policy Toward the Rich Peasants" (December 15, 1935), 73–74. Also "On Tactics Against Japanese Imperialism" (December 27, 1935), 86–102.

36. Schram, "Introduction" to *Mao's Road to Power*, Vol. V, p. lxi.

37. Sheng, *Western Imperialism*, 29. Schram, "Introduction" to *Mao's Road to Power*, Vol. V, pp. lxx, lxxii. Sheng, *Western Imperialism*, 29.

38. Quoted in Schram, "Introduction" to *Mao's Road to Power*, Vol. V, p. lxxxvi. As Schram notes, there are various versions of this telegram. Edgar Snow, *Random Notes on Red China* (Cambridge, Mass., 1957), 2.

Chapter Five: Becoming the Chairman

1. Farnsworth, *Vagabond*, 222.

2. Snow, *Red Star*, 74, 70, 75. John Maxwell Hamilton, *Edgar Snow: A Biography* (Bloomington, Ind., 1998), 76–77.

3. Agnes Smedley, *Battle Hymn of China* (New York, 1943), 168–169. For a description of some of Smedley's "scandalous" interactions with Mao that relies heavily on the gossipy letters that Smedley sent to Snow's wife, Nym Wales, see Farnsworth, *Vagabond*, 289–291.

4. Reminiscences of some of those who were influenced by Snow can be found in Wang Xing, ed., *China Remembers Edgar Snow* (Beijing, 1982). S. Bernard Thomas discusses this in *Season of High Adventure: Edgar Snow in China* (Berkeley, 1996), 156–157. Hamilton, *Edgar Snow*, 222–223.

5. Kampen, *Mao Zedong . . .* , 126. Frederick C. Teiwes with the assistance of Warren Sun, *The Formation of the Maoist Leadership: From the Return of Wang Ming to the Seventh Party Congress* (London, 1994), 5.

6. See Wang Ming, *Mao's Betrayal* (Moscow, 1975), 38. See the discussion in Kampen, *Mao Zedong . . .* , 89. Chang Kuo-t'ao, *The Rise of the Chinese Communist Party*, Vol. II, p. 572. See the discussion in Shum Kui-kwong, *The Chinese Communists' Road to Power: The Anti-Japanese National United Front, 1935–1945* (New York, 1988), 129–130. The quote is from Teiwes, *Formation*, 8.

7. Teiwes, *Formation*, 6.

8. Mao Zedong, "On Protracted War" (May 1938), in *Selected Works of Mao Tse-tung* (Beijing, 1965), Vol. II, pp. 113–132. Braun, *Comintern Agent*, 223–225. See also the discussion in Teiwes, *Formation*, 8.

9. See the discussion in Kampen, *Mao Zedong* . . . , 93–94. Teiwes, *Formation*, 30.

10. Ibid., 8–9.

11. Shum, *Road to Power*, 129–130. Snow, *Red Star*, 77.

12. See Stuart Schram, *The Thought of Mao Tse-tung* (New York, 1989), 61–65. See also the comprehensive discussion of this issue in Nick Knight, ed., *Mao Zedong on Dialectical Materialism: Writers on Philosophy*, 1937 (Armonk, N.Y., 1990), "Introduction," 7–8.

13. Ibid., 37. This cultural preference for the loose citation of sources admittedly can be abused. It is now often used to offer what I think is a faulty cultural explanation of why the Chinese pay little attention to international copyright and intellectual protection laws. See William P. Alford, *To Steal a Book Is an Elegant Offense: Intellectual Property Law in Chinese Civilization* (Palo Alto, 1995), 30–40.

14. Edgar Snow, *The Long Revolution* (New York, 1971), 207. Knight, *Mao on Dialectical Materialism*, "Introduction," 37–38, 40–48. See also Knight, "The Laws of Dialectical Materialism in Mao Zedong's Thought: The Question of 'Orthodoxy,' " in Arlif Dirlik, Paul Healy, and Nick Knight, ed., *Critical Perspectives on Mao Zedong's Thought* (Atlantic Highlands, N.J., 1997), 99.

15. Mao Zedong, in Knight, *Mao on Dialectical Materialism*, "On Practice," 37–38.

16. Mao Zedong, in Knight, *Mao on Dialectical Materialism*, 95. See also Schram, *Thought*, 68.

17. See Joseph Levenson, *Confucian China and Its Modern Fate: A Trilogy* (Berkeley, 1968).

18. Mao Zedong, "On Contradictions," in *Selected Works*, Vol. I, p. 151. I am quoting here the final edited and polished version of the speech. In the original version it is titled "The Law of the Unity of Opposites" and begins, "This law is the basic law of dialectics." Mao Zedong, in Knight, *Mao on Dialectical Materialism*, 154. See also Knight, "The Laws of Dialectical Materialism in Mao Zedong's Thought: The Question of 'Orthodoxy,' " in Dirlik, *Critical Perspectives*, 100.

19. Mao Zedong, "On New Democracy," in *Selected Works*, Vol. II, pp. 339–385. See also Schram, *Thought*, 78, 77.

20. Mao Zedong, "On New Democracy," in *Selected Works*, Vol. II, p. 353.

21. Farnsworth, *Vagabond*, 222. Much of Snow's essay is translated in Janice and Stephen MacKinnon, *Agnes Smedley: The Life and Times of an American Radical* (Berkeley, 1988), 188–192. For an English-language account of an apparently different incident, see Short, *Mao*. He uses the diary of Snow's wife, Nym Wales, who shared a room with Smedley when the two were together at Yan'an, to describe how Lily Wu began flirting with Mao, putting her hand on his knee.

22. See Short, *Mao*, 369–372. Relying on Nym Wales's diary, Short describes the first time (apparently) that Lily Wu began to throw herself at Mao in the pres-

ence of Wales and Smedley. For extensive quotes from both the diary and Smedley's letters on this incident, see Farnsworth, *Vagabond*, 289–292. According to Smedley's account to Snow, it was the CCP that expelled Lily Wu, not Mao (see the MacKinnon account cited in the note above). Short relies on He Zizhen's reminiscences, which were written down after Mao's death. See Wang, *Jinggang du juan hong*, 208–217.

23. Li Zhisui, *The Private Life of Chairman Mao*, trans. Tai Hung-chao (New York, 1994).

24. Wang Ming, *Mao's Betrayal*, 38–52.

25. Snow not only wrote this in interviews at the time but repeated the point in an addendum to the 1944 edition of *Red Star*, 502. "Telegram of G. Dimitrov to the Central Committee of the Communist Party of China on the Occasion of the Interview of Mao Zedong by the American Journalist Edgar Snow" (October 1939), *Kommunisticheskii Internatsional i Kitaiskaya Revolyutsiya* (Moscow, 1986), 284–285. Translated from the Russian by Nirmal Kumar and quoted in Vijay Singh, "Georgi Dimitrov and the Chinese Revolution." See: http://revolutionarydemocracy.org/rdv2n2/dimitrov.htm.

26. Gregor Benton, *New Fourth Army: Communist Resistance Along the Yangtse and the Huai, 1938–1941* (Berkeley, 1999), 529.

27. Ibid., 590.

28. Ibid., 592. "Telegraph of G. Dimitrov to Mao Zedong" (January 4, 1941), *Kommunisticheskii Internatsional i Kitaiskaya Revolyutsiya* (Moscow, 1986), 291. See Singh, "Georgi Dimitrov and the Chinese Revolution." See also Benton, *New Fourth Army*, 593–596.

29. Chen Yung-fa, "The Blooming Poppy Under the Red Sun: The Yan'an Way and the Opium Trade," in Saich and Van De Ven, *New Perspectives*, 263–298.

30. Tony Saich, "Writing or Rewriting History," in Saich and Van De Ven, *New Perspectives*, 315–316. For a discussion of the movement and some of the appropriate documents, see Boyd Compton, *Mao's China: Party Reform Documents, 1942–44* (Seattle, 1966). Saich, "Writing or Rewriting History," in Saich and Van De Ven, *New Perspectives*, 318.

31. Shum, *Road to Power*, 214.

32. David Apter, "Discourse as Power: Yan'an and the Chinese Revolution," in Saich and Van De Ven, *New Perspectives*, 211.

33. As such he was theoretically one of the so-called Returned Students who had studied together in Moscow with Wang Ming and were therefore supposedly inclined to oppose Mao. In fact the idea that these people were a united faction was, as Thomas Kampen has demonstrated, yet another fiction created at this time by Mao with help from Kang Sheng, in order to highlight Mao's supposed independence from Stalin and to discredit Wang Ming as a tool of the Soviets. Kampen shows the lack of unity in the group and exposes the fiction that there were "28 Bolsheviks." See Kampen, *Mao Zedong* . . . Teiwes, *Formation*, 54.

34. Apter, "Discourse as Power," in Saich and Van De Ven, *New Perspectives*, 211. Mao Zedong, "Talks at the Yenan Forum on Literature and Art" (May 1942), in *Selected Works*, Vol. III, p. 70.

35. For a discussion of this whole affair as well as some of the writings of Wang and those criticizing him at the time, see Dai Qing, *Wang Shiwei and 'Wild Lilies': Rectification and Purges in the Chinese Communist Party, 1942–1944* (Armonk, N.Y., 1994), ed. David E. Apter and Timothy Cheek, trans. Nancy Liu and Lawrence R. Sullivan, documents compiled by Song Jinshou. For a discussion of the execution, see ibid., "Introduction," xix, xxiv. For a more detailed and somewhat different discussion of the events leading up to the execution, and Mao's reaction, see Dai Qing's account on pp. 66–76 of this work.

36. Teiwes, *Formation*, 55.

37. Ibid., 33.

38. Teiwes, *Formation*, 57–59.

39. Shum, *Road to Power*, 225.

40. Mao Zedong, "Some Question Concerning Methods of Leadership" (June 1, 1943), in *Selected Works*, Vol. III, p. 119.

41. Ibid., 119.

42. Teiwes, *Formation*, 17, 22. See also Kampen, *Mao Zedong . . .* , 27. Teiwes, *Formation*, 22.

43. Ibid. See also Kampen, *Mao Zedong . . .* , 104.

44. Teiwes, *Formation*, 22. See also Kampen, *Mao Zedong . . .* , 27, 32.

45. Letter of G. Dimitrov to Mao Zedong on the Situation in the Communist Party of China (December 22, 1943), *Kommunisticheskii Internatsional i Kitaiskaya Revolyutsiya*, 295–296. Teiwes, *Formation*, 43–47.

46. See Sheng, *Western Imperialism*, 104.

47. Ibid.

48. Ibid., 106–109, 110–111.

49. Ibid., 103–118.

50. Sidney Rittenberg and Amanda Bennett, *The Man Who Stayed Behind* (New York, 1993), 18–19.

51. "Telegram of J. V. Stalin to Mao Zedong dated 10th January 1949," NSA Archives. See: http://www.gwu.edu/~nsarchiv/CWIHP/BULLETINS/b6–7a2. htm. "Continuation and the end of the preceding telegram of J. V. Stalin to Mao Zedong dated 11 January 1949," in ibid. "J. V. Stalin's telegram to Mao Zedong dated 14 January 1949," ibid. "J. V. Stalin's telegram to Mao Zedong 15 January 1949," ibid.

52. "Telegram of J. V. Stalin to Mao Zedong dated 10th January 1949," NSA Archives. John S. Service, *Lost Chance in China: The World War II Dispatches of John S. Service* (New York, 1974), 373.

53. Mao Zedong, "Minutes, Conversation Between Mao Zedong and Ambassador Yudin" (July 22, 1958), as translated in *Cold War International History Project*, 56–58. From *Mao Zedong Wanjian Wenxuan*, 322–333. This can be

found at: http://www.gwu.edu/~nsarchiv/CWIHP/BULLETINS/b6–7a10.htm. See also Document I, "Mao's Conversation with Yudin" (March 31, 1956) from the Journal of P. F. Yudin (April 5, 1956), in ibid., 65–68. This can be found at: http://www.gwu.edu/~nsarchiv/CWIHP/BULLETINS/b6–7a11.htm. Mao Zedong, "Talk on Questions of Philosophy," in Stuart Schram, ed., *Chairman Mao Talks to the People* (New York, 1975), 217.

Chapter Six: The People's Republic of China

1. Mao Zedong, "Conversation with a Painter from the Soviet Union" (1949), Michael Y. M. Kau and John K. Leung, ed., *The Writings of Mao Zedong, 1949–1976*, Vol. I, *September 1949–December 1955* (Armonk, N.Y., 1986), 55.

2. This is expressed most forcefully in Harrison Salisbury, *The New Emperors: China in the Era of Mao and Deng* (Boston, 1992). See Li Zhisui, *Private Life*, 99–103, 504–507. Li was upset that Mao refused to brush his teeth but instead just washed them with tea, claiming, "A tiger never brushes his teeth. Why are a tiger's teeth so sharp?"

3. Mao Zedong, "Opening Speech at the First Plenary Session of the CPPCC" (September 21, 1949), in Kau, *Writings of Mao*, Vol. I, p. 5. Mao Zedong, "Proclamation of the Central People's Government of the PRC" (October 1, 1949), in Kau, *Writings of Mao*, Vol. I, pp. 10–11.

4. Ibid., 11.

5. See Sheng, *Western Imperialism*, 181.

6. Mao Zedong, "On the People's Democratic Dictatorship" (June 31, 1949), in *Selected Works*, Vol. IV, p. 415. Huang Hua, "Nanjing jiefang chuqi wo tong Stuart de jici jiechu" ("My Contacts with John Leighton Stuart During the Initial Period After Nanjing's Liberation"), in *Xinzhongguo wanjiao fengyun, 1949–1956 (The diplomatic experiences of the New China)* (Beijing, 1990), 22–31. Mao Zedong, "Farewell, Leighton Stuart" (August 18, 1949), in *Selected Works*, Vol. IV, pp. 433–430.

7. "Conversation Between Stalin and Mao" (December 16, 1949), in *Cold War International History Project Bulletin*, 7. A number of years later, when relations with the Soviets had become strained, Mao during a talk with the Soviet ambassador tried to justify this action by asking, "Why did I ask Stalin to send a scholar [to China] to read my works? Was it because I so lacked confidence that I would even have to have read my works? Not a chance! [My real intention] was to get you over to China to see with your own eyes whether China was really practicing Marxism or only half-hearted toward Marxism." See "Conversation Between Stalin and Mao" (December 16, 1949), in *Cold War International History Project Bulletin*, 5. "Conversation Between Stalin and Mao" (January 22, 1950), in *Cold War International History Project Bulletin*, 8.

8. Mao Zedong, "Orders for the Chinese People's Volunteers" (October 8, 1950), in Kau, *Writings of Mao*, Vol. I, pp. 139–140.

9. Mao Zedong, "Oppose the Bourgeois Ideology in the Party" (August 12, 1953), in Kau, *Writings of Mao*, Vol. I, p. 371.

10. Mao Zedong, "Speech on the Victory in Resist U.S. Aggression and Aid Korea Movement" (September 12, 1953), in Kau, *Writings of Mao*, Vol. I, p. 389.

11. Mao Zedong, "Comments on Suppressing and Liquidating Counterrevolutionaries" (September 27, 1950), in Kau, *Writings of Mao*, Vol. I, pp. 136–137. Mao Zedong, "Comments on Suppressing and Liquidating Counterrevolutionaries" (March 24, 1951), in Kau, *Writings of Mao*, Vol. I, p. 178. Mao Zedong, "Comment on Suppressing and Liquidating Counterrevolutionaries" (December 9, 1950), in Kau, *Writings of Mao*, Vol. I, p. 152.

12. Mao Zedong, "Comments on Suppressing and Liquidating Counterrevolutionaries" (March 9, 1951), in Kau, *Writings of Mao*, Vol. I, p. 176. Mao Zedong, "Letter to Huang Yanpei" (February 17, 1950), in Kau, *Writings of Mao*, Vol. I, p. 168.

13. Mao Zedong, "Soliciting Suggestions on the Question of Strategy for Dealing with Rich Peasants" (March 12, 1950), in Kau, *Writings of Mao*, Vol. I, pp. 67–68. Mao Zedong, "Struggle for a Fundamental Turn for the Better in the Financial and Economic Situation in the Country" (June 6, 1950), in Kau, *Writings of Mao*, Vol. I, pp. 100, 101.

14. Mao Zedong, "Letter to Rao Shushi and Others" (March 18, 1951), in Kau, *Writings of Mao*, Vol. I, p. 177.

15. Mao Zedong, "On the 'Three-Anti's' and 'Five-Anti's' Struggles" (November 1951–March 1952), in Kau, *Writings of Mao*, Vol. I, pp. 236, 241.

16. Nicolas Lardy, "Economic Recovery and the First Five-Year Plan," in Roderick MacFarquhar and John K. Fairbank, ed., *The Cambridge History of China*, Vol. XIV (New York, 1987), pp. 149–150.

17. Mao Zedong, "Letter to Huang Yanpei" (September 5, 1952), in Kau, *Writings of Mao*, Vol. I, p. 283. See the discussion in Chapter 5.

18. Roderick MacFarquhar, *The Origins of the Cultural Revolution, 3: The Coming of the Cataclysm, 1961–1966* (New York, 1997), 326.

19. Mao Zedong, "Closing Speech of the Fourth Session of the First National Committee of the CPPCC (February 7, 1953), in Kau, *Writings of Mao*, Vol. I, p. 318.

20. Suzanne Pepper, "Education for the New Order," in MacFarquhar, *Cambridge History*, Vol. XIV, pp. 1209–1210. Mao Zedong, "Speech on the Youth League" (June 30, 1953), in Kau, *Writings of Mao*, Vol. I, pp. 352–353.

21. Mao Zedong, "Letter to Zhou Enlai" (June 14, 1952), in Kau, *Writings of Mao*, Vol. I, p. 269.

22. See the discussion of this affair in Frederick C. Teiwes, *Politics at Mao's Court* (Armonk, N.Y., 1990).

23. See, for instance, Carl Riskin, *China's Political Economy: The Quest for Development Since 1949* (New York, 1988), 58, 53.

24. Mao Zedong, "Criticize the Right-Deviationist Viewpoints That Depart from the General Line" (June 15, 1953), in Kau, *Writings of Mao*, Vol. I, pp. 348–349.

25. Mao Zedong, "Oppose the Bourgeois Ideology in the Party" (August 12, 1953), in Kau, *Writings of Mao*, Vol. I, p. 367. Mao Zedong, "Speech on Mutual Aid and Cooperativization in Agriculture" (October 15, 1953), in Kau, *Writings of Mao*, Vol. I, p. 415.

26. Mao Zedong, "On the Cooperativization of Agriculture" (July 31, 1955), in Kau, *Writings of Mao*, Vol. I, p. 591.

27. Ibid., 601. Mao Zedong, "The Debate over Agricultural Cooperativization and the Present Class Struggle" (October 11, 1955), in Kau, *Writings of Mao*, Vol. I, p. 634.

28. Frederick Teiwes, "Establishment and Consolidation of the New Regime," in MacFarquhar, *Cambridge History*, Vol. XIV, p. 116.

29. Mao Zedong, "Talk on Opposing Right-Deviation and Conservatism" (December 6, 1955), in Kau, *Writings of Mao*, Vol. I, p. 680. Mao Zedong, "Circular Requesting Opinions on the Seventeen Articles on Agricultural World" (December 21, 1955), in Kau, *Writings of Mao*, Vol. I, p. 686.

30. Teiwes, "Establishment and Consolidation of the New Region," in Mac-Farquhar, *Cambridge History*, Vol. XIV, p. 117. Mao Zedong, "Talk on Opposing Right-Deviation and Conservatism," (December 6, 1955), in Kau, *Writings of Mao*, Vol. I, p. 680. Mao Zedong, "Circular Requesting Opinions on the Seventeen Articles on Agricultural World," 688.

31. Mao Zedong, "Talk on Opposing Right-Deviation and Conservatism," (December 6, 1955), in Kau, *Writings of Mao*, Vol. I, p. 680.

32. Ibid., 682.

33. Roderick MacFarquhar, *The Origins of the Cultural Revolution, 1: Contradictions Among the People, 1956–1957* (New York, 1974), 19–25. Lardy, "Economic Recovery and the First Five-Year Plan," in MacFarquhar, *Cambridge History*, Vol. XIV, p. 155.

34. Ibid., 156.

35. See Frederick C. Teiwes, "Mao and His Lieutenants," *Australian Journal of Chinese Affairs* 19/20 (January–July 1988), 7–15. Mao Zedong, "Talks at the Chengdu Conference" (March 1958), in Schram, *Chairman Mao*, 98. For a discussion of what Stalinism entails, particularly in the Chinese context, see Maurice Meisner, "Stalinism in the History of the Chinese Communist Party," in Dirlik, *Critical Perspectives*, 186–188. Although Meisner acknowledges that there is no accepted definition of Stalinism, he emphasizes "the promotion of an autonomous bureaucratic state" dominated by "a monolithic party (and its Leader)," "the pursuit of conservative social policies which aim to create an urban elite of professional managers and technocrats," and such items as "the

personality cult" and the "command economy." See Chapter 3, page 34 for a discussion of the sick leave issue.

36. Mao Zedong, "Talks at the Chengdu Conference" (March 1958), in Schram, *Chairman Mao*, 99.

Chapter Seven: The Great Leap into Cataclysm

1. This is only part of the poem. The translation is from Jerome Chen, *Mao and the Chinese Revolution* (New York, 1965), 346.

2. See Teiwes, "Mao and His Lieutenants." For a discussion of the comparison, see MacFarquhar, *Origins*, 3: *The Coming of the Cataclysm*, 324, 331–332.

3. See Timothy Cheek, *Propaganda and Culture in Mao's China: Deng Tuo and the Intelligentsia* (Oxford, England, 1997), 178–181. Jonathan Spence nicely summarizes this scene in *Mao Zedong*, 142. For an excerpt of Mao's criticisms of the paper, see Mao Zedong, "Criticism of Renmin ribao" (April 1957), in Kau, *Writings of Mao*, Vol. II, pp. 515–516.

4. Mao Zedong, "Comment on Stalin" (April 6, 1956), in Kau, *Writings of Mao*, Vol. II, p. 41. See the end of Chapter 6.

5. MacFarquhar, *Origins*, 1: *Contradictions Among the People*, 46. In 1996, Mao's deputy Chen Yi called Mao someone who "doesn't remember old hatred and evils." See *Wenge fengyuan* (*Cultural Revolution Storm*), no. 4, 1967. Quoted in Teiwes, "Mao and His Lieutenants," 1.

6. Mao Zedong, "On the Ten Great Relationships," in Schram, *Chairman Mao*, 81.

7. Ibid., 72, 75. Mao Zedong, "Talk at Enlarged Meeting of the Political Bureau" (April 1956), in Kau, *Writings of Mao*, Vol. II, p. 69.

8. Mao Zedong, "Reinforce the Unity of the Party and Carry Forward the Party Traditions" (August 30, 1956), in Kau, *Writings of Mao*, Vol. II, p. 114.

9. Mao Zedong, "Talk at Enlarged Meeting of the Political Bureau" (April 1956), in Kau, *Writings of Mao*, Vol. II, p. 70.

10. Mao Zedong, "Speech at the Second Plenum of the Eighth Central Committee" (November 15, 1956), *wansui* version, in Kau, *Writings of Mao*, Vol. II, pp. 188, 189. This quote is from the *wansui* version of the speech, which is presumably the unedited unofficial version. In the official version published in *Xuanji* after editing, Mao supposedly acknowledged that when the Dalai Lama, who was then in Beijing, returned to Tibet he might go into exile. He said the Chinese should not try to stop him: "If a person no longer likes your place and wants to run away, let him go. What harm to us is there if he runs away? There's no harm except that he will curse us. . . . I don't think it is good for a person to be afraid of being cursed." Ibid., 170. Mao said something similar in the unedited version of his speech a few months later, referring not to the Tibetan rebellion but to the Dalai Lama's journey to a conference in India, from which he threat-

ened not to return. See Mao Zedong, "Summary Address for the Conference of Provincial, Municipal, and Autonomous Region Party Secretaries" (January 27, 1957), in Kau, *Writings of Mao*, Vol. II, p. 281.

11. For a discussion of the remarkable variety of criticism that was eventually raised, see Roderick MacFarquhar, ed., *The Hundred Flowers Campaign and the Chinese Intellectuals* (New York, 1960); Merle Goldman, *Literary Dissent in Communist China* (Cambridge, Mass., 1967); and MacFarquhar, *Origins*, 1: *Contradictions Among the People*.

12. Mao Zedong, "Summary Address for the Conference of Provincial, Municipal, and Autonomous Region Party Secretaries" (January 18, 1957), in Kau, *Writings of Mao*, Vol. II, p. 242.

13. Ibid., 234.

14. Teiwes, "Mao and His Lieutenants," 1-20.

15. Mao Zedong, "Summary Address for the Conference of Provincial, Municipal, and Autonomous Region Party Secretaries" (January 27, 1957), in Kau, *Writings of Mao*, Vol. II, p. 281. This is the unofficial *wansui* version.

16. Mao Zedong, "Interjections at Conference of Provincial and Municipal Party Secretaries" (January 1957), in Kau, *Writings of Mao*, Vol. II, p. 290.

17. Mao Zedong, "On the Correct Handling of Contradictions Among the People" (Speaking Notes), in Roderick MacFarquhar, Timothy Cheek, and Eugene Wu, ed., *The Secret Speeches of Chairman Mao: From the Hundred Flowers to the Great Leap Forward* (Cambridge, Mass., 1989), 175, 173.

18. For a discussion of Liu's failure to appear in any of the photographs and of the general lack of enthusiasm of many of Mao's colleagues, see MacFarquhar, *Origins*, 1: *Contradictions Among the People*, 189-196. In a later article, MacFarquhar discusses Liu's presence at the speech but his failure to appear in the picture. See MacFarquhar, "The Secret Speeches of Chairman Mao," in MacFarquhar, *Secret Speeches*, 11.

19. Mao Zedong, "Concluding Remarks at the Supreme State Conference" (March 1, 1957), in Kau, *Writings of Mao*, Vol. II, p. 355.

20. See note 11.

21. MacFarquhar, *Origins*, 1: *Contradictions Among the People*, 223.

22. Mao Zedong, "Concerning Disturbances Among Workers" (May 13, 1957), in Kau, *Writings of Mao*, Vol. II, pp. 541-555. Elizabeth J. Perry, "Shanghai's Strike Wave of 1957," in Timothy Cheek and Tony Saich, ed., *New Perspectives on State Socialism in China* (Armonk, N.Y., 1997), 238.

23. MacFarquhar, *Origins*, 1: *Contradictions Among the People*, 224. Mao Zedong, "Concerning Disturbances Among Workers" (May 13, 1957), in Kau, *Writings of Mao*, Vol. II, pp. 541-555.

24. Mao Zedong, "The Bourgeois Orientation of *Wenhui bao* Should Be Criticized" (July 1, 1957), in Kau, *Writings of Mao*, Vol. II, p. 596. Mao Zedong, "Repel the Attacks of the Bourgeois Rightists" (July 9, 1957), in Kau, *Writings of Mao*, Vol. II, pp. 632-633.

25. Mao Zedong, "Interjections at a Meeting During the Qingdao Conference" (July 17, 1957), in Kau, *Writings of Mao*, Vol. II, p. 638.

26. Benjamin Yang, *Deng: A Political Biography* (Armonk, N.Y., 1998), 140. David Bachman, *Bureaucracy, Economy, and Leadership in China: The Institutional Origins of the Great Leap Forward* (Cambridge, England, 1991), 151.

27. MacFarquhar, *Origins*, 1: *Contradictions Among the People*, 293.

28. Kenneth Lieberthal, "The Great Leap Forward and the Split in the Yenan Leadership," in MacFarquhar, *Cambridge History*, Vol. XIV, p. 299.

29. Frederick C. Teiwes with Warren Sun, "The Politics of an 'Un-Maoist' Interlude: The Case of Opposing Rash Advance, 1956–1957," in Cheek, *New Perspectives*, 172–173. Bachman, *Bureaucracy*, 205. Teiwes's explanation (see note 26) somewhat contradicts that of Bachman. Bachman argues that institutional imperatives led to the Great Leap; Teiwes says it was Mao, spurred on by local leaders. Mao Zedong, "Speech at the Conclusion of the Third Plenum of the Eighth Central Committee, Version II" (October 9, 1957), in Kau, *Writings of Mao*, Vol. II, p. 720–721.

30. MacFarquhar, *Origins*, 2: *The Great Leap Forward*, 16. See also Michael Schoenhals, *Salationist Socialism: Mao Zedong and the Great Leap Forward 1958* (Stockholm, 1987), 1. Mao discusses this in the speech he gave in Moscow. See Mao Zedong, "Speech at the Congress of Communist Parties and Workers Parties in Socialist Countries" (November 18, 1957), in Kau, *Writings of Mao*, Vol. II, p. 78.

31. Bachman, *Bureaucracy*, 206.

32. MacFarquhar, *Origins*, 3: *The Coming of the Cataclysm*, 146. In spite of his post-1976 image as a moderate alternative to Mao, as late as 1962, well after the program had been proven a dismal failure, Liu defended the Great Leap Forward at length in a speech excluded from his posthumously published works. The statement regarding Britain was first made on November 18, 1957. Mao Zedong, "Speech at the Congress of Communist Parties and Workers Parties in Socialist Countries" (November 18, 1957), in Kau, *Writings of Mao*, Vol. II, p. 78. It was repeated more famously in Mao Zedong, "Speech at the Supreme State Conference" (January 28, 1958), in Schram, *Chairman Mao*, 91. Dali Yang, *Calamity and Reform in China: State, Rural Society, and Institutional Change Since the Great Leap Famine* (Stanford, 1996), 34. Yang, *Deng*, 143.

33. See Bachman, *Bureaucracy*, 94–96.

34. Mao Zedong, "Fan langfei fan baoshou shi dangqian zhengfen yundong de zhongxin renwu" ("To oppose waste and conservatism is the central task of the Rectification Movement at present"), from *Renmin ribao* (*People's Daily*), February 18, 1958, as reprinted in *Mao Zedong Sisiang wansui* (Beijing, 1967), 139–142.

35. See Schoenhals, *Salationist Socialism*, 43–66.

36. Quoted in Edward Friedman, Paul G. Pickowicz, and Mark Selden, *Chinese Village, Socialist State* (New Haven, 1991), 218.

37. MacFarquhar, *Origins*, 2: *The Great Leap Forward*, 20–21. Li Zhisui, *Private Life*, 278.

38. Mao Zedong, May 8, 1958, 290. Translated in Schoenhals, *Salationist Socialism*, 56.

39. Li Zhisui, *Private Life*, 247.

40. MacFarquhar, *Origins*, 2: *The Great Leap Forward*, 21–24, 305. "Farewell to the God of Plagues." For the translation, see Chen, *Mao*, 349. See David Lampton, "Health Policy During the Great Leap Forward," *China Quarterly* 60 (October–December 1974), 668–698.

41. MacFarquhar, *Origins*, 2: *The Great Leap Forward*, 81, 78.

42. Mao Zedong, "On the Correct Handling of Contradictions Among the People" (Speaking Notes), in MacFarquhar, *Secret Speeches*, 161. Quoted in Maurice Meisner, *Mao's China and After* (New York, 1986), 223. MacFarquhar, *Origins*, 2: *The Great Leap Forward*, 318.

43. Suzanne Pepper, "New Directions in Education," in MacFarquhar, *Cambridge History*, Vol. XIV, p. 404.

44. MacFarquhar, *Origins*, 2: *The Great Leap Forward*, 82–88.

45. See the discussion in Dali Yang, *Calamity and Reform*, 42–62.

46. See MacFarquhar, *Origins*, 2: *The Great Leap Forward*, 124–128.

47. Ibid., 88–90.

48. See the discussion in Schoenhals, *Salationist Socialism*, 151–152. Mao Zedong, "Talks at the Wuchang Conference" (November 21–23, 1958), in MacFarquhar, *Secret Speeches*, 494–515.

49. See MacFarquhar, *Origins*, 2: *The Great Leap Forward*, 152–153. Mao Zedong, "Talks at the First Zhengzhou Conference" (November 6, 1958), in MacFarquhar, *Secret Speeches*, 448, 469. See also 456–479 for Mao's use of Stalin to argue against the idea of moving ahead with the establishment of a Communist means of production.

50. See MacFarquhar, *Origins*, 2: *The Great Leap Forward*, 152–153.

51. See ibid., 163–170.

52. As quoted in MacFarquhar, *Origins*, 1: *Contradictions Among the People*, 136, 72.

53. MacFarquhar, *Origins*, 2: *The Great Leap Forward*, 225–228.

54. Ibid., 204–206, 170. Li Zhisui, *Private Life*, 311–312.

55. Mao Zedong, "Return to Shaoshan," in Chen, *Mao*, 350. See also MacFarquhar, *Origins*, 2: *The Great Leap Forward*, 187–192. Quoted in Dali Yang, "Surviving the Great Leap Famine," in Cheek, *New Perspectives*, 269.

56. Li, *Private Life*, 314. Mao Zedong, "Speech at the Lushan Conference" (July 23, 1959), as translated in Schram, *Chairman Mao*, 139.

57. Ibid., 131, 143.

58. Ibid., 145. Dali Yang, *Calamity and Reform*, 54–62. Mao Zedong, "Speech at the Lushan Conference" (July 23, 1959), as translated in Schram, *Chairman Mao*, 140.

59. Ibid., 139.

60. Li Zhisui, *Private Life*, 317. MacFarquhar, *Origins*, 2: *The Great Leap Forward*, 234–236, 239.

61. Ibid., 228–233.

62. Mao Zedong, "Speech at the Lushan Conference" (July 23, 1959), as translated in Schram, *Chairman Mao*, 144.

63. Dali Yang, *Calamity and Reform*, 53.

64. Mao Zedong, "Speech at the Lushan Conference" (July 23, 1959), as translated in Schram, *Chairman Mao*, 139. Quoted in Schoenhals, *Salationist Socialism*, 170.

65. See Kenneth Lieberthal, "The Great Leap Forward and the Split in the Yenan Leadership," in MacFarquhar, *Cambridge History*, Vol. XIV, p. 318. For a full discussion of this issue, see also Jasper Becker, *Hungry Ghosts: Mao's Secret Famine* (New York, 1996). Dali Yang, *Calamity and Reform*, 53.

66. Quan Yanchi, *Mao Zedong yu Heluxiaofu* (*Mao Zedung and Khrushchev*) (Jilin, 1989), 126–128. Li Zhisui, *Private Life*, 261.

67. See William Taubman, "Khrushchev vs. Mao: A Preliminary Sketch of the Role of Personality in the Sino-Soviet Split," www.gwu.edu/~nsarchiv/CWIHP/BULLETINS/b8–9a23.htm.

68. MacFarquhar, *Origins*, 2: *The Great Leap Forward*, 298, 293.

69. See Dali Yang, *Calamity and Reform*, 71–81. See also MacFarquhar, *Origins*, 2: *The Great Leap Forward*, 324.

70. MacFarquhar, *Origins*, 3: *The Coming of the Cataclysm*, 105.

71. Mao Zedong, "Speech at the Tenth Plenum of the Eighth Central Committee" (September 24, 1962), in Schram, *Chairman Mao*, 194.

72. Dali Yang, *Calamity and Reform*, viii, 241.

73. MacFarquhar, *Origins*, 1: *Contradictions Among the People*, 133. Friedman, *Chinese Village*, 272.

Chapter Eight: The Cultural Revolution Revisited

1. Richard Baum with Louise B. Bennett, ed., *China in Ferment: Perspectives on the Cultural Revolution* (Englewood Cliffs, N.J., 1971), 2. Snow, *Long Revolution*, 14. This is based on Snow's interview with Zhou Enlai.

2. Mao Zedong, "Talk on Questions of Philosophy" in Schram, *Chairman Mao*, 217.

3. See Andrew Walder, "Actually Existing Maoism," *Australian Journal of Chinese Affairs* 18 (July 1987), 158.

4. Ibid., 160, 162.

5. See Graham Young, "Mao Zedong and the Class Struggle in Socialist Society," *Australian Journal of Chinese Affairs* 16 (July 1986), 41–80.

6. Mao Zedong, "Dui chuan guo wen lian he suo zhu ge xie hui zheng feng de zhishi" ("Instructions for the Rectification of the Country's Cultural Associa-

tions") (June 27, 1964), in *Mao Zedong Sixiang Wansui* (*Long Live Mao's Thoughts*), (Beijing, 1967), 220.

7. Dongping Han, "Impact of the Cultural Revolution on Rural Education and Economic Development," *Modern China*, Vol. 27, no. 1 (January 2001), 59–90.

8. *On Khrushchev's Phoney Communism and Its Historical Lessons for the Future* (Beijing, 1964), 30, 63, 67.

9. "Draft Resolution of the Central Committee of the Chinese Communist Party on Some Problems in Current Rural Work," as translated in Richard Baum and Frederick C. Teiwes, *Ssu-Ch'ing: The Socialist Education Movement of 1962–1966* (Berkeley, 1968), 58–59.

10. Ibid., 70.

11. "Some Concrete Policy Formulations of the Central Committee of the Chinese Communist Party in the Rural Socialist Education Movement," as translated in Baum, *Ssu-Ch'ing*, 105.

12. "Chinese Communist Party Central Document No. (65) 026," as translated in Baum, *Ssu-Ch'ing*, 125.

13. Ibid., 120.

14. Snow, *Long Revolution*, 17, 136. Zhou Enlai disclosed to Snow that Mao had decided to purge Liu at the time he presented his "Twenty-three Articles." As Lowell Dittmer has suggested, this may simply have been a "post hoc explanation by the victors." See Lowell Dittmer, *Liu Shao-ch'i and the Chinese Cultural Revolution* (Armonk, N.Y., 1998), 47. In his only public talk about his motives for launching the Cultural Revolution, Mao noted: "It was at the time of the Twenty-three Articles that my vigilance was aroused." See Mao Zedong, "Talk of the Central Work Conference" (October 25, 1966), translated in Schram, *Chairman Mao*, 270. MacFarquhar, *Origins, 3: The Coming of the Cataclysm*, 433.

15. Schram, *Chairman Mao*, "Remarks at the Spring Festival" (February 13, 1964), 209. Ibid., 203–205. See also in "Talks with Mao Yuan-hsin," in Schram, *Chairman Mao*, 247–248. Actually Mao had been making comments like this for years.

16. Dongping Han, *The Unknown Cultural Revolution: Educational Reforms and Their Impact on China's Rural Development* (New York, 2000), 97. "Decision of the Central Committee of the Chinese Communist Party Concerning the Great Proletarian Cultural Revolution" (Adopted on August 8, 1966), in *Important Documents on the Great Proletarian Cultural Revolution in China* (Peking, 1970), 148.

17. Dongping Han, "Impact of the Cultural Revolution on Rural Education and Economic Development," *Modern China* 27, no. 1 (January 2001), 63–64.

18. Dongping Han, *Unknown Cultural Revolution*, ix.

19. Ibid., 88. See also Pepper, "Education," in MacFarquhar, *Cambridge History*, Vol. XV, p. 416.

20. Pepper, "Education," in MacFarquhar, *Cambridge History*, Vol. XV, pp. 570, 573.

21. "Decision of the Central Committee of the Chinese Communist Party" (May 16, 1966), in *Important Documents on the Great Proletarian Cultural Revolution in China*, 123–124.

22. Di Bai, "Feminist Brave New World: The Cultural Revolution Model Theater Revisited" (Ph.D. dissertation, Ohio State University, 1997), 98.

23. See http://www.sino.uni-heidelberg.de/conf/propaganda/musik.html. This exhibit: "Rethinking Cultural Revolution Culture." The audio-visual materials and this written document were collectively produced and revised by David Carnochan, Barbara Mittler, Sue Tuohy, and Jeffrey Wasserstrom with thanks to the assistance of Peter Alyea, John Fenn, Michael Schoenhals, Sarah Stevens, and Liana Zhou. Workshop 22.–24. 2. 2001 Exhibition 31.1.–28. 2. 2001, Universitätsmuseum Heidelberg, "Picturing Power: Art and Propaganda in the Great Proletarian Cultural Revolution." The website contains the best summary I have seen of the various writings that reassess the culture of the Cultural Revolution.

24. Ibid.

25. Ibid. See also Bonnie S. McDougall, "Writers and Performers, Their Works, and Their Audiences in the First Three Decades," in Bonnie S. McDougall, ed., *Popular Chinese Literature and Performing Art in the People's Republic of China*, 1949–1979 (Berkeley, 1979), 293. According to Richard Kraus's count there were five more operas as well as a piano concerto, a symphony, and a number of other different works. See Richard Kraus, "Arts Policies of the Cultural Revolution: The Rise and Fall of Culture Minister Yu Yaiyong," in Joseph, *New Perspectives*, 233.

26. Vivian Wagner, "Songs of the Red Guards: Keywords Set to Music," *Indiana East Asian Working Paper Series on Language and Politics in Modern China* (Winter 1996).

27. Di Bai, "Feminist Brave New World," 101. For a discussion of the idealistic heroism embedded in the operas of the Cultural Revolution and their attempt to change consciousness, see Ellen R. Judd, "Dramas of Passion: Heroism in the Cultural Revolution's Model Operas," in Joseph, *New Perspectives*, 233.

28. Di Bai, "Feminist Brave New World," 99–100, 184–185.

29. Li Zhisui, *Private Life*, 358–359.

30. Yao Wenyuan, "On the New Historical Play *Dismissal of Hai Rui*," translated in Ralph C. Croizier, ed., *China's Cultural Legacy and Communism* (New York, 1970), 287, 289.

31. MacFarquhar, *Origins*, 3: *The Coming of the Cataclysm* (New York, 1997), 386. Teiwes, *Politics*, lx–lxi.

32. Lowell Dittmer has argued that it is unlikely that Mao initially set out to purge Peng. See Dittmer, *Liu Shao-ch'i*, 55. MacFarquhar has argued the opposite; see his *Origins*, 3: *The Coming of the Cataclysm*, 440–460. During the 1990s Peng, who survived the Cultural Revolution, became the chairman of the Na-

tional People's Congress. He helped implement a system of democratic elections
for village office that gave the peasants some power over their own affairs and
began the process of educating them about the political and economic system in
which they lived.

33. Quoted in Teiwes, *Tragedy of Lin Biao*, 62. Yao Wenyuan, "The Three
Family Village," translated in *The Great Socialist Revolution in China* (Beijing,
1966), Vol. I, pp. 29–69. This article claimed there was a plot by Deng Tuo, Wu
Han, and Liao Mosha, all important figures in the Beijing municipal government, to satirize Mao in a series of veiled attacks. For a discussion of the charges
and their apparent lack of validity, see MacFarquhar, *Origins*, 3: *The Coming of
the Cataclysm*, 249–258.

34. MacFarquhar, *Origins*, 3: *The Coming of the Cataclysm*, 324.

35. Liu Guokai, *A Brief Analysis of the Cultural Revolution*, ed. Anita Chan
(Armonk, N.Y., 1987), 18.

36. Ibid., 23. Mao Zedong, "Speech at a Meeting with Regional Secretaries
and Members of the Cultural Revolution Group" (July 22, 1966), in Schram,
Chairman Mao, 259.

37. Mao Zedong, "Paoda siling bu" ("Bombard the Headquarters") (August
5, 1966), *Mao Zedong sisiang wansui* (June 1967), 420–421.

38. Liu Guokai, *Brief Analysis*, 31–32. For a full discussion of the background
to the Red Guards, see Hong Yong Lee, *The Politics of the Chinese Cultural Revolution: A Case Study* (Berkeley, 1978). See also Stanley Rosen, *Red Guard Factionalism and the Cultural Revolution in Guangzhou* (Boulder, Colo., 1982). Liu
Guokai, *Brief Analysis*, 31–45. Marc J. Blecher and Gordon White, *Micropolitics
in Contemporary China: A Technical Unit During and After the Cultural Revolution* (Armonk, N.Y., 1979). After the present book was at press, an interesting new
essay was published by Andrew G. Walder, "Beijing Red Guard Factionalism:
Social Interpretations Reconsidered," *Journal of Asian Studies*, Vol. 61, no. 2,
pp. 437–471.

39. Liu Guokai, *Brief Analysis*, 31–45.

40. Michael Schoenhals, "The Central Case Examination Group
(1966–1979)," *China Quarterly* (1996), 87–111. For a summary of the deaths of
high officials like Liu, see Harry Harding, "The Cultural Revolution: China in
Turmoil, 1966–1969," in MacFarquhar, *Cambridge History*, Vol. XV, pp. 213–214.

41. As Philip Short succinctly put it: "Unlike Stalin, Mao appears to have
taken no interest in the sordid details of his victims' treatment." *Mao*, 570. Frederick Teiwes has noted that unlike Stalin, Mao did not pore over the list of the
names of his victims. See the interview with Frederick Teiwes by Borge Bakken,
"An Interview with Frederick Teiwes: On the Memoirs of Mao's Physician,"
Nordic Newsletter of Asian Studies, no. 3 (October 1996). Lynn T. White III,
"The Cultural Revolution as an Unintended Result of Administrative Policies,"
in William A. Joseph, Christine P. W. Wong, and David Zweig, *New Perspectives
on the Cultural Revolution* (Cambridge, Mass., 1991), 83–104. For a discussion of
how Chinese intellectuals similarly question the interpretation that just a few

people at the top of their society could be responsible for all this violence and acknowledge that it was the general culture and hatred of the bureaucracy that had developed since 1949, see Perry Link, *Evening Chats in Beijing: Probing China's Predicament* (New York, 1992), 152–154. Tony Saich, "The Historical Origins of the Cultural Revolution," *China Information*, Vol. XII, no. 1/2 (Summer/Autumn 1997), 34.

42. Mao Zedong, "Talk at the Reform Meeting" (October 24, 1966), in Schram, *Chairman Mao*, 267. See Huang Zhang, "The Special Case Inquiry," *Chinese Law and Government*, Vol. 32, no. 3 (May–June 1999), 48–93.

43. Liu Guokai, *Brief Analysis*, 46.

44. Elizabeth J. Perry, *Challenging the Mandate of Heaven: Social Protest and State Power in China* (Armonk, N.Y., 2002), 238–269.

45. Mao Zedong, "Talk at Three Meetings with Zhang Chunqiao and Yao Wenyuan" (February 1967), in Schram, *Chairman Mao*, 277.

46. Liu Guokai, *Brief Analysis*, 46. For a discussion of the differing demands of the various groups of workers who focused on "socioeconomic grievances," see Elizabeth J. Perry and Li Xun, *Proletarian Power: Shanghai in the Cultural Revolution* (Boulder, Colo., 1997), especially 97–117.

47. Perry, *Proletarian Power*, 145.

48. Dongping Han, *Unknown Cultural Revolution*, 70.

49. David Zweig, *Agrarian Radicalism in China*, 1968–1981 (Cambridge, Mass., 1989), p. 41. David Zweig, "Agrarian Radicalism as a Rural Development Strategy, 1968–1978," in Joseph, *New Perspectives*, 73, 78–79.

50. See Xaoxia Gong, "Perpetual Victims: The Persecution of the 'Bad Classes' During the Cultural Revolution," *China Information*, Vol. XI, no. 2–3 (Autumn/Winter 1996–1997), 43–51. For an informative discussion of the rural violence that plagued China in the 1980s with the breakdown of the old collective structures and the increasingly unequal distribution of wealth, see Perry, *Challenging the Mandate*, 290–302. See also Jonathan Unger, "Cultural Revolution Conflict in the Villages," *China Quarterly* (1998), 153, 82–106. Dali Yang, *Calamity and Reform*, 98.

51. Ibid., 101.

52. Ibid., 98–120. For a discussion of the process in which the Dazhai model was severely criticized and abolished, see Tang Tsou, Marc Blecher, and Mitch Meisner, "The Responsibility System in Agriculture: Its Implementation in Xiyang and Dazhai," *Modern China* 8, no. 1 (January 1982). For a discussion of how the criticism was politically motivated and ignored Dazhai's real achievements, see William Hinton, "Mao's Beloved Model Village," *Time Asia* (September 27, 1999), Vol. 154, no. 12. For a fascinating discussion of both the pros and cons of the Dazhai campaign, especially its effect on women, see Xin-An Lu, "Dazhai: Imagistic Rhetoric as a Cultural Instrument," *American Communication Journal*, Vol. 5, issue 1 (Fall 2001). For new developments in Dazhai, see John Schauble, "Iron Lady of Dazhai Restores Her Good Name," *The Age*, April 28, 2000.

53. David Zweig, "Agrarian Radicalism," in Joseph, *New Perspectives*, 78–79. William A. Joseph, Christine P. W. Wong, and David Zweig, "Introduction," in Joseph, *New Perspectives*, 7. Dali Yang, *Calamity and Reform*, 147. See also the discussion in "Introduction" to Joseph, *New Perspectives*.

54. Dongping Han, "Impact of the Cultural Revolution on Rural Education and Economic Development," *Modern China*, Vol. 27, no. 1 (January 2001), 80.

55. Philip Huang, *The Peasant Family and Rural Development in the Yangzi Delta*, 1350–1988 (Stanford, 1990). Dwight Perkins, "China's Economic Policy and Performance," in MacFarquhar, *Cambridge History*, Vol. XV, p. 482.

56. Lynn T. White III, *Unstately Power: Local Causes of China's Economic Reforms* (Armonk, N.Y., 1998), Vol. I, p. 85.

57. Dali Yang, *Calamity and Reform*, 119–120.

58. White, *Unstately Power*, Vol. I, pp. 85–89.

59. See, for example, *Zhongguo tongji nianjian* (*Statistical Yearbook of China*), 1986, 274. Some outside researchers have suggested the rate may have been even higher. Rivkin, for instance, has estimated an annual industrial growth rate for the period of 10.4 percent. See Riskin, *Political Economy*, 185. See also Chapter 9.

60. White, *Unstately Power*, Vol. I, p. 12. See also 12–17.

61. Christine Wong, "The Maoist 'Model' Reconsidered: Local Self-Reliance and the Financing of Rural Industrialization," in Joseph, *New Perspectives*, 183–196.

62. Barry Naughton, "Industrial Policy During the Cultural Revolution: Military Preparation, Decentralization, and Leaps Forward," in Joseph, *New Perspectives*, 166.

63. White, *Unstately Power*, Vol. I, p. 258.

64. Carl Riskin, "Neither Plan Nor Market: Mao's Political Economy," in Joseph, *New Perspectives*, 148.

65. Naughton, "Industrial Policy During the Cultural Revolution," in Joseph, *New Perspectives*, 176.

66. Shaoguang Wang, "'New Trends of Thought' on the Cultural Revolution," *Journal of Contemporary China*, Vol. 8, no. 21 (July 1999), 197–219.

67. Translated in Liu Guokai, *Brief Analysis*, 116.

68. Shaoguang Wang, "'New Trends of Thought,'" 197–219. Lisa Rofel has noted that in the factory she studied, the workers willing to take political action against the autocratic factory authorities, the workers who did not automatically assume that "one gender or another would easily enact those politics," and those more aware of worker creativity were the ones who had come of age during the Cultural Revolution. See Lisa Rofel, *Other Modernities: Gendered Yearnings in China After Socialism* (Berkeley, 1999), 173–187, especially 174–175 for the quotes. For the article by Mao, see Mao Zedong, "The Great Union of the Popular Masses" (July 24, July 28, August 4, 1919), in Schram, *Mao's Road to Power*, Vol. I, pp. 378–389.

69. Lowell Dittmer, "Reconstructing China's Cultural Revolution," *China Information*, Vol. XI, no. 2–3 (Autumn/Winter 1996–1997), 17–18.

70. Xueping Zhong, Wang Zheng, and Di Bai, ed., "Introduction," *Some of Us: Chinese Women Growing Up in the Mao Era* (New Brunswick, N.J., 2001), xxx.

71. Wang Zheng, "Call Me Qingnian but Not Funu," in Xueping Zhong, *Some of Us*, 52.

72. Bill Brugger, "The Cultural Revolution from a Post-1989 Perspective: The Significance of Counterpoint Values," *China Information*, Vol. XI, no. 2–3 (Autumn/Winter 1996–1997), 105.

73. "Introduction," Xueping Zhong, *Some of Us*, xi.

74. Henry Kissinger, *The White House Years* (Boston, 1979), 702–703.

75. See the table in Rivkin, *Political Economy*, 317.

76. Mao Zedong, "Talk at the Central Work Conference" (October 25, 1966), in Schram, *Chairman Mao*, 270–274. See also Michael Schoenhals, *China's Cultural Revolution, 1966–1969: Not a Dinner Party* (Armonk, N.Y., 1996), 5–9.

77. Perry, *Proletarian Power*, 192.

78. Brugger, "The Cultural Revolution from a Post-1989 Perspective," 109.

79. Mao Zedong, "Seal the Coffin and Pass the Final Verdict," as translated in Schoenhals, *China's Cultural Revolution*, 293.

Chapter Nine: An Assessment

1. Paul Pickowicz, "Huang Jianxin and the Notion of Postsocialism," in Nick Browne, Paul G. Pickowicz, Vivian Sobchack, and Esther Yau, ed., *New Chinese Cinemas: Forms, Identities, Politics* (New York, 1994), 61. Pickowicz borrowed the term "postsocialism" from Arlif Dirlik and others who have used it to talk about what they see as the abandonment of socialism by China's new leaders. See Arlif Dirlik, "Postsocialism? Reflections on 'Socialism with Chinese Characteristics,'" in Arlif Dirlik and Maurice Meisner, *Marxism and the Chinese Experience* (Armonk, N.Y., 1989), 362–384. Dirlik's point is that while ideology under Deng Xiaoping was no longer socialist, it was not exactly capitalist either. Paul Pickowicz, "Huang Jianxin and the Notion of Postsocialism," in Browne, *New Chinese Cinemas*, 80. Ben Xu, *Disenchanted Democracy: Chinese Cultural Criticism After 1989* (Ann Arbor, 1999), 196.

2. Pickowicz, however, insists that Chinese feelings of disillusionment with the state should not be blamed solely on the actions of the post-Maoist leadership and should not be taken as a vindication of Maoism. At the same time he acknowledges that this disillusionment began during the Cultural Revolution. I see this as proof that the disillusionment stems from Mao's exposure of the Stalinist party structure during the Cultural Revolution. See Pickowicz, "Huang Jianxin and the Notion of Postsocialism," in Browne, *New Chinese Cinemas*, 62–63. See

Xudong Zhang, "Challenging the Eurocentric View of China and a Post-Tiananmen Intellectual Field," in *East Asia: An International Quarterly*, Vol. 19, no. 1–2 (Spring/Summer 2001), 23–26. Some of these same writers are discussed in Joseph Fewsmith, *China Since Tiananmen* (New York, 1991). For interesting coverage of the de-Maoification that has occurred since 1976, and an interesting perspective on the pre-1990s efforts to prove the compatibility between Maoist and Socialist ideology and China's post-1976 development strategy, see Kalpana Misra, *From Post-Maoism to Post-Marxism: The Erosion of Official Ideology in Deng's China* (New York, 1998).

3. Adapted from the Historical National Accounts of the People's Republic of China, 1952–1995. Prepared by the Joint SSBC–Hitotsubashi University Team and Supported Financially by a COE Grant from the Ministry of Education and Sciences of Japan for the Compilation of Asian Historical Economic Statistics (September 1997). As this book goes to press a spate of articles have been published questioning the official statistics for China's recent growth rate. If some of the authors are correct, Mao's comparative record in promoting industrial growth may be far better than even the official figures suggest, though other writers seem to imply the opposite. See Thomas G. Rawski, "What's Happening to China's GDP Statistics?" in *China Economic Review* (December 2001), Vol. 12, no. 4. This article is also available at: http://www.pitt.edu/~tgrawski/. Rawski contends that though the official figures show a 7.8 percent growth in GDP in 1997–1998, he believes it was really 2.2 percent at best, and more likely negative. Rawski does, however, argue that for some of the period before 1997 China's growth rate may have been higher than stated because China's GDP figures do not account for the growing service sector. The journalist Melinda Liu argues that many of the economic figures since 1992 have been "cooked up by eager-to-please cadres." Melinda Liu, *Newsweek International* (April 1, 2002). See also Carsten A. Holz and Yi-min Lin, "Pitfalls of China's Industrial Statistics: Inconsistencies and Specification Problems," in *China Review*, Vol. 2, no. 1 (Spring 2002). For an overall discussion of the problem, see Nicholas Lardy, *Integrating China into the Global Economy* (Washington, D.C., 2002), 11–13.

4. Mao Zedong, as translated in "Conversation with Wang Hai-jung" (December 21, 1970), *Joint Publications Research Service (JPRS), U.S. Department of Commerce* 52029 (December 21, 1970).

5. See ibid. See the interview with Frederick Teiwes by Borge Bakken, "An Interview with Frederick Teiwes: On the Memoirs of Mao's Physician," *Nordic Newsletter of Asian Studies*, no. 3 (October 1996).

Acknowledgments and a Note on Sources

1. See Michael Schoenhals, "Ghost Writers: Expressing 'The Will of the Authorities,'" in *Doing Things with Words in Chinese Politics* (Berkeley, 1992), 55–77, 114–115. See also the discussion in Geremie R. Barme, *Shades of Mao: The*

Posthumous Cult of the Great Leader (Armonk, N.Y., 1996), 28. *Mao Zedong xuanji (Selected Works of Mao Zedong)*, (Beijing, 1991), four volumes. Mao Zedong, *The Selected Works of Mao Zedong* (Beijing, 1977), five volumes.

2. Takeuchi Minoru, ed., *Mo Takuto shu (Collected Writings of Mao Zedong)* (Tokyo, 1983), and *Mo Takuto shu hokan (Supplements to Collected Writings of Mao Zedong)* (Tokyo, 1983–1986).

3. *Mao Zedong sixiang wansui (Long Live Mao Zedong's Thought)*, (Beijing, 1967, 1969). In addition to the original work published in Beijing, there is also a three-volume text released by the Institute of International Relations, Taipei.

4. *Jianguo yilai Mao Zedong wengao (Manuscripts of Mao Zedong from the Period After the Nation's Founding)* (Beijing, 1987–1991). *Mao Zedong junshi wenxuan (Selected Military Writings of Mao Zedong)* (Beijing, 1981). Feng Xianzhi, ed., *Mao Zedong nianpu, 1893–1949*, 3 vols. (Beijing, 1993).

5. Stuart Schram, ed., *Mao's Road to Power: Revolutionary Writings, 1912–1949*, Vol. I: *The Pre-Marxist Period, 1912–1920* (New York, 1992). Stuart Schram, ed., *Mao's Road to Power: Revolutionary Writings 1912–1949*, Vol. II (Armonk, N.Y., 1994). Stuart Schram, ed., *Mao's Road to Power: Revolutionary Writings 1912–1949*, Vol. III (Armonk, N.Y., 1995). Stephen Averill and Stuart Schram, ed., *Mao's Road to Power: Revolutionary Writings 1912–1949*, Vol. IV (Armonk, N.Y., 1997). Stuart Schram, ed., *Mao's Road to Power: Revolutionary Writings 1912–1949*, Vol. V (Armonk, N.Y., 1999). Stuart Schram, *Chairman Mao Talks to the People: Talks and Letters, 1956–1971* (New York, 1974).

6. Michael Y. M. Kau and John K. Leung, *The Writings of Mao Zedong, 1949–1976*, Vol. I: *September 1949–December 1955* (Armonk, N.Y., 1986). Michael Y. M. Kau and John K. Leung, *The Writings of Mao Zedong, 1949–1976*, Vol. II: *January 1956–December 1957*. Roderick MacFarquhar, Timothy Cheek, and Eugene Wu, ed., *The Secret Speeches of Chairman Mao: From the Hundred Flowers to the Great Leap Forward* (Cambridge, Mass., 1989).

Index

A NOTE ON THE AUTHOR

Lee Feigon is professor of history and East Asian Studies at Colby College, and an associate of the Center for East Asian Studies at the University of Chicago. He grew up in Chicago and studied at the University of California, Berkeley, the University of Chicago, and the University of Wisconsin, Madison. Mr. Feigon has written extensively on Asian and particularly Chinese history and politics, including the book *Chen Duxiu: Founder of the Chinese Communist Party* and articles in the *Atlantic*, the *Wall Street Journal*, the *Nation*, *Barron's*, and the *Chicago Tribune* as well as the *Journal of Asian Studies* and the *American Historical Review*. His most recent books, *China Rising: The Meaning of Tiananmen* and *Demystifying Tibet: Unlocking the Secrets of the Land of the Snows*, were widely praised.

CPSIA information can be obtained
at www.ICGtesting.com
Printed in the USA
LVHW111716230920
666899LV00001B/94

9 781566 635226